"I recommend *Pass, Set, Crush* to anyone associated with volleyball. The skills are shown and explained exactly. I give it a top rating."
> —Tom Selleck
> Two-time USVBA National Champion

"I wish I had had the visual reference provided by *Pass, Set, Crush* when I was giving clinics. Everyone—from junior high kids to adults—would have benefited."
> —Jeff Reddan, Player/Coach
> Seattle Smashers, Professional League
> Four-time Professional All-Star

"Lucas has taken the 'umbrella' approach: he covers in detail the methods that work best in performing volleyball skills. Focus on the these and become a better player."
> —Aldis Berzins
> Olympic Gold Medal, 1984
> World Cup Champion, 1985

"Jeff Lucas' *Pass, Set, Crush* is a well-thought-out, valuable addition to the volleyball enthusiast's library."
> —Bill Neville
> Former USVBA Technique Director
> Olympic Gold Medal, 1984

"*Pass, Set, Crush* is a solid work. Any student of the game will find it worth reading."
> —Chuck Erbe, Former Head Coach
> USC Women's Volleyball Team
> Winner of 4 Collegiate National Championships
> Winner of 3 USVBA National Championships

"...exactly what the learning player or coach needs: an up-to-date, easy-to-follow visual presentation."
> —Craig Thompson
> Former Technique Director
> International Volleyball Federation

"*Pass, Set, Crush* makes the complex skills of volleyball seem simple; I highly recommend it."
> —Debbie Green
> Winner of the Olympic Silver Medal, 1984
> First team All-Pro, 1987

PASS, SET, CRUSH
VOLLEYBALL ILLUSTRATED

Third Edition

by Jeff Lucas

ILLUSTRATED BY STUART MOLDREM

EUCLID NORTHWEST PUBLICATIONS
Wenatchee, Washington

Library of Congress Cataloging-in-Publication Data

Lucas, Jeff, 1946-
    Pass, Set, Crush.

    Bibliography: p.
    Includes index.
    1. Volleyball.   I. Moldrem, Stuart.   II. Title.

GV1015.3.L83 1993   796.32'5   93-3636

Section I title drawing from photo by All-Sport
Section I, Chapter III drawings from photos by J.B. Saunders
Section I, Chapter 4 and pages 133–136 drawings
    from photos by Shelly Field
Page 157 drawing from photo by Diane Williams
Page 163 drawing from photo by Steve Kaminoff
Page 165 drawing from photo by All-Sport (Rick Stewart)
Page 171 drawing from photo by All-Sport (Bob Daemmrich)
Page 185 drawing from photo by All-Sport (Rick Stewart)
Page 187 drawing from photo by All-Sport (Todd Allred)
Page 209 drawing from photo by All-Sport (Joe Patronite)
Page 225 drawing from photo by All-Sport (Tim DeFrisco)
Page 229, 232 drawings from photos by Steve Kaminoff
Page 239 drawing from photo by All-Sport (Ken Levine)
Page 243 drawing from photo by All-Sport (Tony Duffy)
Page 253 drawing from photo by All-Sport (Mike Powell)
Page 259 drawing from photo by All-Sport (Bruce Hazelton)
Page 262, 263 drawings from photos by Steve Kaminoff
Page 339 drawing from photo by All-Sport (Vandystadt)

First Edition 1985
Second Edition 1988
Third Edition 1993

Manufactured in the United States of America
Published by Euclid Northwest Publications
4227 Crestview Street
Wenatchee, WA 98801

ISBN 0-6915088-6-8

To the memory of my father,

Fay Lucas

Pass, Set, Crush has been translated into
French, Italian, Spanish, Japanese and Turkish.
It is the first volleyball book in 25 years to be
translated from English into Japanese.

CONTENTS

FOREWORD

Volleyball is a complex game. The individual skills can be compared in intricacy to the golf swing. Advanced offenses include attack patterns numbering in the hundreds; defenses must prepare themselves to stop all of these attacks.

The game, however, crystallizes to the reader of *Pass, Set, Crush*. The book makes the complex seem simple. Part is the organization; part is the writing; part is the abundant illustrations.

A middle-school kid can read the book and improve his skills. The All-American player and the high-level coach, too, can benefit from the text as an encyclopedia of volleyball.

I worked with Jeff Lucas for scores of hours over 16 months. The result is a book that deserves a place in the library of any player, coach or analyst of the game.

Dave Saunders
Two-time Olympic gold medalist

Introduction to the First and Second Editions

The writer or an athletic technique book is confronted with a dilemma. If the book is to be helpful, it must say, "This is the way to do it." Yet the writer knows that the descriptions cannot be absolutely perfect for everyone; body builds, for example, make a difference. The solution may lie in quantity. What if the writer could bring the reader near to perfect—say, 95 percent of the way? Or, to use an analogy: what if the book could illuminate a *target* called "perfect technique," even though the exact location of its bull's-eye were to remain unknown?

The purpose of this book is to illuminate the target "perfect technique." To this end, I have devoted parts of 10 years, shot 7,000 photos, studied 52 books on volleyball, attended numerous clinics and camps, talked to the best players and coaches in the world and hit thousands of balls.

The technical basis for this book is provided by the performances of the best players in the world. It is they—not the coaches—who advance the volleyball community's knowledge of individual skills. Their bodies, through repetition, simply find the easiest or most effective ways to perform.

* * * * *

The most striking feature of volleyball skills is the importance of the body's center of gravity. In three of the five most important skills, the center of gravity (in the area of the hips) holds the key to either balance or power. Pushing the hips back keeps the forearm passer on balance; positioning them forward gives power to the spiker; and rotating them makes the Asian serve more powerful than the overhand.

The demonstrators include Dave Saunders of the United States Men's volleyball team, winner of the Olympic gold medal in 1984, the World Cup in 1985, the World Championship in 1986, the Olympic gold medal in 1988 and player in the Italian professional league in 1989-92;

Steve Suttich, former U.C.L.A. All-American, former head volleyball coach at the University of Washington, and now professional volleyball clinician; Debbie Green of the United States Women's team, winner of the Olympic silver medal in 1984 and First Team Professional All-Star in 1987 (setter's tip); Shelly Field, formerly Whitman College Volleyball (forearm pass, roll); Cathy Kuntz, Portland State University Volleyball, two time collegiate National Champion and volleyball coach at the University of Oregon (set, collapse); Kari Becker, Eastern Washington University Volleyball and USVBA All-American (other attacks); and Jeff Lucas, Wenatchee Volleyball Club (serve, dive).

The demonstrators were chosen because they were able to show the skills easily. There was no intent to choose male for this skill or female for that. The skills work equally well as performed by either sex.

The illustrations—pencil on coquille board—were drawn by Stuart Moldrem, professional painter and sports illustrator for the *Seattle Post Intelligencer* for 35 years. Many of the illustrations are sequences; all of these are arranged from left to right. The demonstrators are all right-handed. The left-hander needs to reverse the images and substitute "left" for "right" and vice versa.

The book assumes that the reader knows the way volleyball is played, for example, that the object of the game is to put the ball on the opponents' floor, that each team is allowed three contacts of the ball, that serves are usually received on the forearms, etc. Watching a match should give the reader enough knowledge to follow the book.

The first three chapters cover, in order, the contacts in a typical offensive play: the pass, the set and the attack. This arrangement also corresponds, not coincidentally, to the book's title. The following chapters and sections are ordered roughly by the importance of the skills covered.

Introduction to the Third Edition

The third edition of *Pass, Set, Crush* contains the former book and more than 250 pages of new material.

Section I covers the skills, the former book. Section II addresses the acquiring or the learning of the skills. Section III integrates the skills into the game. Section IV formulates the team's offense and defense at three levels of play.

The third edition includes 45 pages of charts, which delineate the team's serve-receive formations, plays, blocking patterns and backcourt defenses.

The third edition continues the "Volleyball Illustrated" tradition of its predecessors. The combined old and new illustrations total more than 840.

Pass, Set, Crush's artist, Stuart Moldrem, rendered many of the new illustrations from photos of the best teams and players in the world. Thousands of these photos were considered; the winners and their drawings exhibit athletic perfection.

The book embodies one change over traditional treatments of offense and defense: left is left and right is right. This means that the left-side hitter, for example, is referred to as the right when viewed by the defense.

Linear measurements are metric. The most common references are 15 centimeters, which equal 6 inches, and 30 centimeters, which equal 1 foot. One meter equals about 40 inches.

* * * * *

Dave Saunders provided more help in the formulation of the new material than can be described. His credentials are beyond reproach: he operated in the world's most sophisticated volleyball systems for more than a decade.

Saunders explained, over the course of sixteen months, the intricacies of team offense and defense with patience, good humor and an eloquence gained from teaching the game. He also edited. "Consider me your bodyguard," he said more than once.

Doug Partie shared the middle-blocker's perspective; Jeff Stork and Laurel Brassey, the setter's; the coaches of the U.S.A. national teams, Terry Liskevych and Fred Sturm, provided both verbal and written information on their team's systems; Debbie Hunter and John Kessell offered insight from the USVBA.

Expert information is only as good as the writer who transforms it. Mistakes are mine.

* * * * *

Kari Becker designed the book. The elegance of her choices is evident on every page and every court.

Patsy Everson cleaned the book's language and grammar.

* * * * *

Jim Holcomb, Marilyn Stewart, Bob Eller, Tom Byrne, Merle and Anne Dowd, Hartwig Petersen, Doug Beal, and Tom Tait helped with the first and second editions, now Section I.

SECTION I: THE SKILLS

    Skill, more than any other factor, influences the team's success. The skilled team that has never played together beats the unskilled team that has.

    Players and coaches at all levels address fundamental movements first.

CHAPTER 1: THE PASS

The forearm pass is a method of bouncing the ball from both forearms (**1**). The combination of ball and forearms makes the skill unique in North American sports. It is primarily used in serve-receive and, thus, starts the team's offense.

1

In its short history experts have asked one main question about the forearm pass: How can the passer move quickly into a hard serve and still make a soft pass? For many years leg straightening was thought to be the secret (2). But leg straightening is slow. This means that the player must start her passing motion early. She must commit herself to the ball while it is still a distance away. Last moment adjustments are difficult for her.

2a   b

3

The present-day passer uses a short armswing (3). Her legs do not move during the pass, nor does any part of her body (except her arms). Arms are quicker than legs. With an armswing, the passer can wait until the last moment to start her passing motion. She is like the baseball batter with "quick wrists"; she does not need to swing until she has the best possible idea where the ball is going.

There is a further advantage to the armswing pass. Since the passer's whole body is still, including her head and eyes, she can watch the ball more closely. The passer slows or stops her forearms to make a soft pass.

4

Ready

A good ready position is high and relaxed (4). A bent or low position is tiring and hurts a quick start. A good ready position is also compact. The passer keeps her hands on or near her body. Her feet are side-by-side and spread, but not too much. She bends her knees slightly.

Balance is all-important. The passer who has perfect balance when the ball is served gets a quick and controlled start. Weight held on the front part of the feet (so that the passer can push with her toes) helps balance. So does positioning the hips slightly to the rear. A slight shifting of the weight from side-to-side, or a slight sway of the upper body, or a slight up-and-down movement also helps.

Getting to the Ball

The Foot Position

The player wants to pass with a foot position that brings, above all, stability. The best passers in the world have found that the most solid is like the police officer's in shooting a pistol: side-by-side, flat on the floor and wide (5). Pointing the toes and knees slightly inward, which locks the hips, makes the position even more stable.

The stride position—one foot in front of the other—allows only the front foot to be flat on the floor; it is not as solid as the side-by-side.

5

The passer's first job, once she sees the ball coming to her, is to move her feet to the ball (6). Once arrived, she will position them side-by-side, as mentioned. Feet go before arms. Sometimes it seems natural for the passer's arms to reach toward the ball first. The player then ends up going to the passing spot with her arms held out (7). This is a mistake. Arms held out slow the passer's movement to the ball.

Three more points:

1. The passer watches the ball all during her movement to the passing spot.
2. She carries most of her weight on the front part of her feet.
3. She lowers her body slightly for better balance.

7

6

8

The Bounce

When the ball is going to arrive nearby, the passer makes a series of quick bounces to adjust her position (8). She keeps her feet side-by-side and holds her arms comfortably away from her body for balance. The front part of her feet does the springing.

The Side-Step

The bounce turns into a side-step when the passer moves to her side (**9**). She leads with the foot nearer the passing site and follows with a skip-step (**a, b**). The passer completes the movement with her feet in the side-by-side position, ready either to pass or to make another side-step (**c**).

Both bouncing and side-stepping allow the passer to face the serve as she moves and also to stop easily.

9a

b

c

9

The Cross-and-Run

When the ball is served more than two or three steps away, the passer needs to cross-and-run (**10**). She leads with the foot nearer the passing site, as in the side-step, but begins to turn her foot and her body toward the ball (**b**).

10a   b

The passer's second step makes the cross (c). It completes her turn away from the server; her hips have rotated 90 degrees. Her toes point to the side.

The cross helps the passer to speed up. She can run for the ball once she is turned. Running is faster than side-stepping. However, running makes stopping more difficult.

c

11a b

The Hop

In order to stop from a run, the passer needs to hop (**11**). The hop turns her body back toward the server and places her feet in the side-by-side position (**c**).

The player also needs to hop after moving forward. This can be difficult, especially when the serve is very short. For an extremely short serve, it is smoother to make the pass with one foot in front of the other. This is also the case for a high serve or a free ball.

Most serve-receive formations do not require the passer to move backward more than a step. A bounce or two brings her into position in this case.

In order to get to the ball, the forearm passer:

1. Moves her feet first
2. Hops into passing position
3. Places her feet
   a. side-by-side
   b. wider than her shoulders
   c. flat on the floor

c

12

The Pass

The best way for the passer to join her hands is by interlocking her fingers at the first knuckle (12, 13). She relies on the heels of her hands— they are pressed together—to square her forearms. Unlike other grips, inter-locking fingers leaves the forearm muscles relaxed. This means that the passer can move her arms at their quickest. Relaxed forearm muscles bring the greatest gains in quickness when the passer reaches to the side (13).

13

Once the passer has a good hand clasp, she needs to position her forearms. There are three things that help make her passes accurate:

1. The passer locks her elbows so that her arms do not bend. This allows her arms to work as one.
2. She rolls her forearms outward, turning the flat part of her forearms toward the ball.
3. She holds her forearms as close together as possible, making double hits less likely (**12, 13**).

14

A good body position is low for balance (14). The passer bends her knees and pushes her upper body forward at the waist. She straightens her back by pushing her hips to the rear. Hips pushed back are all-important in keeping the passer balanced: she is solid from the beginning to the end of her pass.

Hips held forward round the passer's back (**15**). This means that her head and shoulders are too far back for balance. The passer with a rounded back falls backward during or after the pass.

The only time the passer draws her hips forward is in handling topspin: digging a hard spike or receiving a topspin serve (**16**). Her arms need to be nearly vertical to keep the topspinning ball from climbing straight up or, worse yet, jumping backward. Hips held forward balance her arms in their nearly vertical position.

15

16

17

The arms swing from the shoulders to meet the ball (17). The armswing is short: the hands move only a few centimeters and then stop at about 45 degrees to the floor. This is the best arm angle for passing most serves. The player may swing *through* a slow, easy ball. But swinging through a hard serve usually results in a high or hard pass. These passes are difficult to set. When the serve is coming fast, the passer waits until the last minute to start her armswing. She tries to watch the serve as long as possible.* Then she moves her arms quickly forward and, in order not to hit the ball too hard, pulls them back just after contact. The ball touches the forearms one third to one half the distance from wrist to elbow.

Here are the main points for the forearm pass. The player:

1. Presses the heels of her hands together

2. Locks her elbows

3. Rolls her arms out and holds them near each other

4. Bends her knees and her waist

5. Pushes her hips to the rear

6. Holds her body and her head still

7. Uses a short armswing, stopping near 45 degrees

8. Touches the ball seven to ten centimeters above her wrists

*The passer does not "look the ball into her forearms." Tilting her head forward or looking suddenly downward interferes with her vision. She simply watches the ball as long as she can without making quick head or eye movements.

CHAPTER 2:
THE SET

18

The set or overhand pass is a method of pushing the ball upward with both hands (**18**). It is the most accurate pass in volleyball and the main tool of its magicians, the setters.

The best setters contact the ball near their foreheads. They stay in contact with the ball as it moves toward the target. They continue to touch it until their arms are straight. These setters have a soft, but commanding "touch." A soft but commanding touch is the result of two things: wrists that spring (soft) and arms that squeeze (commanding).

19

20

Getting to the Ball

As in forearm passing, the setter must first move her feet to the ball (**19**). She can either side-step or run. She will never move backward if she can help it. There is too great a chance to be whistled for holding. The player arrives facing the target, with the ball directed toward her forehead (**20**). Her shoulders are square—at a 90 degree angle with a line drawn to the target. From this position both arms can push in the same way.

21   22

Ready to Pass

The Feet

There are two positions for the feet: *stride* and *side-by-side*. The stride position is like a short walking step (21)*. The feet are shoulder width apart. The front foot is flat on the floor; the heel of the rear foot is raised. In the side-by-side position, both feet are in a line 90 degrees to the target (22). They are close to each other—only a few centimeters apart—and flat on the floor. The toes point toward the target.

*Invariably the setter positions her right foot forward. This allows her to turn easily from left to right, from facing her teammates as they pass to facing down the net as she sets. In most of the illustrations (Fig. 21, for example), the setter's *left* foot is forward. The reason for this is to keep the left-to-right format of the illustrations and still show both legs of the setter.

23a   b

The stride position is used almost all the time. When the setter is standing, she steps forward into the stride, shifting most of her weight to her front foot (**23a, b**). She bends her knees slightly, and then straightens her legs as she pushes the ball upward (**b, c**). Leg straightening adds force to the set.

c   24

    When the setter is running, her last step takes her into the stride (24). In this case the stride helps her to slow down. As in a standing start, her front leg carries most of her weight.

    The setter almost always uses the stride. She needs balance as she steps or runs to the ball.

The side-by-side foot position gives extra power (**25**). Both the player's feet are under her weight instead of mainly the front one (**a**). Her legs are near to each other throughout their length, working in exactly the same way. They push forcefully as one (**b**).

The side-by-side setter tilts her body toward the target during the pass for the greatest power (**a, b**).

The side-by-side foot position is limited to players who do not need to chase the ball. These are usually not setters, but spikers playing the back row. They need to make a long set, but do not need the balance or stopping power of the stride.

25a   b

26

The Body

The setter bends her knees before making the pass, as mentioned. This gives her legs a chance to push. But there is one time when the setter wants to push with her legs very little: when she is in position to set two or more hitters (**26**). In this case, she wants her body to be nearly motionless so that she can fool the blocker about where she intends to set. Her body is upright as she receives the ball; she waits as long as possible before starting her setting motion.

The setter tilts her head upward, watching the ball (**26**). Her back is straight and vertical. She holds her hands about 15 centimeters in front of her forehead while she waits for the ball. She does not move her head; her eyes follow the ball to her hands.

The set or overhand pass ready position is now complete. The setter has:

1. Moved her feet to the ball
2. Directed the ball toward her forehead
3. Faced the target
4. Positioned her feet in stride
5. Bent her knees
6. Tilted her head upward
7. Positioned her hands about 15 centimeters in front of her forehead

27a   b

The Pass

The Arms

The arms do only one thing in the set: they push the hands (**27**). The push, however, is important; it gives the setter a solid contact of the ball, a commanding touch. The setter's arms push her hands *inward* as well as forward (**27a, b**). This allows her to squeeze the ball, keeping it from straying to the left or right.

The setter's elbows are held very wide at ready (**27a**). Wide elbows put her arms in a plane, making for a direct squeeze (**28**). Wide elbows also position the passer's wrists for the greatest flex (to be discussed).

At the start of the pass, the setter's forearms move toward the ball like arrows (**29a, b**). Her hand is the tip of the arrow; her elbow is the tail. This means that her hands and arms travel at an inward angle—about 45 degrees—until clamping the ball. Each hand touches the *side* of the ball (**29b**).

Once the setter's hands are firmly touching the sides of the ball, they change direction. First, they were moving toward each other; now they move toward the target, straight forward (**30a, b**). The ball's resistance—not the player's effort—brings this change of direction.

31a   b

The setter continues to squeeze the ball as her hands and the ball move forward (31). Her elbows do not rotate or twist; they stay in a plane throughout the pass. Her hands are driven from a few centimeters in front of her forehead to full arm extension (d).

Should the setter pull her arms back as the ball arrives? No. A simple inward push works better. There are three reasons for this:

1. Pulling back must be timed with the ball's speed. Each ball arrives at a different speed, and some are spinning. It is impossible to be in time with every one.

c   d

2. Pulling back is slow. It takes extra time to pull back and then to push. This is important to the setter. She wants to pass quickly so that opposing blockers have little time to move into position. Also, hitters time their approaches by the setting motion. A quick motion means fewer timing errors between the hitter and the setter.

3. Pulling back causes referees to sit up and take notice. The touch time is very long, so referees call fouls more strictly.

32a   b

The Wrists

A soft touch on the set can seem like magic to those who do not have it. But a soft touch only means that the ball changes direction in the player's hands *gradually* (**32**). Her wrists and, to a lesser extent, her fingers do the work.

The setter's wrists work as springs. In other words, they flex when the ball pushes on them (**b, c**). The setter does not need to think about the flex; the action is automatic. She does need to hold her hands gently back, without stiffness in either her hands or wrists (**a**). This is important, since every beginning player wants to tense the muscles of her hands and wrists toward the ball. Wrists held rigid do not flex.

33   **34**

There is one more thing the player does to gain wrist flexibility and a soft touch. She positions her wrists so that the ball pushes them squarely back (33). "Squarely back" means that the arriving ball tilts her hand neither toward her thumb nor her little finger. Wide elbows, both at ready and during the pass, keep the player's wrists square as the ball pushes on them (33, 34, 35, 36).

35

36a   b

37a   b

38   39

The Hands

Once the setter's elbows are wide and her wrists square, she needs to open her hands to receive the ball. "Open" is important. The player holds the fingertips of one hand together and then opens her fingers gently; this motion gives her the hand position she wants at contact with the ball (**37a, b**). Her hands are cupped, her fingers slightly curled (**38, 39, 40, 41, 42**). There is firmness, but it comes from opening her fingers, not from tensing them forward. Tensed fingers do not flex.

The setter holds her hands about 15 centimeters in front of her forehead (40, 41, 42). The left is held exactly like the right (39). Her index fingers are nearly in a line and about 20 centimeters wider than they will be on the ball (38, 39).

40

41

42

43 a   b   c   d

The Entire Motion

The player intending to set or overhand pass raises her hands early—as soon as she knows the ball is coming to her (**43a**). She starts moving her arms early, too, well before the ball touches her hands (**b**).

Once the setter has started moving her arms toward the ball, she must put up her biggest fight. The muscles of her arms are working, pushing her hands toward the ball. But the muscles of her hands are not. The setter must hold her hands gently but firmly back.

The problem becomes acute just before and during the player's touch of the ball (**c**). Her hands want to *do* something to the ball. They cannot. They must let the ball act on them. The doing is in the arms.

The ball first touches the pads of the fingers, on the fingerprint. It pushes the fingers back, spreading them about the ball (**d**). The ball sinks deep into the setter's hands, finally touched by the length of her fingers and the pads of her thumbs. The setter's wrists are also pushed back by the force of the ball. This is the important instant: hands and wrists are flexing automatically—backward—as the arms move forward.

e   f   g   h

By this time the ball has stopped moving toward the player and is about to reverse its direction and head for the target. This is the moment that the setter puts the greatest pressure on the ball. Her hands, on each side of the ball and pushed by her arms, squeeze it firmly.

Now the ball is moving away from the player (e). The setter's hands and wrists rebound so that they stay in contact with the ball as it moves away. Pressure on the ball is still inward, though less and less so (f).

The setter continues to touch the ball until her arms are nearly straight (g). The last contact is made with the tips of the fingers.

Since the player has avoided tightening her wrists during the pass, her hands turn outward as the ball leaves (h). The player's arms are straight and parallel at the end of the motion, about a ball's width apart (44). The ball leaves cleanly and without spin.

When the arriving ball is high or spinning, the setter needs greater resistance. She must start her hands toward the ball sooner, giving them greater speed at contact. She must also firm her hands and wrists. Both of these changes help to keep the ball from breaking through her hands. They also decrease the setter's spring of the ball, which does not sink so deeply into her hands.

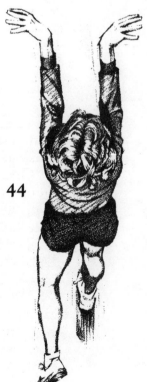

44

44

46a   b   c

The Back Set

The setter can pass the ball to a teammate behind her, that is, to back-set (46). She receives the ball in exactly the same position as in setting forward (a). She contacts the ball in the same place—in front of her forehead (b). She springs and squeezes the ball as in front setting, but for the back-set quickly pushes it over her head (c). Her shoulders move backward with her arms; her hips move forward. As in front setting, she stays in contact with the ball as long as possible.

The Jump Set

The setter can combine her overhand pass with a jump (**45**). There are three times when she will want to do this:

1. The pass from her teammate is high and long. She jumps to keep from touching the net.

2. She wants to quicken her attack. She jumps in order to set the ball sooner, before it falls.

3. She is in the front row and likes to attack the second touch. She jumps so that her opponents do not know what she will do—attack or set.

Jumping brings two differences to the set:

1. There is a delay between the leg push (jump) and the pass itself. This means that the rhythm is different than in setting from the floor: "jump," then "set." The entire motion takes more time.

2. The setter has less power in midair. She cannot push with her legs as she can on the floor.

45

I. Here are the main points of the set or overhand pass. The player gets ready to receive the ball by:

1. Moving her feet to the ball
2. Positioning her forehead in the ball's path
3. Facing the target
4. Positioning her feet in stride
5. Bending her knees
6. Tilting her head upward
7. Positioning her elbows wide
8. Holding her hands
   a. back
   b. open
   c. 6 inches in front of her forehead
   d. nearly horizontal (index fingers point slightly upward)

II. Once the player is ready, she:

1. Starts her arms before the ball arrives
2. Pushes her arms inward
3. Touches the sides of the ball
4. Allows the ball to spread her hands and flex her wrists
5. Straightens her arms to full extension
6. Stays in contact with the ball as long as possible
7. Straightens her legs as her arms push the ball outward

47

CHAPTER 3:
THE SPIKE

The spike is a method of smashing the ball into the opponents' court (47). There is no other athletic skill—in any sport—quite like it. Why? Because the player must hit the ball as hard as he can *while in midair*. He can't push on the floor for power, as in throwing. This means he must use his body in a special way: against itself.

The player uses his body "against itself" both by bending and twisting in midair (47). His lower body—especially his hips—makes the base against which he does this. The position of the player's hips is most important in developing power in midair.

48

To Pike or Not to Pike

"To pike" means to bend forward at the waist. Piking is common among spikers (**48**). In fact, a good pike has been thought to show that the hitter has smashed the ball with all his power. Quite the opposite is true. The pike represents power that was not given to the ball.

Newton's third law of motion says that for every action there is an equal and opposite reaction. Applied to the spike, this might read: The harder the spiker hits the ball, the more his body stops at contact.* Said in another way, the spiker whose body stops cold at contact has hit with power (**49**). The hitter who pikes has not.

How does the spiker avoid piking? Or, how does he generate enough power that contact stops his body cold?

1. The spiker must time perfectly the motions of his body, hitting arm and hand. They move in a sequence, like the uncoiling of a whip.

2. The spiker must hit the ball when his body is perfectly straight.*

Hitting the ball with a perfectly straight body is important in developing power. It is also difficult to do. The secret is in the spiker's hips: they must snap quickly forward during the jump. The hitter whose hips have not snapped forward during the jump has no chance to bring them forward once he is in the air. What snaps the hips forward? The spiker's body position *before* he starts his jump is most important. He must time his armswing well. Also, he must draw his hips back. He must cock them. Hips that have been cocked can snap forward during the jump. A timely armswing and a cocking of the hips are the keys to power in the spike.

*For further explanation, see the Appendix to Chapter III.

49a   b

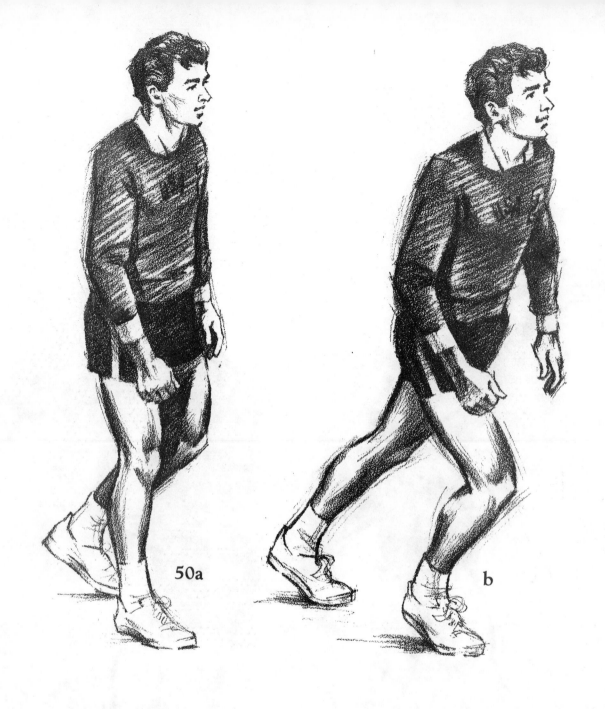

50a   b

Getting to the Ball

Ready

The ready position for the spike is like the distance runner's: one foot leads the other (a). There is one big difference, however. The spiker holds all his weight on his front foot, allowing him to start upright; the runner distributes his weight more evenly, leaning forward at the start. The right-handed spiker positions his right foot forward.

The right-hander wants to contact the ball slightly in front of his right shoulder. His run brings him into position to do this.

48

c   d

The Steps

The spiker makes a four-, three- or two-step run to the ball. The four-step is standard and easiest to learn. Players who need to be quicker simply drop one or both of the first two steps (at a loss of speed in the run).

The right-handed spiker starts his four-step run with a quick step to the rear using his left foot (**a, b**). It is as if he is stepping forward with his right foot — though his right does not leave the floor. This quick step backward allows him to start nearer the point of his attack, but still gives him a "step" with his right for extra speed. His right foot is counted as Step 1 of the four-step approach (**b**).*

Step 2, taken with the left foot by the right-handed spiker, is longer than Step 1 (**c, d**). The spiker increases his speed during Step 2.

*The spiker who is already moving takes a full step with his right foot in the course of his run.

51a

b

COUNT	STEPS
1	right
2	left
3	right/left

Step 3, taken with the right foot, is long and quick (**a, b**). It speeds up the approach. Step 4 brings the spiker's left foot into position next to his right for the jump (**c, d**). It is also quick. The player can count evenly "one-two-three" during his four-step approach. The last two steps—one after the other—occur in the time it takes to say "three."

50

c   d

45°

Steps 3 and 4 put the player's feet side-by-side. His toes point about 45 degrees to the right of the target (**d**). His body, too, has turned to the right, toward his hitting hand. The turn is important. The spiker wants to position his hips in the air at this 45 degree angle.

52a

The Armswing

The armswing gives the spiker a higher jump. He throws his arms upward and his body follows. But the armswing plays an even bigger role in a successful spike. A well-timed armswing helps the spiker to bring his hips back on Step 3, so that he can snap them forward during his jump. The spiker then can hit the ball when his body is straight. He does not pike. The spiker gives all of his power to the ball.

Most spikers' armswings are late. Late means that the player does not have time to swing his arms fully forward and up. He must stop his armswing and quickly raise his arms to hit. Without a full armswing, it is difficult for the spiker to move his hips back and then forward. He pikes, losing power.

The timing of the armswing is determined early in the approach – during Step 3 (**a, b**). At this point the spiker's arms swing backward as his body speeds forward. Step 3 is where the hitter is likely to have trouble: his arms do not want to move in the direction

opposite to his body. The spiker allows his arms to swing as far to the rear as possible (**b**). His shoulders limit his armswing to the rear.

The spiker's arms stop their backswing just before his right foot hits the floor (**b**). This is an important point in timing the armswing and the steps.

The spiker's arms swing forward with power during Step 4. They move in a straight line, crossing the spiker's body near his hips (**c**). His arms are slightly forward of his hips as he starts his jump and horizontal in the middle of it (**d**). They swing above his head as he leaves the floor (**e**). His arms are nearly straight throughout their swing.

The forward and upward swing of the spiker's arms helps to tilt his upper body: his hips move forward and his shoulders back (**c, d, e**). This allows him to hit the ball when his body is straight, using all of his power.

53a   b

The Hips

The spiker's backward armswing starts the tilting of his upper body—bringing his hips back and his shoulders forward (**53a**). The spiker must now continue the motion, bending his body forward at the waist.

As the spiker starts his armswing forward, his hips continue to move to the rear (**b**). His shoulders dip toward his knees. He bends severely at the waist; his upper body and his thighs make a sharp angle. The spiker's back is arched, increasing the effect of his bend (**b**).

This is the most important moment in the spike. The spiker has coiled his body. His hips are cocked back, ready to snap forward. His shoulders are down, ready to drive upward and back. His back is arched. He is now in position to hit the ball with maximum power. His body will be perfectly straight at contact.

As the spiker's arms swing forward, his hips also move forward (**c, d, e**). His shoulders, on the other hand, start moving to the rear. His torso is nearly vertical during the upward thrust of his legs (**c, d**).

By the time the spiker has left the floor, his hips have snapped forward. They are set in the air (**e**).

54

The Foot Action

The spiker's hips move sharply forward as he jumps. His feet reflect the movement of his hips. They roll forward on the floor like rolling pins—heel to toe (**a, b, c, d**).

The spiker's right heel hits the floor first (**a**). His right toe quickly follows (**b**). His right heel leaves the floor, continuing its rolling action (**c**). Now his left foot joins in, touching down (**c**). By this time the spiker's hips have driven far enough forward that *only his left toe* touches the floor. His left heel never contacts the floor (**c**).

Now the toes of both feet roll forward together (**d**). The spiker continues the rolling action even as he leaves the floor (**e**). It is as if he is trying to keep his toes on the floor, pointing them downward as he jumps (**e**). This corresponds to the snap of his hips; they are now well ahead of his shoulders (**e**). He can now arch his back in the extreme without piking during his hit.

The player's feet hitting the floor can be counted evenly "heel, toe, toe." The spiker pushes equally hard with the toes of both feet, giving him a square jump.

54

55

The Jump

The spiker wants to jump so that his body is vertical in the air (55). Jumping with a forward lean means that he cannot reach as high; he contacts the ball lower (54). He may, however, fly forward during his jump (like the long jumper in track). A fast run brings a forward jump of from one half to one meter—but with the body vertical. The spiker's feet and hips point to the right of the target during the upward part of his jump.

I. In order to time his run, the spiker:
    1. Lengthens and quickens Steps 3 and 4
    2. Swings his arms backward during Step 3
    3. Finishes his arms' backswing just before Step 3 touches down
    4. Counts his four-step approach 1-2-3

56a   b   c

II. In order to position his hips in the air, the spiker:

   1. Times his backward armswing to stop just before his right foot hits the floor
   2. Thrusts his hips backward, dips his shoulders and arches his back during Step 3 (**56a**)
   3. Points his feet (and his hips) 45 degrees to the right of the target on Steps 3 and 4 (**b**)
   4. Rolls his feet forward as he swings his arms (**b**)
   5. Pushes himself upward with the front part of his feet, heels raised
   6. Jumps with an equal push from the toes of both feet (**b**)
   7. Tilts his shoulders to the rear as he jumps
   8. Swings his arms well forward and above his head (**c**)

III. In order to jump high, the spiker:

   1. Swings his arms as far to the rear as possible (**a**)
   2. Times his arms so that they lead his body into the air (**b**)
   3. Keeps his body upright during his jump
   4. Swings both of his arms above his head (**c**)

57a   b

Cocking the Hammer

The spiker's feet have left the floor; his hips are set in the air (a). He arches and twists his upper back (b). His left hand remains above his head, seeming to reach for the ball, as he arches and twists. His right arm draws back. The spiker bends his elbow to the extreme and moves it as far to the rear and as high as possible. This arm position is often called the "bow-and-arrow," for its similarity to archery.* His entire arm is held above his shoulder; his right hand is held palm-down and slightly out. Now the hitting motion, which is very similar to throwing, begins.

*The term "bow-and-arrow" is *approximate*. There are important differences between the spiker's arm position and the archer's: The spiker's right elbow is cocked well above the line of his shoulders (b). The archer's elbow stays in line with his shoulders. The spiker's left arm angles upward from his shoulder line (b). The archer's left arm lines up exactly with his shoulders.

58

c

d

The Hit

The spiker's body begins to straighten and to untwist (**c**). Now three things happen at once:

1. His left arm moves downward toward his body
2. His right hand drops back, sweeping above his ear (**c**)
3. His right shoulder drives forward, leading his arm into the ball (**c**)

His elbow does not move ahead of the line of his shoulders. This is important. The spiker who pushes his elbow farther ahead is uncoiling his arm too early. The spiker's elbow remains high throughout his motion.

The spiker's arm unbends at the elbow as he turns into the ball. When his arm is straight—pointing upward—his wrist snaps (**d**). His hand contacts the ball directly over his right side and slightly in front of his shoulder. His fingers are spread. His body faces the target. The spiker's body is straight at contact (**d**). His hips and shoulders make a vertical line. His hand is moving at its fastest. He is solid in the air.

58a   b

The Whip

How does the spiker get power? By whipping his body. This means that he accumulates speed at its tip. The spiker's body can be seen as a series of four movable parts (**a**). His torso (heaviest) moves first (**b**). His upper arm moves next (**c**). His forearm follows (**d**). Finally the lightest part, his hand, moves into the ball (**e**).

c   d   e

Each part in turn *slows down* as its energy is transferred to the next part. His torso slows as his upper arm speeds up (**c**). His upper arm slows for his forearm (**d**), which in turn slows for his hand (**e**). These transfers accumulate great speed; his hand snaps like the tip of a towel or whip.

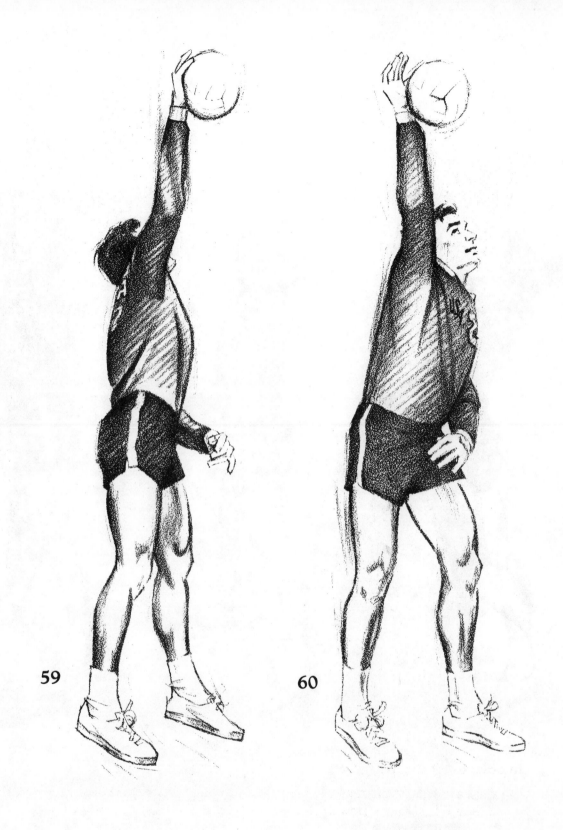

59   **60**

The player spikes the ball from as high as he can reach (**59**). This means that his hitting arm is nearly vertical at contact. How does he keep his arm nearly vertical and hit the ball down at different angles? By adjusting the location of his wrist snap (**60**). A change of an inch or two forward or back does not move his arm far from vertical. But it changes the angle of his hit a great deal.

61a   b

In order to hit the ball as hard as possible, the spiker:

1. Leaves his left arm pointing upward as his right draws back
2. Keeps his right elbow above his right shoulder during his draw-back and his hit (61)
3. Leads with his shoulder, elbow and wrist in order
4. Hits the ball as high as he can reach
5. Makes contact when his body is perfectly straight
6. Snaps his wrist over the ball
7. Spreads his fingers about the ball at contact
8. Faces the target both at contact and during his finish

d

b

c

The Finish

The spiker gives up a great deal of his energy to the ball at contact: his entire body either stops or slows down. His torso stops. Its final position is straight and vertical (62). His arm continues forward, but much more slowly. It finally stops near his side (c). This is his "follow-through" position. The spiker lands with his toes pointing directly toward the target.

63a   b

There is a final point about body rotation. The player jumps facing 45 degrees to the right of the target (**a**). He arches and twists; then he straightens. His torso develops its greatest power on return to its 45 degree position. But the spiker does not hit the ball facing to the right of the target. His body continues to rotate—past the 45 degrees—so that the spiker is facing the target when and after he hits (**b**). Why does his torso move past its position of greatest power? Because the whip does not end with his torso. It must go through his arm and hand. This takes the added time.

* * * * *

In the top row of the following sequence note the spiker's armswing, the backward and then forward movement of his hips and the tipping back of his shoulders. In the bottom row note the spiker's whip—the starting and stopping of his hips, the same for his shoulders and the stopping of his elbow before contact.

64

66

65a   b

Note the turn of the spiker's hips (**a, b**), the rise of his elbow toward the ball (**c**), the severe tilt of his shoulders at contact (**d**), the rigidity of his whole body after the hit (**e**) and the straight-forward action of his arm on its follow-through (**e**).

At the instant of touch
All is quiet.
The torso does not budge;
Neither do the legs,
Nor the head.
There is no resistance from the ball.
No pressure at the elbow,
No bump at the shoulder,
Not the slightest vibration
Anywhere in the body.
And no work.
Selected contractions,
Long since past,
Have done it all:
Hand speed
Beyond the imaginable,
Beyond control.
And the ball,
Astonished,
Makes a fast trip.

67

CHAPTER 4:
THE SERVE

The serve is a method of throwing the ball and then hitting it over the net to start play (67). It is the only skill in volleyball in which the player has complete control of the ball. The server stands alone outside the court, waiting for a signal from the referee. His serving motion is slow. For these reasons, volleyball players usually have more mental problems with the serve than with any other skill.

The ball can be served so that it travels with or without spin.

68

Most spinning serves are hit with topspin (**68**). These curve downward in a smooth path. This means that the receiver of a spinner knows where it will go. To counteract the receiver's advantage, the server usually tries to serve hard. Serving hard leads to mistakes.

A spinless serve changes direction in midflight, dancing through the air (70). Eddies behind the ball do the trick.

When the ball moves slowly, the air behind it swirls in two large, symmetrical eddies (69a). The symmetry keeps the ball in a straight path.

As the ball increases speed, the two eddies become less stable. They oscillate, that is, they swing from side to side (69b). The oscillating eddies exert a force on the ball so that it, too, swings.

The ball that moves very fast does not swing. The eddies in its wake become symmetrical again, losing the power to move the ball from side to side.

The spinless serve, called a "floater" for its oscillations, is the favorite at all levels of play.

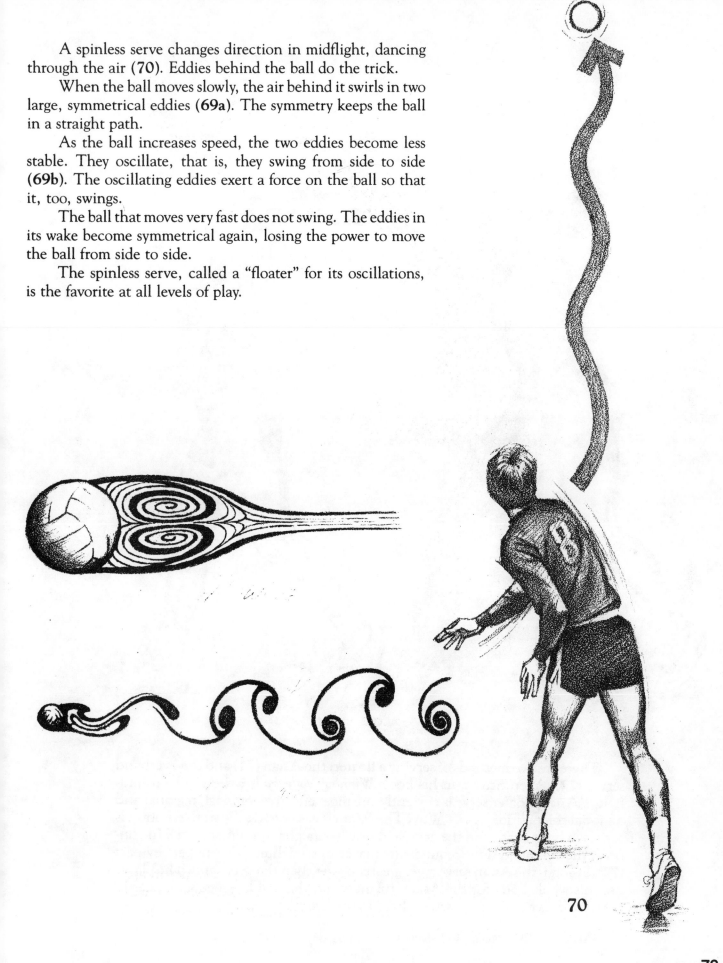

70

71

72

There are two methods of serving a floater: the Asian (71) and the overhand serves (72). Allen Scates, in his book *Winning Volleyball*, writes: "The roundhouse [Asian] floater serve is currently the most effective for local, regional and national competition . . . ."* Why? The Asian is easier to do. First, the motion is simple: a body turn with the arm held nearly straight throughout (71). In contrast, the overhand serve requires the player to straighten his arm part by part (72). Second, the Asian serve gives greater power than the overhand. The player uses his whole body for the Asian, turning into the ball like a golfer or batter (71). He does not have to work as hard as the overhand server.

*Allen E. Scates, *Winning Volleyball*, Allyn and Bacon, Inc., 1976, page 15.

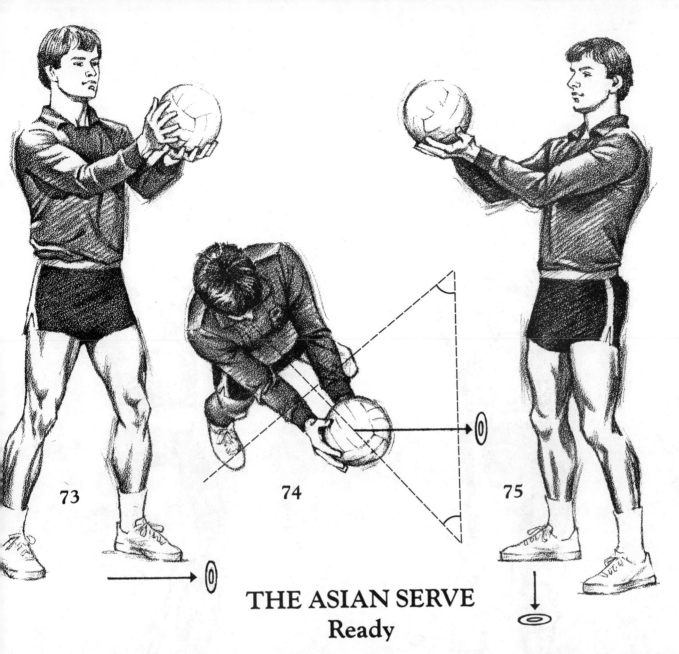

THE ASIAN SERVE
Ready

In the ready position, the Asian server's body is motionless and firm (**73**). His feet are flat on the floor, side-by-side and about shoulder width apart. He faces about 45 degrees to the right of the target (**74**).* His toes are at the same 45 degree angle. His weight is even. The player's knees are slightly bent, his back straight (**73, 75**).

The server locates the bottom of the ball directly in front of his breastbone (**73, 74, 75**). His left or lifting hand holds the ball from underneath. The server does not grip the ball. He cradles it, using the pads of his fingers for balance. His right hand rests lightly on the back of the ball (**73, 74**).**

The server's left elbow points down (**75**). It is bent, but not so bent that it touches his side. It rests a few inches in front of his body (**74**). This elbow position is important because it locates the ball the right distance from the server's body. From here he can lift the ball straight up. His right elbow, too, is comfortably bent (**73**). The server looks at the ball.

*Facing 45 degrees to the right of the target at ready allows the server to turn his body forward for contact. This means the greatest possible power. See page 83.

**Starting with the right hand on the ball helps the server to focus. It also helps in timing, since both hands can move from this position at once.

76a   b

The Coil

The Asian serve begins with three separate motions. The server's left hand lifts the ball, his right hand draws back and his left foot moves forward (a, b). These motions all start at once (they also end at once).

c

d

The Lift

The server lifts the ball with a smooth vertical motion (76). His hand stays in contact with the ball as long as possible, then releases it without spin (c). At the release, the server's arm is nearly straight. The ball rises from his hand about 15 centimeters only (d). Why so low? High throws turn small throwing mistakes into big ones. The ball must not be thrown lower than 15 centimeters, however. The server does want to hurry the motion of his serving arm.

77a   **b**

The Right Hand

The server's right hand draws away from the ball at the start of the lift (**a, b**). His arm straightens as his hand reaches back (**c**).

His arm continues to move backward until it can go no further, stopped by his shoulder (**d**). His hand is now a few inches past the line of his hips. His shoulders rotate, too, until they, in turn, are stopped by his torso (**d**). His chest faces 90 degrees to the right of the target.

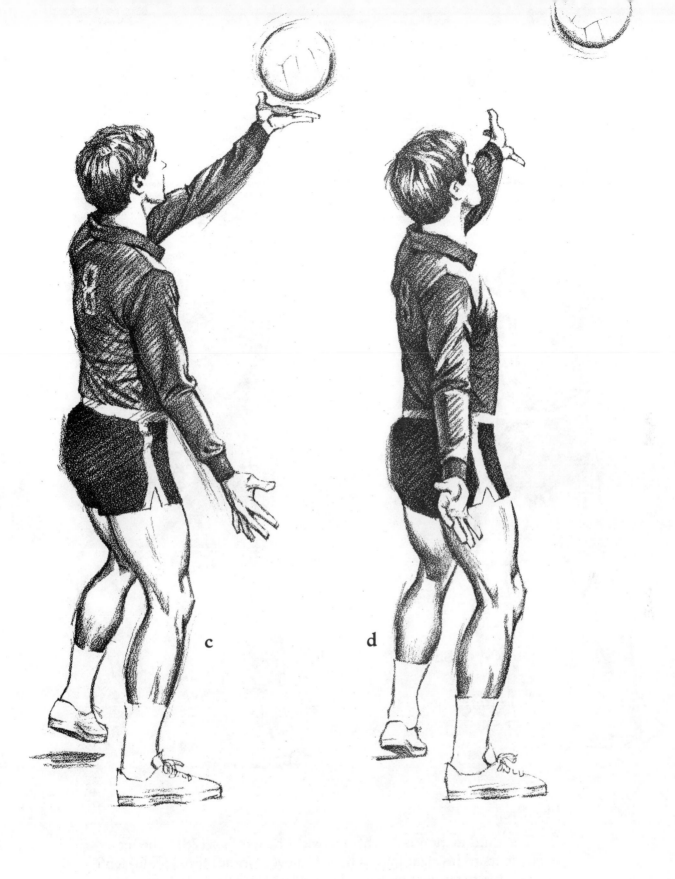

*Note that all of the server's weight has shifted to his right foot (**d**). He is coiled, ready to move into the ball.*

78a   b

The Step

The third motion is a light step with the left foot (78). The server's weight shifts to his right foot as his left moves forward (a, b). The step is short—seven to ten centimeters only—and in a line about 45 degrees to the left of the target (this is the same line set by his ready position—page 75, Fig. 74) The server has almost no weight on his left foot at the end of the movement; only his toe, pointing toward the target, touches the floor (d). The server's torso *does not* move forward with his left foot—he does not want to start his weight shift too soon.

c   d

The server's body is coiled, ready to move into the ball (**d**). Both his serving arm and his right shoulder have rotated as far to the rear as possible. His weight has shifted to his back foot.

The player's serving hand has stopped about 30 centimeters in back of his right hip (**d**). It faces slightly back and is ready to contact the ball.

The server's elbow, wrist and hand are straight and firm. This does not change throughout the hit. His elbow can be a trouble spot. He does not want to lock it, to extend it all the way. To most servers, locking means that the arm is bent back, not straight. Also, it hurts to hit the ball with a fully extended elbow.

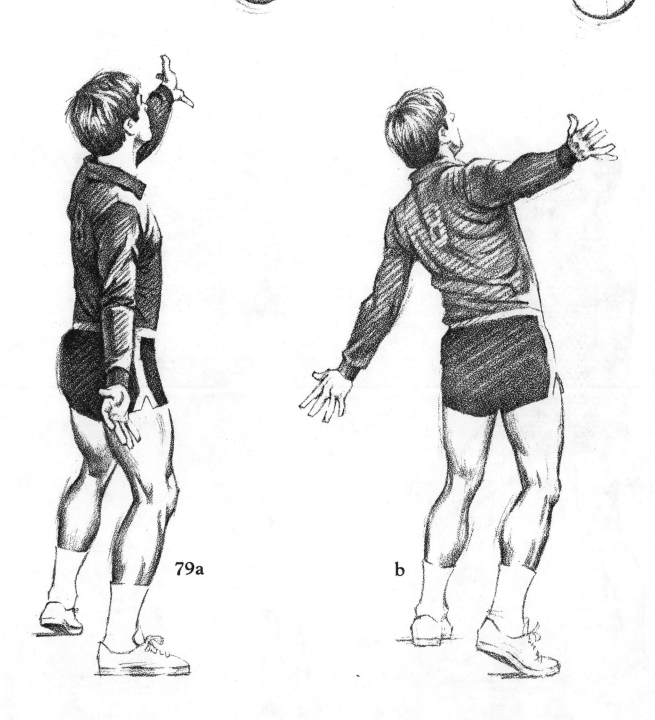

79a   **b**

The server's hand is ready to contact the ball (**79a**). It bends slightly where the fingers attach to the palm—at the big knuckles (**80**). The bend allows the player to hit the ball on the meat of his hand—both the heel and the edge. It also helps to stiffen the server's wrist, preventing waggle. Furthermore, the bend keeps the palm-side of his knuckles from sticking out and interfering with a clean hit. Each finger is straight; they are also spread (**79c**).

*The server who tries to contact the ball with his arm more nearly vertical breaks the straight line made by his arm and shoulders. This means less power.

**The server does not need to stop his hand to avoid spin. The ball springs quickly away. The path of his hand after contact has no effect on the flight of the serve.

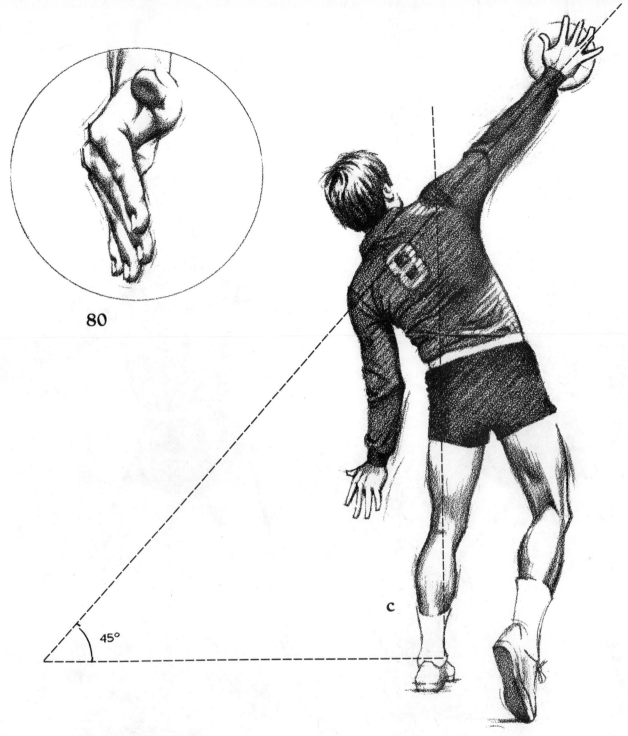

80

45°

c

The Body Turn

The server rotates his hips and shoulders into the ball (**79**). As his body turns, he shifts his weight from his back foot to his front one. The forceful turn of the server's body—accompanied by the weight shift—is the basis for the power of the Asian serve.

At contact, the server's body faces the target (**c**). His shoulders, arm and hand are in a line about 45 degrees to the floor.* His hand is moving fast.

The server contacts the exact center of the ball (**c**). His hand follows a line drawn through the ball's core (a diameter line). The slightest mistake puts spin on the ball.**

81a   b

The Weight Shift

The server's right hand rises, and his left hand drops as he moves into the ball (81). His shoulders reverse their angle, turning his arms like the vanes of a windmill (a, d).

The server's left foot—still pointing toward the target—steps firmly down at the beginning of his weight shift (a, b). As his weight moves forward, his front leg straightens (b, c).

At contact, the server's front leg has locked (**d**). All of his weight has moved to his front foot; only the toe of his back foot touches the floor. The left side of the server's body has stiffened. His leg, body and right arm make a vertical line (**d**). The server continues to watch the ball at contact.

Note that the server's right shoulder leads his hand (**c**). This is important in whipping the ball, discussed on the next page.

82a   b

The Whip

The server moves into the ball with a strong turn of his shoulders (82).
Before contact, the line of his arm lags that of his shoulders by about 30
centimeters (measured at his hand) (a). When the server's shoulders are nearly
facing the target, he slows their turn (b). His arm speeds up, acting like a whip.
This whipping motion adds power to the Asian serve. At contact, the server's
shoulders and arm make a straight line, square to the target (b).

83

After contact, the server's arm continues to whip, crossing the line of his shoulders (c).

The server's arm has given up a great deal of its energy to the ball at contact. It sweeps—slowly—across his body as the ball speeds away (83). The player's left foot continues to carry all of his weight at the finish of the motion. His torso is locked against his left hip. The server is balanced, ready to take his position on the court.

84

85

I. In order to start his motion efficiently, the Asian server:

    1. Points his feet 45 degrees to the right of the target, shoulder width apart
    2. Distributes his weight evenly
    3. Cradles the ball in front of his breastbone
    4. Locates his left elbow a few centimeters in front of his body
    5. Looks at the ball

II. To tee the ball in the air, the server:

    1. Raises his left hand vertically
    2. Stays in contact with the ball as long as possible
    3. Allows the ball to rise from his hand about 15 centimeters only

III. To shift his weight into the ball, the server:

    1. Transfers all of his weight to his right foot
    2. Raises his left foot
    3. Moves his left foot slightly forward, 45 degrees to the left of the target
    4. Touches his left toe lightly to the floor
    5. Points it toward the target

IV. To drive the ball with little effort, the server:

    1. Rotates his hips and shoulders into the ball
    2. Shifts his weight to his front foot
    3. Straightens his front leg
    4. Raises and whips his arm into the ball
    5. Drops his left arm

V. At contact, the server:

    1. Hits the exact center of the ball with the meat of his hand
    2. Faces the target
    3. Makes, with his serving arm and his shoulders, a line about 45 degrees to the floor
    4. Locks his front leg

THE OVERHAND SERVE

86

The overhand serve is like the Asian in many ways. The timing—from beginning to end—is exactly the same. The lift of the ball is the same. So are the step and the weight shift. The hand and wrist position does not change from the Asian nor does the contact point of the ball. The biggest difference is in the bends at the elbow and shoulder (86). These mean more effort and, therefore, greater chance for error for the overhand server.

87

88

Ready

In the ready position, the server's body is solid. He faces about 45 degrees to the right of the target (**88**). His feet are flat on the floor and slightly wider than his shoulders. His right foot points in the same direction as his body — about 45 degrees to the right of the target (**88**). His left foot points slightly to the right of the target. He carries more weight on his right foot than his left (**87**). His knees are slightly bent, his back straight.

The server locates the ball directly in front of his right shoulder (**88**). He cradles the ball in his left hand at shoulder height (**87**). His right hand rests on the back of the ball, helping him to focus. His left arm is comfortably bent. The server looks at the ball.

89

The Coil

Like the Asian serve, the overhand begins with three separate motions. The server's left hand lifts the ball, his right arm draws back and his left foot moves forward (89). These motions all start at once and also end at once.

90a   b

The Lift

The overhand server lifts the ball with a smooth vertical motion, just like the Asian server (**a, b**). His hand stays in contact with the ball as long as possible, then releases it without spin (**c**). The ball rises from his hand less than 30 centimeters—just like the Asian.

c

d

The Right Hand

The server's right hand draws away from the ball at the start of the lift (**a, b**). His elbow remains high as it leads his arm back. His arm continues to move until it is stopped by his shoulder (**c, d**). Both his upper arm and his forearm are nearly in line with the target. His palm turns slightly outward.

91a　　**b**

　　The server draws his elbow as far to the rear as possible (**a, b, c**). The player's right forearm angles slightly upward toward the ball at the end of his drawback (**c**). His arm is now coiled, ready to unfold like a whip.

　　The server arches his back *very little* during the drawback of his arm. A large arching movement interferes with both the vertical lift of the ball and a complete drawback of the player's elbow.

c

d

The Step

The server takes a light step forward during his lift of the ball (91). As he steps, his weight shifts to his right foot (a, b). The step is about 30 centimeters long and directly toward the target. His left leg is slightly bent when his foot touches down (d). His torso moves forward only slightly with the step.

92a   b

The Hit

The Body Turn

The server begins to rotate his hips and shoulders into the ball (**a, b**). His right shoulder, just like the spiker's, leads the way. His left arm moves downward and his right hand sweeps back.

98

c

d

The server's elbow rises toward the ball during his body turn (c). Like the spiker's, his elbow does not move ahead of the line of his shoulders. He does not want to uncoil his arm before he has finished his shoulder turn.

At contact, the server's body faces the target (d). His arm is bent (unlike the spiker's). A bent arm allows greater firmness at the shoulder and more control. His hand is held as if it were Asian serving—with a slight bend at the big knuckles (page 83, Fig. 80). He contacts the exact center of the ball; his wrist is firm.

The Weight Shift

As the server moves into the ball, his weight shifts from his back to his front foot (93). His front leg straightens; his body becomes increasingly firm.

His elbow rises toward the ball (a, b, c). When his elbow is in line with his ear, his arm begins to straighten (c).

100

c   d

At contact, the server's left leg carries all his weight; it is firm (**d**). His shoulders are square to the target. His forearm is vertical, with a slight bend at the elbow.

94a   b   c

The Whip

The overhand server drives his elbow toward the ball (a). His elbow slows, allowing his forearm to speed up (b). His forearm continues to speed up until contact. His arm does not straighten entirely—completing its whip— until the ball is on its way (c). By this time his arm is going slowly. Its motion has been transferred to the ball.

95

At the finish of his motion, the server carries his entire weight on his left foot; his right toe rests lightly on the floor. His right hand has followed the ball forward so that his arm angles downward. The server is perfectly balanced.

96

97

98a b

THE TOPSPIN SERVE

The spinner can be an effective serve (98). The server overpowers his opposition; even when the ball is contacted solidly by the passer, it sometimes spins away. Use of the spin serve has increased in recent years, particularly in combination with a jump.

The spin server must bend his back for power (a). This takes time and means that he must lift the ball high. The ball rises about a meter from his hand (a). As in serving the floater, the player transfers all of his weight onto his front foot as he contacts the ball (b). His left side—leg, hip and torso—is firm. Unlike in serving the floater, his arm is straight at contact (b). It is also vertical. As in spiking, the server snaps his wrist over the ball, giving it topspin. The server finishes his motion with balance.

99a   b

THE JUMP SERVE

The jump serve is a variation of the spinner (**99**). The server jumps well into his own court before contact. He is closer to and higher above his opponents than the conventional server. This means a larger target. However, the jump server, who uses a very high lift of the ball and a powerful jump, has a great chance of making an error.

The server uses the same four-step approach as in spiking. This includes a full armswing. He measures his steps so that he jumps near the baseline.

The server cradles the ball in both hands as he starts forward (**a**). He lifts it high and in front of him on his second step (his left foot). Now he continues as if he were spiking. There is one difference: he jumps as far forward as possible, landing well inside his own court (**b**).

I. In the ready position, the overhand server:

1. Faces 45 degrees to the right of the target
2. Positions his feet flat on the floor
3. Puts more weight on his back foot than his front
4. Holds the ball in front of his right shoulder

II. At the start of the motion, the server:

1. Lifts the ball straight up
2. Draws back his right elbow
3. Steps forward with his left foot

III. The server must remember, above all to:

1. Draw back his right elbow as far and as high as possible
2. Drive his right shoulder forward
3. To keep his elbow in line with — not ahead of — his shoulder turn
4. Press his left foot firmly down at contact
5. Bend his right elbow slightly at contact

CHAPTER 5: THE BLOCK

The block is a method of driving an attacked ball back into the opponents' court (100). It takes place next to the net and is volleyball's first line of defense. The blocking motion is simple and, compared to the spike, effortless. It gains strong results from staying, that is, from holding its position. The blocker's hands remain over the net—stuffing the ball—after the spiker's hand has gone. The most powerful block stems from a powerful spike.

100

101

Ready

The blocker positions his feet side-by-side, the width of his shoulders or wider (101). They are flat on the floor with his weight on the front part. He holds his hands comfortably above his shoulders, palms forward. He spreads his fingers and bends his knees slightly. His back is straight. He watches his opponents' attack as it develops.

The Block

When the player has decided it is the time and place to block, he quickly lowers his weight (**a**). His hips move backward; his back is straight. When his knees are near a right angle, he pauses, ready to jump. His face remains vertical; he does not look down or change the angle of his head.

The blocker jumps vertically (**b**). His arms straighten, firming from shoulder to fingertip. He shrugs his shoulders so that his biceps approach his head on either side. Shrugging narrows the distance between his arms. His thumbs angle up; a distance less than the ball's diameter between them keeps the ball from going through.

102a

b

c

111

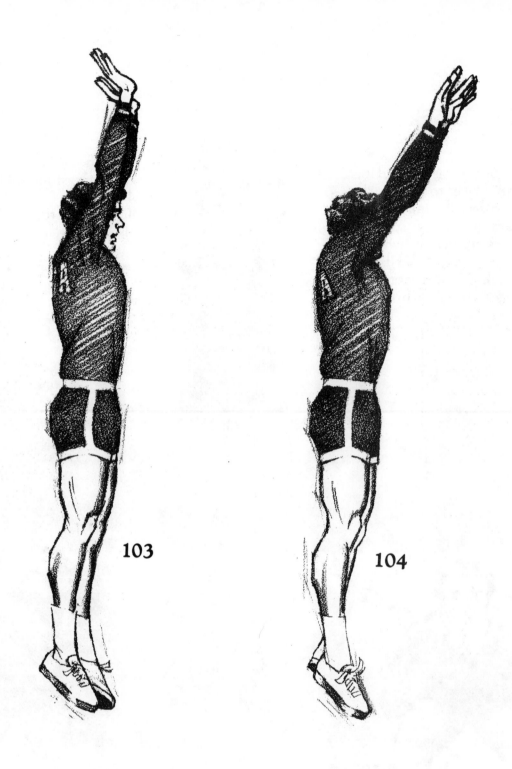

103

104

The blocker who cannot reach over the net angles his hands back (103). He *soft* blocks, that is, he deflects the ball upward so that his backcourt teammates can make an easy play.

The blocker who can reach over the net angles his arms forward as he jumps, penetrating the plane of the net (104). His torso, shoulders, arms and wrists are firm. The player bends his wrists neither forward nor back, but aligns them with his arms throughout the block.

106a   b   c

Getting to the Ball

The Side-Step

    Side-stepping is the easiest and most controlled way to move to the ball (106). The blocker faces his opponents throughout the movement. Outside blockers almost always use the side-step to adjust their position.

Cross-Over Step

Side-steps are too short for the middle blocker, who must quickly travel 10 feet or more. He needs a cross-over step. He leads with the foot nearer the blocking site and follows with his cross-over (**a, b**).

107a   b

The blocker turns his right foot toward the net as he arrives in his blocking position (**c**). This allows him to complete his turn easily (**d**). He jumps facing the net (**e**). His hands remain in front of his body, ready to slide up and over the net, throughout his movement to the ball.

c

d

e

The Spike Approach

Stopping and turning toward the net before the jump brings control. But it also keeps the blocker from using all of his forward motion to gain a higher jump. For this reason shorter middle blockers (and some outside blockers) use a spike approach. The blocker once again starts with a short step (**a**). This time he follows with a long running step and a spike armswing, keeping his side to the net (**b, c**).

108a

b

The blocker does not face the net when he jumps; rather, he angles his side toward it (**d**). He turns slowly in the air, facing his opponents at the top of his jump (**e**).

Most of the time the three steps of the spike approach bring the player into blocking position. If he must cover more distance, he adds an even number of steps to his approach: two, four or more.

c

d

e

109

CHAPTER 6:
THE BACKCOURT

110

The backcourt player must control an attacked ball that has passed his team's block. He is the last line of defense and can often save a rally. There are four defensive techniques that make his job easier. The dig allows the player to receive a hard spike. The roll, dive and collapse allow him to throw himself onto the floor to retrieve the ball. A spectacular save in the backcourt, more than any other play, can inspire a team (110).

111

THE DIG

The dig is a method of receiving a hard spike, usually with the forearms (111). The term originated, according to legend, from beach volleyball. Saving a ball meant "digging" into the sand. A dig can be made with one or both forearms.

112

113

Moving

The backcourt player wants to position himself where he thinks the ball will arrive. As his opponents' attack unfolds, he is in constant motion, trying to find just the right spot to receive the ball. He moves forward, back, left or right. He takes small steps, large ones or runs at full speed.

When his opponents attack only with soft shots, the backcourt player can keep his body high and relaxed as he moves (112). This allows him to move his feet quickly to the ball, as in receiving serve. He can cover a large section of court and still arrive under control. He is also in a good position to re-

ceive a high, off-speed shot with an overhand pass.

When his opponents hit the ball hard, the backcourt player must coil his body and spring for the ball. Springing is very quick, but less controlled than receiving the ball in a high, relaxed position. To be ready to spring, the player must lower his body during his movement (113).

A low body position not only coils the player's body for the spring but shortens his distance to the floor. This makes it easier to receive spikes hit low. The defender can still spring upward to dig a high attack.

114a   b

The Hop

The defender has lowered his body and adjusted his location on the court. He faces the attack. Now he makes one more move to obtain the greatest chance to dig a hard spike. He makes a short hop toward the attack (**a, b**). The hop helps the digger to spring or explode toward a hard hit. But it also leaves him in good position to make the other moves required to defend his area: to collapse, dive or roll.*

When the defender guards against a multiple attack, he does not know when or from what direction the spike will come. In this case he must make a hop for each possible spike, meaning a series of hops during one attack.

*The collapse, dive and roll are discussed separately from the dig. Their emphasis is in throwing oneself to the floor without pain. The emphasis in the dig is in receiving the ball, particularly when the player can stay on his feet.

The hopper lands slightly before the ball is hit (**c**). His feet are side-by-side and wider than his shoulders. His body is at its most coiled upon landing. Now he begins to uncoil (**d**). He moves his weight upward and slightly forward. He rises slowly. He has not yet started to spring, but his legs are pushing him toward the attack. He has perfect balance.

The defender who faces a quick offense, and who has multiple responsibilities, may not leave the floor to prepare for a hard spike. He descends, without hopping, in order to rise thereafter. He does so for each possible attack.

115

116

The Spring

At the instant the defender sees the attack, he makes his spring.* He can move in any direction. When he has positioned himself in the ball's path, the defender pushes upward and receives it on both forearms (115). He draws his arms toward his body. They are nearly vertical; this prevents the spiked ball—arriving with hard topspin—from jumping backward. The player thrusts his hips forward for balance as he moves upward. He does not need to clasp his hands. He does, however, press the heels of his hands together so that his arms are square.

*Occasionally the defender will not need to spring. He will have guessed perfectly the path of the attack. In this case he only needs to straighten his body and bring his forearms together. He remains still and balanced throughout his move.

117

118

When the ball has been hit outside the midline of his body, the defender would like to move in front of it (116). This allows him to see the ball well and to keep his arms square and still. But on the hardest hits, the digger does not have time to move in front of the ball. He must pivot quickly on the foot furthest from the ball as he spins his shoulders (117). This brings his arms swinging toward the path of the ball.

The player tries to keep his arms together during their swing. This gives him a controlled, two-arm contact of the ball (117). But when the ball is hit very hard, or is almost out of reach, the player's arms may split (118). The defender has less control with split arms but can move his leading arm more quickly. The digger wants to face his forearms as much as possible toward the front.

119

When the ball is hit a distance from the digger, he must take a short step toward it (**119**). He does not have time to receive the ball with both arms. He must spring with one arm extended, hoping to deflect the ball upward so that a teammate can help.

126

120

121

Emergencies

When the ball is hit near the defender's face, he must bring his hands up to protect himself. He can dig the ball with his hands up, but the contact must be very clean to avoid a foul. The quickest way is to use an open hand (**120**). The defender holds his hand palm-up. This deflects the ball upward.

Sometimes the player will have time to raise both hands (**121**). In this case he can clasp them by cupping one over the other. Contact is made on the edges of both hands. Two-handed contact is firmer than one-handed, resulting in greater control and fewer fouls.

122

Receiving the Off-Speed Attack

Not all attacks that intend to result in a hard spike do so. When the defender has determined that the ball will not be hit hard, he rises from his low posture **(122)**. This allows him once again to move his feet quickly, covering a large section of the court with control. Raising his hands puts him in position to receive a high ball with an overhand pass.

123

124

Special Contacts

When the defender is chasing a ball off the court, he must pass the ball over his shoulder. He angles his hands backward by curling or "jaying" his wrists at contact (123). He must also "jay" his wrists when he is chasing a ball toward the net or when he needs to get up a ball that has been hit at a steep angle.

When the ball is low and almost out of reach, the digger can use the "pancake." He flattens his hand firmly on the floor, allowing the ball to bounce from it (124).

The Range of the Dig

131a   b   c

The defender continues to cover the court even after he sees that the ball has been hit away from him. Now he must play rebounds from his teammates.

The defender has hopped into digging position, facing the attack (a). The ball is hit past him, for example, on his right. He has one more hop to make: a spinner toward the arrival site of the ball (b). The defender keeps his body low throughout his hop, landing in digging position (c). He is ready to receive a ball driven toward him or to run for a ball deflected off the court.

132

THE DIVE

All floor skills—the dive, the roll and the collapse—allow the defender to stretch his body horizontally without hurting himself. The dive differs from the other two in that it starts with a powerful jump—the diver flies through the air (132). The dive requires the upper body strength to do a push-up or two and is the most tiring floor skill. Men usually prefer to dive rather than to roll.

133a   **b**

The player runs toward the ball (**a**). The right-hander would like to take off with his left foot (**b**). This allows him to reach farther with his right hand. He lowers his body on the last step; he also draws back his arms in readiness for their drive toward the ball (**b**).

134

c

As he pushes off, he kicks his rear foot into the air, bringing his body horizontal (c). His back is arched, his head up. When he needs to play the ball forward or up, he makes contact with the back of one hand (c). If the ball is not too far away, he may clasp his hands and contact the ball on both forearms. This brings greater control. If he needs to hit the ball sideways or back over his shoulder, he uses his thumb and index finger together (134).

135a   b

The player's hands touch the floor (**a**). He continues to keep his head and feet up; his body forms a letter "C." He pushes with his arms, lowering his body gently to the floor. His chest touches first, followed by his stomach and then his hips. His hands push to the rear, helping him to slide (**b**). Now the diver must bring himself quickly to his feet in order to continue play.

The player can dive directly from the ready-to-dig position as well as from a run. In this case the dive acts as a recovery from a spring. (The full dive sequence is shown on pages 142 and 143.)

136

136

THE ROLL

The roll is the only method of "going to the floor" that brings the player back to her feet (136). The player's use of her momentum does the trick. She does not resist her momentum as in diving or collapsing. She simply guides it. This makes the roll the least tiring of the three floor skills. Women more often roll than dive.

137a   b

To retrieve a ball to her left, the player takes a short step toward the ball with her left foot (**a**). This starts her momentum. After a skip step, she takes a long step toward the ball (**b**).* She draws back her contact hand in readiness for its reach for the ball. Her opposite hand is held out for balance (**b**).

*She does not need a skip step when she is already running toward the ball.

c

The roller falls toward the ball (c). She allows her weight to move over and past her front foot. Her leading knee turns inward to avoid hitting the floor. She reaches toward the ball, contacting it with the heel, the back, or the thumb and index finger of her left hand.

139

138a   b

After the touch, the player slides the heel of her hand lightly along the floor, easing her body down (**a**). Her side—from her hip to her hand—touches the floor (**b**). Both knees are bent. She rolls on a diagonal line across her body—from her left hip to her right shoulder (**a, b**). Her right arm stays near her side on the floor, with her hand held palm up. This is important. If her arm or hand strays, it can resist her momentum.

c

d

The player's right knee leads her body over; the toe of her right foot touches the floor (c). Her left foot follows, still on the diagonal line. Her left arm helps to support her as she returns to her feet (c). She finishes with balance, ready for the next play (d).

139

140

142

141

The roller is not restricted to movement to the side. She can roll in any direction that she can step, including directly to the front (141).

144

142

143 a

b

c

THE COLLAPSE/SPRAWL

The collapse drops the defender quickly to the floor to receive a hard spike (**142**). It is a shortened version of the sprawl, which in its complete form includes a step and support from one arm (**143**). The collapse is used for the hardest hits but is limited to those arriving nearby; the sprawl is generally used for softer hits arriving a distance away.

In order to collapse, the defender springs forward, allowing her weight to fall (**142**). She digs the ball—preferably with both arms—as she drops. The inside of one knee touches the floor in a bent position; the other knee and leg stay straight. The player's hands and forearms break the forward fall of her upper body.

In order to make a full sprawl, the right-hander starts toward the ball with a quick right step (**a, b**). Her foot moves on a line to the right of the ball's path (**b**). She allows her weight to fall, putting her left hand down for support (**b**). Now she stretches herself toward the ball, pushing hard with her left leg (**c**). She contacts the ball on the back of her hand. Her right knee has turned outward; her left hand and right forearm support her upper body.

The Range of the Collapse

* * * * *

    The distinctions among the floor skills—dive, roll and collapse—are becoming more and more blurred. Present-day players combine the use of all three. The sprawl is shortened to the collapse, as mentioned. The roll becomes a slide when the defender does not somersault; support from one hand adds a part of the sprawl. By far the most widely used combination involves the dive and the sprawl. The defender jumps toward the ball as in diving but touches down one hand, one forearm, one knee or a combination of all three.

148

CHAPTER 7: OTHER ATTACKS

151

The spike, volleyball's most powerful shot, is the preferred attack by any player who can do it. But other attacks are useful, too. The floor spike is an easy attack for the beginning player. The dump drops a ball into the opponents' court on the second touch. The tip and chip shots each trick opponents who are expecting a hard spike. The wipe-off gives the attacker an alternative to being blocked (151).

152

THE FLOOR SPIKE

The floor spike is a method of hitting the ball into the opponents' court without a jump (152). It is like the overhand serve in all ways but two: the floor spiker must adjust her location before the hit, and she usually hits the ball with topspin (Chapter IV).

153a   b   c

Getting to the Ball

The right-handed attacker positions her feet in stride by stepping forward with her left foot (a). She points her left hand toward the ball and draws back her right elbow.

The spiker moves to the hitting spot with a series of left steps followed by skips (a, b). This allows her to arrive at the hitting spot with her left foot leading (c). The spiker bends her knees as she moves to the ball; she keeps her arms ready to hit throughout.

154a   b

The Hit

The spiker's right elbow is high at ready (a). At the start of the hit, she moves her hips and her weight forward (b). Her front foot is flat on the floor. Her hitting arm moves exactly as it would for the overhand serve or the spike (page 59).

154c

d

The spiker's shoulder and elbow drive toward the ball (c). Most of her
weight has now moved onto her front foot.

The spiker hits with a controlled wrist snap, putting topspin on the
ball. All of her weight is on her front foot at contact; her hitting arm is bent
for greater control.

155

The Finish

After the hit, the spiker's arm continues to move slowly toward the target (**155**). She finishes her motion with all her weight carried on her left leg, which is straight. She is balanced, ready for the next play.

156

157

THE TIP

The tip or dink is a soft, fingertip push of the ball from a spike approach
(156, 157). It is intended to surprise a defense that expects a hard- driven spike.
The tip is the easiest shot in volleyball.

The approach for the tip is like the spike approach in every way (Chapter III).
At the peak of the attacker's jump, she reaches as high as possible and touches
the ball with all five fingers (156). She pushes the ball softly, using her entire
arm. Her wrist and elbow move very little.

THE DUMP

The dump is a surprise tip by the setter (**158**). Since it takes place on the second instead of the third touch, it greatly changes the rhythm of a team's offense. The dump often catches the opponents off guard.

The setter jumps exactly as if she were going to make a set (**158**). She wants the ball to fall toward her forehead, as usual. She holds her hands in setting position. As the ball nears her hands, she quickly raises her left hand, turning its palm toward her opponents. She touches the side—not the bottom—of the ball; the pads of her fingers make contact. A smooth wrist flip drives the ball over the net (**158**). Her right hand does not change its position throughout the tip.

The setter wants to disguise her intentions as much as possible. Jumping whenever she is near the net helps her to confuse her opponents. Jumping even creates doubt when the setter has rotated to the back row (from which rotation she cannot legally attack a ball above the net).

158

159a

THE CHIP

The chip or spin-dink is a short attack shot that spins from the spiker's palm (159). It is harder to control than the tip, but it happens fast and looks like a spike. It is the spiker's most deceptive shot.

The approach for the chip is exactly like that for the spike. The player jumps high, arches her back and pulls her right elbow back as far as possible (a). From this position she raises her hand straight up from her shoulder (b). Her hand is rounded like the ball.

b

c

The player makes contact behind, not underneath the ball; she gets only a "piece" of it (c). This means that she can move her arm quickly upward but send the ball a short distance only. Her entire hand touches the ball: palm, fingers and thumb. Her arm continues to straighten and finally stops at full extension (c).

161a

THE WIPE-OFF

The wipe-off uses the blocker's hands. When the ball is set close to the net, the blocker has the advantage. She can reach over the net and smother the attack. But a smart attacker pushes the ball into the blocker's hands and out-of-bounds (161).

The attacker uses a spike approach and jump. Her reach for the ball can be compared to the tip: she uses all five fingers to touch the ball; she contacts it as high as possible (a). High contact gives the blocker less chance to push the ball down.

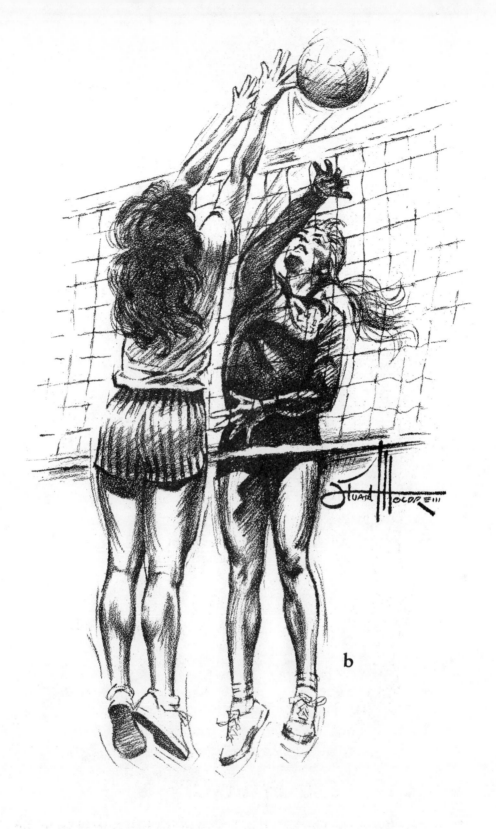

b

The attacker directs the ball toward the blocker's hand nearer the sideline (a). She pushes the ball firmly, keeping her hand on the ball. At the touch by the blocker, the attacker turns her hand and sweeps the ball out-of-bounds (b). She must be careful to withdraw her hand quickly to avoid touching the net.

SECTION II: LEARNING

How does the athlete learn a technique? Or how does he learn to move efficiently? The answer is "practice." Repetition brings improvement. But some players practice all their lives and experience little advancement in their technique. Others improve but not to the extent that their practice would warrant.

The player can learn quickly. In order to do so, he must know how his body learns, what conditions bring the fastest improvement and how to create those conditions. He must know how to practice.

CHAPTER 1: THE IDEAL

The best way to understand motor or movement learning is by imagining a player who practices and learns under ideal conditions. "Ideal" means perfect and also fanciful. No player can realize the conditions set forth.

The student is an average club player learning to spike. He practices with three elements: a demonstrator, a robot that can direct his body through the spiking motion and two of the best teams in the world.

The Demonstration

The demonstrator is one of the best spikers in the world (164). He has perfect technique; he spikes the same way every time.

The student watches from a spot that is perpendicular to the line of the demonstrator's approach. The demonstrator starts from the observer's left and hits to the observer's right. The demonstrator hits in line with his approach.

The ball is thrown to the demonstrator the same height and distance each time, 90 degrees to the line of the spike. There is no net.

The conditions eliminate anything that detracts from the clarity of the demonstration. The student sees only the spike.

The student watches the entire motion, allowing the whole to register. He pays particular attention to the rhythm. He imagines that he is inside the demonstrator's skin, that he moves as does the demonstrator. He does not pay attention to the particulars: the demonstrator's feet, for example, or his left or right arm.

164

The player wants the demonstration to impress his right brain, which deals with wholes. The right directs the player's movements when he is not thinking. In a match, for example, the player is conscious of the ball, the other players, the net, the court boundaries. He is not conscious of his movements except in the context of the game. His right brain tells his body what to do.

The player who can watch a demonstration does not apply words to the skill. He does not discuss it, read about it or analyze it. He does not send verbal messages to his body during practice. He does not recall cues. These processes utilize the left, or analytical, side of his brain, which competes with the right.

The Magic Machine

The magic machine is a robot that the student wears like a suit. It can lead the player through the movements of the perfect spike. The machine allows the player to feel the skill, that is, to watch himself. The feel, called kinesthesia, is the student's most important reference.

Consider the player learning to spike under common conditions. He deviates from his current technique and hits the ball harder. He makes a fortuitous mistake. His body feels different during the spike. He feels the unusual motion and the power that results.

The player tries to find the spike again. He attempts to duplicate its feel. Eventually he does. And again; this time it doesn't take as long. He performs the new technique frequently, then all of the time. He has learned through kinesthesia.

Kinesthesia is fine. A demonstrator performing the serve for a photographer conceded that about 25% of the serves felt perfect: he had hit the ball squarely, transferred his weight on time and maintained balance and rhythm.

Almost all of the photos looked perfect. It was difficult to differentiate one from the other. The camera had not been able to capture what the demonstrator had felt.

The player directed by the machine can attain the feel of the perfect spike either when he forgets or when his left-brain interferes. He does not have to find it through trial and error.

The Good Teams

The player joins a scrimmage between the two international-level teams. He plays his usual position. He adopts the sophisticated role, however, required by the international team's offense and defense.

The club player cannot keep up with the pace of the scrimmage. His opponents' attack develops so quickly that the ball seems to fly out of nowhere. His opponents' spikes, especially those aimed at his head, scare him. He bumps into his teammates running the offense. He cannot remember the signals. When he does have an idea of where to go, he can't arrive on time; the distance is too great. The student is flumoxxed, paralyzed by the speed of what's happening around him.

After several minutes of confusion, the game slows somewhat. The student bumps his teammates less frequently. He makes an assignment in the offense. He touches the ball.

The student transfers to a game at his usual level. He finds it slow. He has no difficulty following even the quickest plays. He finds himself more aware of what's taking place outside his area. He sees more than he had before.

The student's evolution accords with the following axiom: the athlete who confronts conditions beyond his limits extends those limits. The club player, by joining the scrimmage between the international teams, has extended his capacity to see, to organize what he sees and to react.

There are, in other sports, examples of this principle. The sprinter is pulled faster than he can run on his own. The ballerina's foot is moved by her instructor in a *battement* more rapid than she can accomplish without help. The tennis player is challenged by an opponent more skillful than he.

The difficult scrimmage is what the best teams in the world—in any sport—seek but seldom find. What team can extend them in practice? This axiom also explains why coaches attempt to duplicate match conditions in team drills, and why they espouse these drills in clinics.

165

The Perfect Clinic

The club player has two hours per day to devote to one thing: learning the spike (**165**). Once again, the three elements assist: the demonstrator, the machine and the two teams.

The student warms up with light running and pepper. In the manner described above, he watches the demonstrator perform ten spikes.

The student spikes ten balls. The conditions are the same as the demonstrator's: the ball is thrown perpendicular to the spiker's approach; the ball follows the same arc each time; the spiker approaches and hits in line.

The demonstrator spikes ten more as the student watches; the student spikes ten more. They alternate ten-and-ten until each has hit thirty. The hitting doubles as warm-up.

The student gets into the machine, which takes him through thirty spikes, the first ten at half speed, the second ten at three-quarter speed and the last ten at full speed. Each repetition includes the approach, the jump and the hit.

On the first five spikes of each ten, the student allows himself to be moved by the machine; he remains passive, concentrating on the feel of the skill. On the second five, he tries to move himself although the machine does not change its motions.

He goes to the line for ten more spikes. He recalls the feel of his movements when he was directed by the machine. He continues to watch the demonstrator between spikes.

Fifteen more in the machine, five passive and ten active, all at full speed.

The student continues to alternate the machine and the line. He increases the number of active spikes in the machine and also the difficulty of his spikes on the line. He adds a setter and a net, then a block, then a pass to the setter. He joins the game. After several rallies, he's back in the machine for three or four spikes.

He ends his work-out by scrimmaging for about twenty minutes with the better players. The first half of the scrimmage is at normal game rhythm. In the second half, a seventh player on each team starts the new rally with a quick serve after the former rally has ended.

The same plan is followed every day, with the time in the machine reduced as the skill becomes easier. The time spiking under more difficult conditions—net, block, etc.—and the time scrimmaging increase.

* * * * *

The ideal clinic forces the student, through the demonstration and the machine, to experience perfection. He sees it and he feels it. It also challenges the player to perform in increasingly difficult circumstances. It forces him to duplicate his learning with greater and greater distraction.

This interplay between the perfect and the difficult enhances learning in the real world. By adopting a similar, but practical, program, the student can maximize the effectiveness of his practice and increase the speed of his improvement.

CHAPTER 2:
AN ATTAINABLE PROGRAM

No player can reproduce the learning conditions discussed in Chapter 1. But she can learn quickly. She must bring the conditions of her practice as close to the ideal as possible.

The attainable program reflects the principles of the ideal: the demonstration, the feel or kinesthetic sense of the movement and the supranormal challenge. Attainable means that the average club or high school player can implement the exercises; and she can do so without a coach, a gymnasium or a net.

This chapter covers the pass, the set, the spike and the serve, which are the easiest to practice either alone or with a partner.

The Cost

The player must consider how much she wants to improve. There are costs connected with the learning process:

1. The player must take time from playing. Most of the exercises are controlled; the ideal practice may include two players only, each helping the other to improve.

2. The player experiences "in-between" periods during which she cannot do what she is trying to learn. Nor can she duplicate her old technique.

Most athletes have experienced the frustration of trying to change an ingrained movement. A player often gets worse before she gets better.

A high school coach, for example, had just reached the point where she could spike the ball into the court whenever she wanted. She went to a volleyball clinic and found that her foot-plant was different from the standard (her left foot went down first).

Because the coach wanted to demonstrate the spike to her players, she changed. She struggled for a year, "just one step off," before she could perform the footwork without thinking.

Other players cannot sacrifice their current performance for improvement in the future. Years later they do what their bodies found the day they stepped on the court.

The player who considers embarking on a program of improvement may wonder about the consequences of failure. If she does not succeed, will she have lost the opportunity to return to her old technique? The answer is "no."

After learning, the player has two ways to perform the technique: the old and the new. She can always return to what she had been doing. She more likely returns to the old when it is not desired. Avoiding the old is a constant fight.

Watching the Demonstration

167

The easiest part of learning a skill is watching it performed well (**167**). The demonstration registers on the player's right brain, which, in turn, directs her body.

The inexperienced player benefits the most from the demonstration. She is not locked into one way of performing. She can change and she can mimic. Her coach, furthermore, can take advantage of this. Either the coach or a skilled player can demonstrate. The demonstration works best when it occurs before the players work on the skill.

The player without a coach to demonstrate must seek a good demonstrator. The best ones play for the national teams. In the U.S.A., the student can visit the National Team Training Center in San Diego. There are also periodic exhibition tours by both the men's and the women's teams.

The best college players can serve as demonstrators. A university team may allow the observation of its practice. It also stages matches and tournaments. Recording a practice or a match allows the player to retain what she has seen.

The female does not need to confine her search for a demonstrator to other females. Nor does a male need to seek other males. The best players of either sex perform in similar ways; the degree of skill is the main factor.

The best time to watch the national team (or a college team) is during its warm-up to a match. A spot close to the court makes the players' movements immediate and visible.

In warm-up, the players perform perfectly. They are focused but relaxed; everything is easy. The match, in contrast, brings pressure that disrupts their technique. Serves force them off-balance, passes miss the target and fast sets do not allow perfect contact.

Watching the Spike

The advantage of watching during warm-up is especially true of the spike. Before the match, the players perform as if they were demonstrating for a book. During the match, they do not. They contend with the block. They fake, which means hitting away from their power. They hit imperfect sets.

In a game, the hitters pike, especially when they turn the ball right to avoid the block. The best players in the world do not pike under controlled conditions.

Watching the Set

Warm-up is also the time to watch the set. The best vantage point is close to the setter, preferably behind her.

The skilled setter's rhythm is different from most other players'. The setter waits to start her motion. Even when the ball arrives from a distance away, it seems to touch her hands before she makes the set. The setter's touch is fine. The average player cannot wait to start her motion as do the best players in the world.

168

Watching the Pass

The student benefits from seeing a demonstration of the pass. She must be aware, however, that there is a difference in technique between passing the ball back and forth and serve-receive.

In passing the ball back and forth, the player steps forward and takes a long, slow swing at the ball (**168**). In receiving serve, the player hops into the side-by-side foot position and uses a short, quick armswing.

Often the serve is so tough—even in warm-up—that it jams the passer. She falls backwards, off-balance, after making the pass. She may extend her legs, resulting in a jump away from the ball. These moves are to be avoided, not emulated.

Watching the Serve

The manner of performing the serve is the same in warm-up as in the match. In both cases, the server has complete control. The observer, however, may be able to move closer to the demonstrator during warm-up than during the match. This is a benefit.

The observer may also find it easier to register the serving motion in her memory outside of the excitement of the match. Warm-up allows the observer to watch several serves in a row.

* * * * *

How does the student maximize the benefit of her watching? She watches the whole movement and pretends that she is inside the demonstrator's skin. She tries to be aware of the rhythm. She does not focus on the parts of, or try to analyze, the skill.

Watching Oneself

The club or school player must enact—to the extent that she can—the experience offered by the magic machine (Chapter 1). In the magic machine, the student was led, at proper speed, through the skill. She could feel the motion. She then tried to duplicate the feel and, therefore, the skill on the court.

Without the machine, how does the player practice to maximize her motor learning?

The player must gain an idea of how she wants to perform. She can watch the best players in the world, attend a clinic or read a book on volleyball technique.

Finding the technique to emulate is easy. Getting the body to perform it—just once—is difficult.

The player must see herself. Perhaps she has a coach who helps her in this regard. The coach observes and tells the player what she does; the coach may also move her into position. This does in a primitive way what the magic machine did.

Most players don't have a coach, let alone one who muscles them into position. How, then, does she see herself? She takes a look.

The pass gives a good example. The player wants her arms to finish at a 45-degree angle to the floor. She takes a look after the pass. She must slow the drill or structure her practice to allow for this.

The player checks herself in a mirror. Sometimes there is a reflective surface at the practice site. Otherwise, the player watches herself before a mirror at another site, memorizes the feel and brings the memory to practice.

The mirror is especially helpful in learning the set. The player positions her hands by checking an illustration in a book and her reflection in a mirror. She observes her hands directly and memorizes their look. When she returns to practice, she can position her hands without the mirror.

The player can ask someone to watch. The observer must be told what to verify.

The player can check herself with a recording device. This offers the most accurate observation. It is not convenient, however, and can disrupt practice.

The File

The player must guide herself—in lieu of the magic machine—through the motions of a skill. In order to do this, she sends messages to her body from her left, or analytical, brain.

Sending messages means that she tries to move herself into position. She tells herself to swing her arms more quickly on the spike, to lift the ball slowly on the serve, to relax her wrists on the set or to hop into passing position.

Since her goal is to feel the perfect technique, she must adjust her practice to the lowest level of difficulty at which she can do the skill. The lowest level means the simplest or most basic form. The lowest level for the pass, for example, is performing without the ball. One level higher is performing while watching the ball, but not touching it.

Sometimes the student cannot perform the skill even in its basic form. She must divide the skill into parts. She divides the spike, for example, into the approach and the hitting arm. She practices these separately. Likewise, she raises her hands into setting position without worrying about footwork; she draws back her elbow to serve without being distracted by the lift.

Once the player performs the parts of the skill perfectly, she combines them into the whole.

Learning means an interplay between the successful and the unsuccessful performance. The player performs successfully at a low level and moves up. If she fails two or three times at the next higher level, she moves down. After reminding herself, she tries again at the higher level. This is the rhythm of the practice.

The player looks forward to advancing. She must be patient, however. It is better to spend too much time at a lower level than to advance too quickly. The player can lose what she has gained.

There is no player in the world who does not benefit from an occasional review. Coaching a clinic offers the player a chance to do this. She must demonstrate perfectly for her students. She must forget about the ball and concentrate on how her body moves.

* * * * *

The student can make a model of the learning process. The idea is "brain-to-body-to-brain." The "brain-to-body" part refers to the player's sending a message to her body. She tells it to move in a certain way.

Once the player has succeeded—and has felt the motion once—the feel registers in her brain. This is the "body-to-brain" part of the learning process.

The player can think of her successful repetition as having started a "file" in her brain. Each perfect repetition registers in the file. After enough registrations, the file directs the player's performance of the skill.

The idea of a file in the player's brain works as an incentive to perform the skill, at any level, perfectly. Every repetition means she is one step closer to performing without thinking.

Personal Practice

The player can practice the serve, the pass, the set and the spike, either by herself or with a partner. She needs a wall against which to work.

In the first practice session, described below, the player is alone; in the second, she has a partner.

A gymnasium is a benefit but not a necessity. The drills can be performed on a paved surface, on grass or on dirt. Hard-packed sand is better than soft. A net inhibits learning, especially among inexperienced players.

The player advances through as many levels of learning as the limitations allow. Included is a checklist by which she, or her partner, can evaluate her success.

169

When the Player is Alone

The player works on the serve, pass and set. If she finds a thrower, she can also spike.

The player warms up then addresses the serve. Without serving the ball, she checks her starting position. She verifies that her weight is on her back foot and that her right hand is well-positioned in relation to her body and the ball.

The player practices her lift of the ball, again without serving. She checks that she does not drop her hand before starting, that the lift is straight up and that she extends her left arm as far as possible.

The player ascertains the height of the net on the wall and finds a corresponding mark. She serves against the wall from the proper distance (169).

She notes that her elbow draws back high, that she transfers all of her weight to her front foot at contact, that her arm goes straight forward and that she ends with balance. Balance means that she can stay in her finishing position, without taking a step, for two or three seconds.

All of the foregoing practice can be checked, that is, watched by the player herself.

In order to practice the pass, the player hops into position and completes the arm-swing—without the ball (**170**). She baseball-throws the ball against the wall, passing the rebound. The best throwing distance is about five meters. The player passes the ball about halfway to the wall. These distances are comparable to the those of the serve and the pass on the court.

The player avoids passing against the wall in a series. Serial passing means a harder armswing than is appropriate for the rebound (representing the serve). Furthermore, the throw, being accurate, allows the player to position herself to pass.

The pass is one of the easiest skills for the player to check, especially with a mirror. She can note her arm position at the start and the finish, her body angle and her balance.

170

The player sets against the wall (**171**). This is efficient—lots of repetitions in a short time—but tires the neck. The player throws overhand against the wall, setting the rebound. The ball arrives faster, increasing the difficulty of the drill.

The player positions herself with a wall in front and one to her right. She throws against the front wall, turns and sets to the side. This duplicates the left-to-right turn she makes on the court. When the player positions herself six-to-seven meters from each wall, the drill is challenging.

During the player's wall practice, she checks the starting position of her hands. During the setting motion, she checks the width between her hands, the spring of her wrists and the time that her hands stay on the ball.

171

172

The player practices her spike approach (172).

From a standing position, the player hits against the floor and the wall. Facing slightly left makes it likely that her spiking arm ends on the right rather than the left of her torso.

Tossing the ball for each wall spike offers more control than hitting against the wall in a series. The player tosses the ball high (much more so than in serving) so that she has the time to bend her back, raise her left hand and draw back her elbow. Lifting the ball with both hands, rather than one, provides a more accurate toss.

What does the student check in her no-partner spiking practice? For her approach she notes that her plant to jump faces 45 degrees to the right of the target. For wall spiking, she checks that her left arm points to the ceiling and that her right arm finishes by her right side.

When the Player has a Partner

A partner offers the ideal way to practice skills. The partner not only throws the ball for passing and spiking, but she also observes. She can check the player's positions and movements more easily than the player can herself.

For the serve, the partner checks the player's starting position, the lift, the step, elbow movement and balance.

In order to observe the lift, the partner stands to the right of the server. From here she can watch the server lifting the ball vertically. Hooking the ball—flipping it backward—is apparent.

The observer determines that the server's weight does not move forward until contact and that she finishes with all of her weight on her left foot (173). Finishing with a right step shows an error in weight transfer.

173

In order to practice the pass, the partner throws from about ten feet away. She puts enough arc on the ball to give the passer time to move. She throws beside the passer. The passer watches the arrival of the ball. She hops into position and swings her arms, timing their movement with the throw. The passer does not touch the ball.

The partner throws to the receiver, who passes the ball halfway to the thrower. This duplicates the relative distances on the court. The partner increases the distance until she is at least fifteen meters away, comparable to the length of a serve.

The partner baseball-throws for accuracy; this means that the passer experiences the rhythm of the serve but does not have to chase errant balls.

174

Once the player has passed 30-40 thrown balls, the player receives serves. A good server can deliver two-thirds of her serves accurately enough that they can be passed with balance.

The player avoids concern about where her passes go; she attends to the position and movements of her body. This is the only time she has the opportunity to do this; she must make the most of it.

What does the partner check? She notes whether the passer makes a pronounced hop (**174**). Stepping is the enemy.

The partner verifies that the passer receives the ball on the midline of her body and not in front of one leg or the other. She checks the passer's balance and, more important, the quickness of the player's armswing.

To practice the set, the partner throws the ball in front of the setter, forcing her forward (175). The setter moves through the ball, as she often does in a match.

The partner checks the setter's hands in their ready-to-set position. She notes that the setter's hands are wide at the initial touch and stay wide and in contact with the ball throughout the set.

175

176

For the spike, the partner stands ninety degrees to the spiker's approach and throws high and accurate.

The partner checks the position of the spiker's feet. She tells the spiker if her body is vertical in the air, if her arms swing above her head and if the ball is located in the right position in relation to the spiker's head (176). This is especially helpful to the spiker who hits across her body, an error that reduces the spiker's range and power. Most important, she tells the spiker if she pikes.

The Challenge

The player must put herself into volleyball experiences that are beyond her capacity. The more challenged she is—to the point where she loses the skill that she had acquired in less trying circumstances—the greater the benefit.

A practice or a scrimmage with more experienced players offers an opportunity for the player to extend her limits.

The experience does not have to reproduce game conditions, however. The player or coach can design drills that are mentally and physically trying.

Players can be forced, for example, to pass a long, flat and spinless serve to their setter, then to spike the resulting set crisply into the court. As the ball is spiked, the coach serves to the next player.

When the receiver does not send a good pass to her setter, she immediately receives another serve. The serves continue until the passer is successful.

A player in this drill occasionally receives seven or eight balls in a row before producing a pass that can be set. The setter, in the meantime, tries to help her teammate by chasing and setting the errant passes.

Twenty spikes into the court by the whole team finishes the drill.

The server in this drill is also extended. Her goal is to serve hard and quickly—but also accurately. A ball more than a step or two from the receiver cannot be passed; it is a wasted chance.

In a short time, the server delivers fifty or sixty balls as hard and as accurately as possible. Serving in a match becomes easy after this experience.

Rapid-fire drills extend the player. In these, the player is forced to set or attack in a series.

The player may set twenty or thirty balls in rapid succession. She may set a series of balls that are high, spinning or arrive from afar. She may set the balls a long distance. She may set from a low or a high position, or from deep in the court (**177**).

The spiker may attack, drop back and attack again through several repetitions. Passing to the setter or chasing down a ball in the backcourt increases the difficulty. The spiker may hit a series of sets that are high and long. Or a series that starts deep in the court.

177

There are two final points to consider regarding the learning of athletic skills: the value of beginning the skill in a new way and of spacing the player's practices.

1. If the player has been performing for a long time and is trying to change habits, she must find a new way to begin the skill. If she begins the skill as she always has, her habit will continue.

   If the player's problem is a too-long armswing in passing, for example, she must bring her arms together in a new way. Bringing the arms together is usually not important, but for this passer, it initiates her problem.

   If the spiker's armswing is late, she avoids swinging her arms backward for a time. She holds them near her side as she makes her approach to hit. In this way, she avoids the old feel and creates a new one from the beginning.

2. In general, the more the player practices, the better she will be. But if her practice time is limited, she spaces her workouts uniformly. Time between workouts can be considered "clearing the mind."

   Uniform spacing also applies to the yearly schedule. If the playing season is in the fall, she attends a camp or clinic in the middle of the off-season. If the only camps are in the summer, she attends at the beginning of the summer; the least beneficial time is immediately before the season.

CHAPTER 1:
CHOICES, ACTIONS

The player has learned the skills. She performs them at full speed. She may have difficulty, however, integrating the skills into her play on the court; she may move inefficiently from one action to another; she may be unsure about which actions to use and when to use them; and she may have difficulty recognizing bad habits that arise from time to time.

The following essays address these difficulties. They include court movement in passing and setting, shot selection in spiking, trouble spots in serving and tactics in blocking.

Passing: The Wait

The good passer waits. She waits to commit her feet to a spot on the floor; she waits to commit her arms to the ball. She does not move until she has the best possible idea of the ball's path. She can make adjustments when the ball is near.

The passer who waits must also be quick. Waiting gives her less time to move. The learning player can check, and perhaps improve, her quickness in three areas: her ready position, her foot movement and her armswing.

The Ready Position

The ideal ready position allows a quick first movement (**180**). The player, despite bending at the knees and the waist, stands high more than she crouches. The emphasis is on balance and comfort.

The biggest mistake—and a frequent one among the inexperienced—is for the player to lower her body a great deal. This is both tiring and slow.

A low body is useful in digging, when the player springs for the ball. In receiving serve, however, the player is not required to spring. Her first goal is to adjust her position on the court. She must move her feet.

A low starting position requires the receiver to rise or straighten her body before she goes. If she does not rise, that is, if she moves to the ball with her body in a lowered position, she cannot fully extend her legs. She is slow.

180

Receiving the serve in tennis, where the player moves her feet first, makes the best comparison. The tennis player is not only high at the moment of the serve, but she is also heading higher. She is on the rise, already moving. This allows her to direct her momentum quickly either left or right.

Inexperienced volleyball coaches often teach a low starting position. The slower the player's natural reactions, the more likely she is to be forced to crouch at ready.

Coaches sometimes treat the player with slow reactions as if she were lazy. The coach "cures" this laziness by forcing her down. In the lower position, she must work harder. She must expend more effort to support her weight with her legs bent. The effect on her quickness is the opposite of what the coach had planned: she is either slow getting started, slow moving to the ball or both.

To check which body position is quicker, the player side-steps ten or twelve feet at full speed, first in a low position and then in a high. The player can time herself if she cannot sense the difference.

The Foot Movement

The player has taken a ready position that allows her a quick start. She must make a quick transition from her start into passing position.

An example that illustrates the passer's movement includes a hard and spinless serve arriving within a step or two of her starting position. The ball is clearly hers to pass. A serve that arrives farther away changes the rhythm of her movement somewhat, but the principles are the same.

181

182

The opponents serve. The receiver watches the ball start its flight. When she sees where the ball is heading, she adjusts her position. How? By bouncing (181). She makes a series of quick jumps, with both feet working together, toward the location the ball is heading for.

(When the ball is farther than a step or two away, the player's bounces become side-steps. These do not allow fine adjustments of position but are faster).

In bouncing, the player's feet do not stay in the air for long, nor do they stay on the floor for long. She moves her feet as quickly as she can without losing her rhythm. In this way, she can both change her location and face the ball. She maintains perfect balance.

Her series of quick bounces may lead her in more than one direction as she refines her sense of where the ball is heading. She makes as many bounces as she can.

Finally, she can adjust her position no longer. The ball is near, about half-way between her and the net. She must commit herself to a passing position.

Her last bounce takes her deeper, lowering her body into passing position (182). Her feet have remained side-by-side throughout her movement to the ball.

The rhythm is "Bounce, bounce, bounce, HOP," where the "hop" drops her into passing position. The hop takes more time because of its depth.

If she had placed her feet in stride, she would have had to do so early. She would have lost a bounce or two and the last-moment adjustments they provide.

If she had not only placed her feet in stride (page 2), but also extended her legs into the ball as well, she would have been forced to start the entire passing motion even earlier.

Doesn't the stride position give better balance? Yes, if the player is either standing on a rocking boat or moving as she makes the pass.

There is no reason to move during the pass. The bunter does not move as she contacts the ball. There is a good reason not to: the player sees the ball more clearly when her eyes are still.

The player has gotten a quick start, adjusted her location at the last moment and dropped quickly into the passing position. She is perfectly balanced, ready to move her arms into the ball.

The Armswing

The passer brings her arms together. They are slightly steeper than they will be at contact. She waits, her arms ready to pass, watching for the ball to change direction.

When the ball does change direction, she responds with a quick arm adjustment. For a serve that is moving quickly left, right, and back again, her arms move with it. She "wiggles" her arms in front of her. The arm wiggling can be used as a self-evaluation by the passer. If she never finds herself following a serve in this fashion, she is committing her arms too soon (unless her opponents never serve a spinless ball).

183

Finally, she can wait no longer. She makes a short, quick swing into the ball and stops her arms (183). The move is more of a jab than a swing.

If she had a choice, she would not move her arms at all. She would wait like the bunter, who makes fine adjustments of her bat as long as she can see the ball.

But the passer must move her arms a few centimeters into the ball, committing herself earlier than the bunter, in order to send the ball to the net.

The passer who swings her arms farther than a few centimeters, however, is committing herself too soon. She would do as well to position her feet in stride and pass the ball with leg extension.

The receiver has started quickly toward the passing site. She has dropped quickly into passing position and has moved her arms, likewise quickly, into the ball. She has given herself the greatest opportunity to pass well.

Setting: Movement

The setter overhand passes with dexterity and precision (**184**). She delivers the ball from great distances, from a jump, from the floor, from off-balance. She back-sets when her momentum is forward. Her touch is magical.

Delivery and touch, however, are only the most apparent part of the skill. Moving well on the court is the other. For the beginner, efficient movement may be the difference between setting a teammate or offering the opponents a free ball on the second touch.

The beginning or inexperienced setter has two problems: (1) she cannot overhand pass well and (2) she doesn't know how to move on the court.

The first problem requires time and thousands of repetitions of the overhand pass. The second can be solved with coaching or understanding.

The inexperienced setter's difficulty in movement begins during the serve. Like all setters, she waits at the net as the ball flies toward her teammates (**185**). She waits too long.

The beginning setter must move away from the net, toward her teammates, before the ball is passed.

Why? Inexperienced passers seldom send the ball to the net. The ball drops between the passer and the setter, near the center of the court. If the setter, waiting at the net, does not move until she sees the ball passed, she is late.

184

185

The inexperienced setter stands at the net when a teammate passes. The ball arcs toward the three-meter line. The setter sees where the ball is heading and rushes to it. She takes a direct route and arrives with her back to the net (186). Her momentum is toward the baseline. She has only one choice, a long and dangerous backset. Usually she abandons setting in favor of forearm passing the ball over the net.

When receiving the ball from poor passers, the setter must move as the serve flies toward her receivers. She determines which player in the W will pass and adjusts her arrival position.

In general, the setter side-steps or runs to a position one third to one half of the distance between the passer and the passer's target. (187, 188, 189, 190, 191). She does not go directly. She takes a roundabout route, a big C, so that she arrives facing the spot where her attacker will be set.

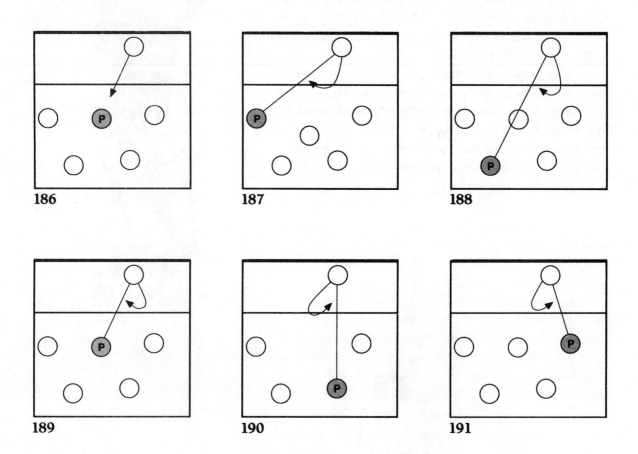

186   187   188

189   190   191

Now there are three possibilities:

1. The ball is passed nearly straight up so that, in order to make the set, the setter needs to continue her retreat from the net. She calls "help" and lets a teammate set.

2. The ball is passed near the waiting setter, in which case she sets the outside hitter as planned.

3. The ball is passed well; it arcs toward the net. The setter side-steps toward the net and sets with her momentum moving toward the hitter.

This is volleyball at its most primitive. Setters at all levels, however, make such moves at times.

What happens as the team improves and a greater number of its passes arrive near the net? The setter does not deepen as much. When a poor passer receives serve, however, the setter moves deep into the court. This insures at least a release set.

The setter may have a receiver who consistently passes well. For this receiver, she remains at the net, giving herself the opportunity to set hitters other than left-front.

Even the good passer gets in trouble. She is jammed by a hard serve, takes a ball in a teammate's area or runs forward to pass a short serve. The setter must make a decision: do I stay or go?

This is a question of reading (Chapter 2). All setters are forced to read at one time or another. The only person who can answer the question of where to go is the setter herself.

As the team gets better, its setter stays at the net, anticipating a pass that allows her to set three hitters. She faces her teammates and rotates her body from left to right as she sets (**192**). This is the same turn that she made as a beginner in taking a roundabout route to her setting spot. Now the turn is compact, occurring as she sets the ball.

192

The setter's facing her passers and turning offers the setter four advantages:

1. She can see all her passers.

2. She can orient herself so that the passed ball flies toward the midline of her body, where she can see it best.

3. She can watch her spikers' approach to hit as the pass arcs toward her. She senses their location and speed and, therefore, can time her set.

4. The body rotation conserves time. She waits at the net for the perfect pass and, if it doesn't come, she runs to the errant pass and turns toward her release hitter.

The rotation during setting has three disadvantages, however, all related to handling the ball:

1. The movement itself—a quick turn—is disorienting.

2. The setter's hands do not work in the same way. Her left hand moves in a greater arc than her right; it exerts more pressure on the ball.

3. The setter often cannot square her body with the net.

(It is important to note that the setter always wants to square herself with the net. This is the only position from which she can both set and see the opposing middle blocker, whose movements, up, left and right, may determine to which spiker she sets.)

One more point: some setters hold up their right hand while waiting for the pass "as a target for the passers." This hurts.

The passers don't need any more target than that provided by the setter's body. If they pass well enough to differentiate between a few centimeters, then they can aim for the setter's forehead.

More important, this levitating arm slows the setter's movement unless she pulls it down. Holding the arm up and then pulling it down is an unnecessary and distracting movement.

Spiking: Shot Selection

Spiking is difficult. The attacker must not only hit the ball squarely in mid-jump but also must avoid opponents who are trying to stuff the ball into his face (**193**). How does the attacker evolve from merely hitting the ball into the court to choosing the right shot?

The answer lies in following the learning player from one degree of skill to the next, as his attacking skill and his vision improve.

(The shots to be discussed exclude the tip, which, as volleyball's easiest shot, is regarded as part of every player's arsenal.)

193

The learning player is a left-side spiker who hits the ball into the court most of the time. He follows the play, gets into position to hit and spikes the ball. He is blocked.

The spiker has used all his mental or visual capacity in watching the ball and hitting it squarely. During his spike, he sees only the ball.

At this point the spiker must play more matches, expanding his ability to organize what he sees.

Once the spiker has capacity to spare, he can decide where he intends to hit before the play begins. This takes the form of hitting the line once in a while, especially after the player has determined that his opponents are leaving the line open.

The rookie's first hit down the line in competition always follows a decision made before the ball is served (except for accidents). This is not deceptive since the spiker usually makes his approach in the direction he plans to hit. It does, however, bring another shot to the attention of the blockers.

Another way for the spiker to mix his shots is to "hit the ball that is set." In other words, he hits the angle on inside and perfect sets, the line on those set outside. This decreases the likelihood of getting blocked.

("Hitting the ball that has been set" does not work for the set that arrives outside of the antenna. It must be hit on the angle; the line offers no space. The spiker can adjust to this condition.)

The spiker cannot train himself to advance to the next stage, that is, to see the block. He can, however, assure that his spiking technique allows him to face his target.

Some spikers hit across their body, that is, they face right and hit left. No matter how long these spikers play, the block never comes into view. This is not a deficiency in organizing what they see; they are looking away from the block when they hit.

In general, the spiker must face the direction he hits (194). This not only offers the most power but allows the player to see the court before, during and after his hit.

194

The spiker's first view of the block cannot be described. One match he sees nothing but the ball; the next match his vision includes the movement of the players in front of him. This usually occurs in the middle of a tournament or match, when the player is processing information well.

The player's vision of the action is not consistent from one day—or one tournament—to another. It rises and falls in clarity as does the player's ability to do the other things required to perform well, that is, to pass, set, hit and play defense.

Once the player begins to see the block, his opportunities increase.

One of the easiest ways for the attacker to keep two shots (line and angle) in mind during competition is to approach the angle but think, "I'm going to hit the line."

The spiker has two possibilities. If the outside blocker has given him the line, he can do what he is thinking, that is, turn and hit the line. If the line is closed, he can hit the angle, the direction of his approach.

As the player's vision of the court increases with play, he refines his choices. He sees not only the positions of the blockers, but their edges, meaning their arms and hands. He also sees the blockers sooner, which gives him time to judge their eventual position.

Now he can retain the option of hitting the line, adding the possibility of using the blocker who is not covering the line well. He aims at the blocker's outside hand. A hit off the blocker's hand means a point by deflection; a miss means an unobstructed line shot.

The angle brings more interesting possibilities.

The spiker watching the middle blocker can work the angle with three main shots. He bases his choice on the middle blocker's mistakes. The middle blocker may overrun the outside blocker, arrive late, form a block that is not square or fail to reach over the net.

When the middle blocker crowds his outside hitter, a common mistake, the outside hitter cuts just inside the middle blocker's hands. The spiker may include the edge of the middle blocker—his inside arm or hand—in the target. If the middle blocker likes to sweep his arms to the inside, the hitter must allow for this.

When the middle blocker is late, the attacker spikes just inside the outside blocker's hands, gaining a large part of the court as a target. Once again, he must be aware of the outside blocker's sweeping his arms toward the center of the court.

When the middle blocker does not square his hands to the net, or does not reach over the net, the spiker can hit right at the middle blocker. This likely leads to a blocking error.

All of these attacks benefit from the spiker's hitting the ball as high over the net or as deep into the opponents' court as possible.

OUT-OF-BOUNDS

IN-BOUNDS

195

A high or deep ball is not spectacular but conservative. A mistake by the spiker leads to a deflection from the top of the blockers' hands. Sometimes these result in a point; other times they are saved by the opposing diggers. They are almost never stuffed, resulting in a lost rally, by opposing blockers.

A spike on a sharp downward angle is dangerous. Sometimes it results in a spectacular point; other times it is stuffed.

A deep set can be a problem when the block is well-formed. The target is bounded on the lower side by the blockers' hands and on the upper side by the opponents' baseline (195). The spiker must squeeze the ball into this area.

The player expands the target by including the top half of the blocker's hands. Anything hit this high deflects from the blocker's hands and, at the least, disrupts the backcourt player's digging rhythm. It may gain a point out-of-bounds.

Once the hitter has considered the top of the blocker's hands, he needs to concentrate on the back line. With experience, he can sense its location surprisingly well.

Hitting directly toward the corner of the court increases the upper limit of the target. Now the spiker has a free zone in which to hit, bounded by the middle of the blocker's hands and the back court line.

This leads to an auxiliary point. The soft spike for deep sets is one of the most underrated shots in the game. There are two ways in which the spiker can benefit from this shot:

1. If the spiker takes what appears to be both an aggressive approach and jump, he freezes the backcourt players in their digging, that is, low stances. They cannot move their feet quickly.

2. The spiker who has a good sense of the court can place the ball close to the line. Diggers often do not make a play, thinking the ball is out.

When the attacker decides to soft-spike, he focuses his attention on the back line. He forgets about the block and the net. Neither of these presents a problem; his spike, having some arc, ought to go over both.

The hitter who soft-spikes must forget about a fake that involves turning away from the angle of his approach. A rotation fake reduces his ability to imagine the opponents' baseline.

Serving: Three Trouble Spots

It is not unusual for players and coaches to overlook serving technique. Serving is one of the easiest skills in volleyball; most players, even beginners, can serve into the court.

Players and coaches seldom accord serving practice as much attention as the other skills. Yet the serve represents an attack. A hard, spinless serve scores points and disrupts an opponent's offense.

There are three trouble spots in serving technique: the server does not lift the ball precisely; he does not step in a way that maximizes his whip; and he does not position his contact hand in a way that lends control.

The Lift

The lift in serving is more important than it would seem (196). It tees the ball for the team's first attack of the rally. The server would like to tee the ball as deliberately and as precisely as the golfer tees his ball. Or he would like to lift the volleyball with the same care as the punter releases the football.

How does the server lift the ball precisely? First, he takes his time. After positioning himself behind the back line, he quiets his body and his mind, checks his opponents' serve-receive formation and focuses on the ball.

Second, he takes a starting position that, from the beginning of the lift to the end of the serve, requires him to move the minimum amount possible. Every extra motion brings a chance of error.

196

The player positions his lifting hand exactly under the ball, about shoulder height (197). Holding the hand lower, a common mistake, means that the hand travels farther and faster than necessary.

The player's left hand does not squeeze the ball but cradles it. His entire hand touches the ball: his palm, the length of his fingers and his thumbs. The sense of control originates from the pads of the fingers and the pad of the thumb surrounding the ball.

The server wants the ball to be stable within his left hand without help from his right. To test this, he removes his right hand from the ball and moves his left hand in any direction; the ball remains in place.

197

The player's right hand rests lightly behind the ball (197). The right hand adds stability to the ball but does not change its position on the server's left hand. A server who forgets that the ball rests on his left hand often evolves into holding—and then lifting—the ball with both hands. This is not precise. If the right hand is removed, the ball must not fall or even move.

There is a benefit from starting the serve with both hands on the ball: it allows the player to concentrate, to focus on the ball.

Both hands on the ball also help in timing. The player starts his serve by moving three things: his left hand up, his right hand back and his left foot forward. Each part moves at a comparable speed and rhythm.

When the server starts with his right hand separated from the ball, he must move his lifting arm before his serving arm. With the right arm ready to serve, there is a temptation to rush the lift.

Separation leads to another problem. The right hand, already drawn back, must move quickly once the ball is in the air. Starting the movement of the right arm gradually, in rhythm with the lift, is smoother.

The server positions the ball directly in front of his right shoulder with his left elbow bent. When the ball is lifted straight up, it is "teed" so that, once the server has taken his step, it is slightly forward of his right shoulder (198).

The lift is slow and as smooth as the server can make it. The server's hand stays in contact with the ball as long as possible. His lifting arm finishes straight (198). The lift reduces the time that the ball is in the air, out of his control.

The player attempts to lift the ball as a machine would, the same every time. The benefit from this precision cannot be overestimated. The player can now move his serving arm forward as he does the lift: the same every time.

The ball seems to freeze in the air. The alternative can be compared to swinging at a golf ball that is suspended and blowing in the wind.

198

What are the common mistakes in the lift?

1. The server does not move with deliberation. He steps to the back line, bounces the ball two or three times and throws. He does not quiet his body or settle the ball into his lifting hand.

2. The server allows the ball to spend too much time in the air. Starting with the ball too low, or lowering it immediately before lifting, leads to a quicker, and often higher, lift. So does positioning the ball too far forward. An extended lifting arm does not give the leverage that a bent elbow does. The server lowers his hand before raising it.

3. The server lets the ball leave his hand before his arm is fully extended, which means less control.

4. The server pauses after drawing back his right hand. The throw must be high.

5. The server hooks the ball with his fingertips. The resulting lift does not rise vertically but arcs toward the server.

The Step

The server wants to whip his body, that is, to speed up and then slow his torso, shoulder, elbow and hand in succession. The step starts the process by accelerating and slowing the player's torso.

The server who steps well can shift his weight at the moment of contact. His foot descends and his weight transfers at once. This shifting of the player's weight firms his body and provides the basis for its whip.

When the server starts the weight shift before contact, he cannot finish it decisively. The shift unravels slowly, dissipating power. The player is out-of-balance.

What are the actions of the player who does not step and shift his weight well?

1. The server tips his torso and his weight forward. His torso and his hips do not align vertically.

2. The server needs both feet on the floor for balance. He cannot lift one or the other from the floor without falling.

3. The server's left heel does not touch the floor. Or his heel touches and then rises. In either case, he finishes his motion teetering on his left toe.

4. The server follows his motion with a right step. The server usually steps forward but may step right or back.

5. The server does not contact the ball squarely; his hand does not slow after contact.

199   200   201

The player who shifts his weight well maintains perfect balance throughout his serve. His torso aligns with his hips (**199, 200, 201**).

The player can stand on his right foot, without falling, before shifting his weight; he can stand on his left, without falling, after shifting his weight (**199, 201**).

The Contact Hand

The server wants to contact the ball with as much flat hand-area as possible. The greater the flat hand-area, the greater the control.

A common mistake is straightening the hand from the wrist through the fingers. This means that the contact surface is the heel of the hand, the equivalent of a straight line.

Bending the hand at the big knuckles allows not only the heel of the hand to contact the ball but a portion of the edge of the hand and the fleshy area below the thumb as well (**202**). The straight line of the heel has become a "U." The U lends control and stability to the contact as a tripod does to the camera.

The player can press his hand on a flat surface, such as a table, to experiment with hand positions. First, he straightens his hand, aligns it with his wrist and presses it onto the table. He notes what parts of his hand touch the table. Next, he bends his hand at the big knuckles and presses it down, again noting what parts touch the table.

Touching the table reveals the flat hand-area. In serving, the ball compresses and enfolds the player's hand. The contact area is greater.

202

Blocking: Increase the Odds

The blocker faces poor odds. The best blockers win rallies less than 10% of the time. Said in the converse, the spiker wins more than 90% of his confrontations with the block.

There are two reasons for the blocker's odds. First, he can't wait; he must commit himself before the spiker (a later jump notwithstanding). The first to commit in athletics loses. Second, the blocker cannot protect the entire court, even when he blocks with a teammate. The best-formed block leaves space around and above it. The spiker with a perfect set can hit away from the block.

So why block? The block reduces the spiker's range. The spiker must be aware of the block and include it in his plans; he may be forced to use an undesirable shot. Furthermore, the blocker's opposition is immediate and formidable. He presides over the net. He may contact the spiker. When the blocker stuffs the ball, he dominates. The spiker may feel as if the building has fallen on him.

The alternative to blocking—digging with four or five players— holds little chance of success. Skilled attackers hit the ball hard and steep. Backcourt players cannot stop them.

Despite the poor odds, the player can assure that his block has a positive effect. He can block well, which means that his technique, timing and tactics are sound.

Technique

The blocker who faces the spiker one-on-one offers the best illustration of blocking proficiency (**203**). The blocker positions himself close to the net. He keeps his hands and arms less than the ball's diameter from the net during his jump and block (**203**). This insures that the ball will not fall between himself and the net.

The blocker's hands are small compared to the area to be protected. The blocker increases the protected area by reaching into the opponents' court (**203**). This is often called *penetrating* the plane of the net; it is one of the blocker's greatest benefits.

The blocker who cannot penetrate the net because of either height or jump deficiencies *soft* blocks (**204**). The soft-blocker angles his hands backward. He points the palms of his hands toward the spiker's contact point with the ball. He tries to slow the spike so that a backcourt player can control the ball.

Soft-blocking does not result in immediate points or side-outs. It has three advantages, however. (1) By presenting a flat hand toward the ball, the blocker protects a greater area of the court than in attack (penetrating) blocking. (2) The upward angle of the soft-block reduces deflection errors by keeping the ball in the air longer. (3) Soft-blocking, by sustaining its backward hand angle, minimizes the effect of the blocker's mistimed jumps. The blocker can deflect the ball both before and after the peak of his jump.

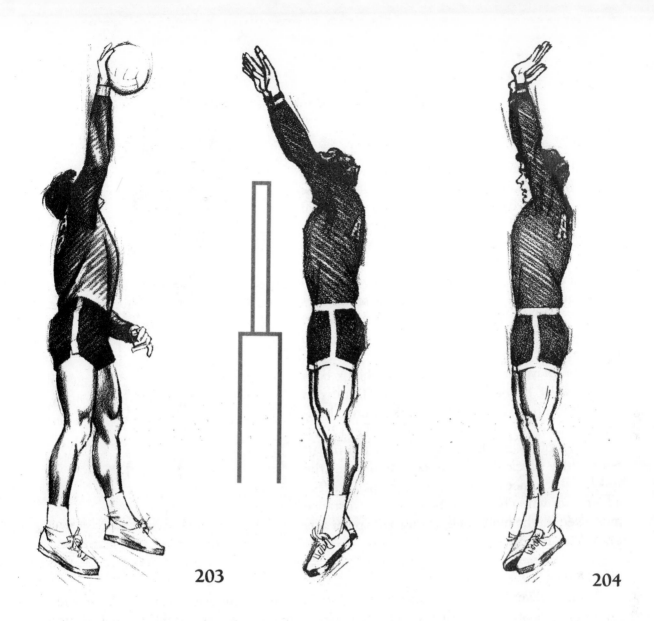

203

204

Timing

The blocker must time his jump in order to intercept the ball without mistake. He bases his timing on the depth of the set.

For a set near the plane of the net, the blocker jumps a micro-second later than the spiker. For a set that falls one-half meter from the net, the blocker jumps as the spiker's hitting arm goes back.

For a set that falls one meter from the net, the blocker jumps as the spiker's hitting arm moves forward, that is, into the ball. For a deep set, the blocker jumps after the spiker has contacted the ball.

Tactics

The blocker positions himself in line with the hitter's approach and attack. He watches the hitter, not the ball. The blocker's most frequent mistake is the failure to avert his eyes from the ball, according to one U.S. Volleyball Association expert.

When does the blocker avert his eyes from the set and watch the spiker? When the set reaches its peak. After the peak, he reads the hitter. (Chapter 2 contains a discussion of reading the opponents.)

The player tall enough to attack-block does so whenever he has positioned himself and can time his jump.* When he has not positioned himself perfectly, he reaches toward the spiker (205).

The blocker who has positioned himself poorly may block. His presence may distract the spiker. His chances of intercepting the ball are few. The player who chooses to block in this instance must execute the block well, in case the spiker hits toward his hands.

205

The blocker in poor position may soft-block, which reduces errors. Does the out-of-position blocker benefit the backcourt players by protecting a section of the court? Perhaps. A blocker may intercept an errant attack to win the rally, as mentioned. Most of the time, an attack toward the well-out-of-position blocker lacks power. On these attacks the blocker can mistime his jump and deflect the ball to the floor. The blocker makes a greater contribution by staying down and allowing the backcourt to play the ball.

* * * * *

The blocker attack-blocks when the set is near the net. Against an opponent who likes to hit the ball off the block and out of bounds, the blocker may withdraw his hands at the last moment.

*On quick sets, the reading middle-blocker may not jump. He bases his decision on where he expects the set to be delivered. See Section IV, Chapter 6 on read blocking.

The Outside Blocker

The team's defensive strategy determines whether the outside blocker positions himself near the sideline, near the center of the court or between the two. He adjusts his position with side-steps (206).

In blocking, the outside angles his hands toward the interior of the court. This is called blocking *outside-in*. The palm of the blocker's outside hand angles inward. This reduces the area protected by the block, but ensures that the blocker does not deflect the ball out of bounds with a solid contact. The ideal inward angle is slight.

The team's plan determines whether the outside blocker protects the line or the angle. In protecting the line, the blocker positions his inside hand in front of the ball. In protecting the angle, the blocker positions his outside hand in front of the ball.

When the outside blocker has not positioned himself perfectly, he reaches in the direction of the attack. The blocker reaches toward the sideline only if his hands penetrate the net and do not face out of bounds.

206

The Middle-Blocker

The middle-blocker either *commits to* or *reads* the quick attack. In committing, he jumps with the quick hitter and tries to stuff the attack. In reading, he tries to discover, from watching the setter, where the ball will be set. He wants to stop the middle attack without losing the possibility of blocking near the sideline.

The commit-blocker jumps high. He attack-blocks, that is, he reaches over the net to stuff the ball. When the set goes outside, the commit-blocker usually does not have the time to form a double-block with his teammate.

The read-blocker neither jumps high nor attack-blocks—unless he thinks that the quick hit is imminent. He jumps low and soft-blocks. When the set flies to the sideline he closes with the outside blocker.

Closing means that the middle blocks near enough to his teammate so that the spiker must go around or over the blockers' four hands (207). The distance the middle-blocker travels depends on the outside-blocker's location. The middle plants his outside foot 10-15 centimeters from his teammate's inside foot. He jumps vertically so that he does not drift into his teammate.

207

Like the outside-blocker, the middle transfers his vision to the spiker as the set peaks.

The middle who is late joining his teammate on the outside reaches to close the gap. If he is later, he soft-blocks. If he is still later, he reaches with one hand. If he is too late to reach with one hand, he covers the tip.

When the middle sees that the opposing outside hitter will angle the attack inside the block, the middle reaches toward the inside. He may do so either with his inside hand or with both hands. It is not unusual for the outside-blocker to reach toward the center of the court in concert with the middle.

Occasionally the middle blocks a high set near the center of the net. When the blocker confronts the spiker one-on-one, the blocker may spread his arms. He tries to stop the spike angled either left or right because most experienced hitters do not hit straight-ahead.

CHAPTER 2: THE READ

208

The world class back-court player is a whirlwind of movement as her opponents' attack unfolds (**208**). She is bent over, making a multitude of quick steps. First she moves forward, then back, then left, then into a small hop and spring as the ball is spiked. What is she doing?

She is reading. She is watching her opponents' attack, deciding where the ball and, in turn, she will go.

She makes these decisions before the ball has been attacked by her opponents, that is, without perfect knowledge. She makes a series of fast, informed guesses.

For many players, reading is the most fun part of volleyball. Its nature is uncertainty; it offers a continual challenge to the thinking player.

The longer the defender plays the game, the better she becomes at discerning what will happen before it does. The experienced reader may find herself saying, "If I had seen that rebound twice before, I would have known what spot to cover."

The reader responds to a probability, a likelihood that something is going to happen. The probability is based on elimination. A poor pass, for example, eliminates a set to the middle hitter, making a set to the right-hitter likely. A set outside the antenna eliminates the line shot, making a sharply angled shot likely. As each micro-second of the play goes by, the reader eliminates certain events and concentrates on others. She improves her chances of making the play.

The player reads her opponents, her teammates and the ball itself.

The Opponents

The defender begins reading before the serve. She checks the number of hitters in the front row, the height of the blockers, and who is switching where.

The more challenging reading, however, begins with the serve. The defender, by watching the opponents' set, the angle of the spiker's approach and other clues, gains a picture of where the attack will arrive. She positions herself accordingly.

The best way to follow the process is by considering one defender. Right-back in a perimeter defense is a good example; she has multiple responsibilities (**209**). Once right-back's decisions are clear, the process can be applied to all backcourt players.

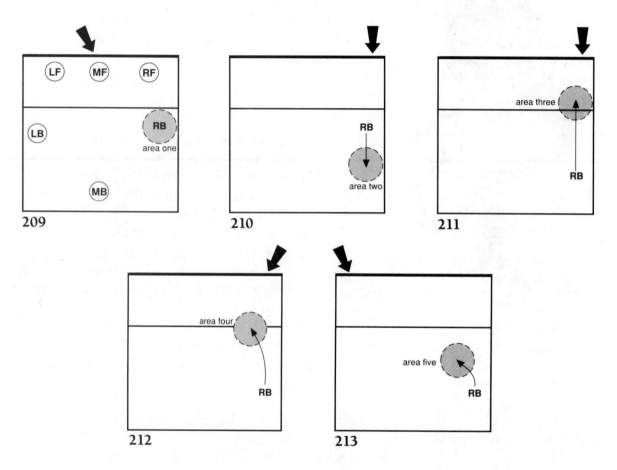

209   210   211

212   213

Right-back in a perimeter defense must cover a quick attack, a line spike, a line tip, a crosscourt attack from the left sideline and, perhaps, an angled chip from the right sideline.

Her movements follow a forward-back-forward pattern that may include adjustments along the way. She starts near the right sideline, about one meter deeper than the attack line, "area one" (**209**). She faces the opposing quick attack.

For an attack by the right hitter, the right-back deepens, positioning herself about three meters from the baseline, "area two" (**210**). She moves forward again to a position either behind her blocking teammates, "area three" (**211**), or toward the interior of the court, "area four" (**212**).

For a crosscourt attack by the left hitter, the right moves a few steps forward and toward the interior of the court, "area five" (**213**). She faces the hitter.

Right's goal is to eliminate from consideration the attacks that are impossible or unlikely. This is easy when her opponents make a big mistake. It is less easy when her opponents make a small mistake and impossible when they make no mistake.

The reads can be divided into the poor pass, the poor set, the right attacker, the setter, the quick attack, the play-set and the left attacker.

The Poor Pass

A pass beyond the court's boundaries eliminates the possibility of a hard spike along the net. The right-back moves into her spot in the free ball formation. (Section IV, Chapter 2 contains a discussion of the standard W free ball formation.)

A pass straight up eliminates anything but a high set by an opposing backcourt player. The set flies to the right- or left-front hitter. The defender retreats to area two (**210**).

A pass two-to-three meters from the net—but handled by the setter—likely eliminates a middle and left attack. Again the right-back retreats. The designated setter sets quicker than the back-row setter, so the defender moves quickly.

The Poor Set

The poor passes described above result in sets that usually fly to the opposing right hitter. The right-back positions herself in area two (**210**). She reads.

A deep set often means that the attacker soft spikes crosscourt or shoots the ball in the same direction. The defender rises from her digging position, ready to move.

A tight set leads to tips, since the hitter's alternative is to be blocked. The right-back has tip responsibility; she must move to the expected landing site during the set (**211**). If she waits until the ball has been touched, she is late: a well-tipped ball falls quickly to the floor.

A set that draws the outside hitter toward the center of the court eliminates a line shot. Even a straight-ahead attack, 90 degrees to the net, is unlikely since the hitter usually faces a well-formed block. The defender drifts toward area four (**212**). If the inside set is deep, the attacker usually soft-spikes or hits off the block. If the set is not deep, a tip in the middle or on the line is probable. The right-back moves before the ball has been touched by the attacker, watching for the soft spike, the carom off the block or the tip.

A set outside the antenna eliminates a spike down the line and probably, because of the distance, a tip. The likely shot is a spike to the opposite corner; the spiker wants to use the court's depth. The defender moves forward, facing inward (**212**).

A set both outside the antenna and close to the net brings only one possibility: a sharply angled, crosscourt spike. The right moves to the attack-line and watches for a carom off the block. It often falls near to the center of the court (**212**).

The Right Attacker

The setter delivers the ball to the right hitter and the defender moves to area two (**214**). The set is perfect, meaning that the defender cannot eliminate shots on the basis of the set. She turns her attention to the spiker.

The defender watches the spiker's entire motion. This includes, in order, the direction of the spiker's approach, the line of her body, the rise of her arm and the movement of her hand (**215**).

The spiker who makes a mistake in her approach cannot deliver a hard spike. The most common mistakes are an early arrival or an arrival in which the set falls behind the spiker. In either case, the attacker soft-spikes or delivers a free ball. The digger rises, ready to move.

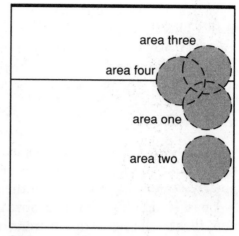

214

The spiker who approaches without error almost always attacks in the direction of her approach. When she does not, she turns her body to attack, usually from an angled approach to a line shot. She may approach the line and hit the angle, but this is uncommon; it costs power.

The line of approach is the reader's most useful clue. When the spiker approaches parallel with the sideline, she almost always attacks the line, that is, toward the right-back. The defender readies herself for a hard spike.

When the spiker approaches the angle, as she usually does, she can turn and hit the line. The following rule governs her change: the farther the spiker moves toward contact, the more difficult for her to change.

All attackers commit themselves; some do during their approach, others at the time of their jump. The best do not commit themselves until their arm moves into the ball. The defender considers each attacker and assesses her skill and range.

The defender fixes on the angle-approaching attacker, whose commitment to the angle increases throughout her motion. The defender rises and moves smoothly from area two to area four as the commitment increases (**214**).

The defender who concludes that an angled attack is certain moves directly to area four. She faces the interior of the court. She attends caroms from the block, particularly those that dribble into area three or four (**214**).

The experienced spiker may not turn in order to attack away from the line of her approach. She may change the movement of her spiking arm. This is more deceptive, that is, more difficult to read. The spike, however, does not travel as fast.

215

The defender sees two changes from the spiker's conventional swing: a hit directed across the spiker's body to the defender's right and a shot turned to the defender's left.

The clue to an imminent across-the-body spike is the position of the set in relation to the spiker's shoulder. A set arriving on the right (as the defender sees it) of the spiker's shoulder can easily be spiked right.

The opposite is true for a ball that is likely to be hit to the defender's left. On this shot, the spiker's arm sweeps over her head before contact.

An on-hand spike of a fast, horizontal set is likely to be hit to the defender's left if the spiker swings early, which is typical. It is likely to be hit to the defender's right if the spiker swings late. The results are the opposite for an off-hand spike.

If the spiker lowers her elbow, she has begun to chip (215). Raising her hand without lowering her elbow means she will tip.

The defender who allows her concentration to rise from the spiker's arm to the spiker's hand has an advantage over the defender who cannot do this. She may gain a lean toward the attack. Sometimes this is enough.

The Setter

A pass that arrives within a meter of the net means that the setter can use three attackers. The defender may eliminate one or two hitters by reading the setter who telegraphs her sets.

The setter most often gives away her back-set:

1. She may receive the ball high or far back.

2. She may lean or begin her tilt early.

3. She may place her feet farther under the ball in receiving the pass.

For setting outside, the setter may bend and straighten her legs more than usual. For setting the middle, particularly the quicker sets, the telegraphing player often stiffens her body before receiving the pass.

The Quick Attack

When the pass is high and forces the setter into the net, a one-handed, quick set to the middle hitter is probable. This is especially true for a setter who is too late to receive the ball with a balanced jump-set. The defender faces the middle-hitter in area one.

When the pass is perfect and the setter does not telegraph her sets, the defender can eliminate nothing. She expects all possible attacks.

The defender positions herself in area one. She readies herself to receive a quick attack from the opposing middle. The most dangerous quick set arrives between the setter and the right sideline. This ball is attacked from a short distance away and likely heads directly toward her.

The quick attack to the immediate right of the setter is likely hit to the defender's left, in accord with the direction of the middle-hitter's approach. The quick attack to the immediate left of the setter, however, is likely turned back to the defender's right. The middle-hitter has more in-bounds space on the right. Furthermore, the middle-hitter may face two blockers on the left; she turns the ball away from them.

The defender facing the quick attack from area one digs any ball hit on, or to the left of, her midline. The ball to her right is out of bounds.

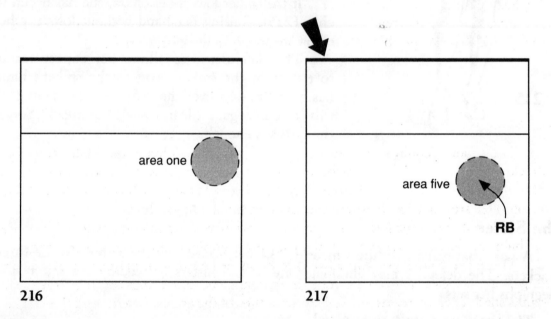

216   217

The Play Set

The defender remains in area one (216) for a play-set near the center of the net. The spiker's approach may limit her range of attack. The defender adjusts. Sometimes the set draws the hitter either left or right, away from her expected attack-point. In this case, the set is likely attacked in the direction that it draws the attacker: a set on the left is hit left, a set on the right, right.

The defender facing a play-set hitter who has a perfect set and an entire range of attack must hold her position in area one. As with the quick attack, she digs the ball arriving to her left and allows the ball to her right to fly out of bounds.

214

The Left Attacker

The left attacker usually directs the ball cross-court. The defender moves two–three meters forward and toward the interior of the court. She faces the attack in area five (**217**).

The left attacker approaches parallel with the sideline, giving herself the opportunity to hit the line. She rotates her body to hit the angle. The left who approaches on the angle almost certainly hits in the same direction; turning away from the angle is difficult.

* * * * *

The defender considers her teammate/blockers, whose movements may change her plans. No-block, for example, may mean that the backcourt player stays in a deep position even though the set is tight. The attacker probably spikes regardless of where the set arrives.

No-block may mean that the defender protects herself. The right-back, for example, positions herself in area one. When the opponent attacks between the setter and the right sideline, the right-back is near the attack. A consistently late-arriving middle-blocker in this instance can be unsettling to the defender.

A tall blocker who reaches deep into the opponents' court may cause more tips than an average blocker. A split block may require an adjustment left or right.

* * * * *

The reader requires orthodoxy in the opponents. This is especially true for the attacker. The attacker whose technique includes hitting across her body, for example, is difficult to read. She hits away from both the angle of her approach and the direction she is facing. Her arm motion, furthermore, is often hidden by her body.

This spiker has the advantage for only a few plays. The defender who is familiar with the habit reads the spiker more easily; the poor technique limits the spiker's range.

The most challenging attacker hits in an orthodox way, giving herself maximum range. She avoids commitment until the last moment. She brings surprises; the defender thinks she's "got her this time," only to see a turn of the attacker's wrist and the ball falling in the defender's court.

Reading the opponents is not confined to the defense. The setter reads the opposing blockers as her team attacks (218).

The setter's view of the blockers depends on the pass. A pass that arrives deep in the court offers no opportunity to watch the blockers. The setter faces away from the net. Even when she can turn toward the net, both her movement and the distance prevent her from detecting the blockers' small telegrams. The setter, furthermore, has fewer targets from deep in the court. She cannot set a quick to her middle hitter, for example.

A pass that arrives near the net offers the best chance to read. In order to see the blockers, the setter turns her shoulders 90 degrees to the net as the pass arrives. She does not look directly at the blockers but sees them in her peripheral vision. Some setters turn their head for a moment to note the position of the middle-blocker's feet.

The setter gains the greatest advantage from the blocker who drifts to the side of the pass. The blocker moves early; the setter has time to absorb this movement and deliver the ball away from the blocker.

The setter can see the opposing middle-block jump to stuff a quick set in the middle. She sets another hitter. She can also see the middle who starts to move. The middle either remains in place or takes a step right or left. The setter directs the ball away from the blocker's movement.

218

* * * * *

The setter's clearest view of the middle-blocker arises when her quick hitter approaches about halfway to the left sideline. The middle-blocker defends in front of, and a distance from, the setter's eyes. The setter can see the middle-blocker's movements and also those of the left-blocker who positions herself to help. She directs the ball away from the quick hitter. A backset to the right sideline is a good choice.

The setter who knows the tendencies of the opponents has an advantage. Some teams commit themselves to stopping the quick attack in the middle. The setter delivers the ball to the combination hitter. Other teams try to stuff the middle on occasion, but prefer to double-block the outside hitters. The setter delivers the ball to the quick attacker.

Teammates

Reading one's teammates offers a benefit that reading one's opponents does not: it increases the sense of *team* through one player helping another. When a player with a supreme effort turns her teammate's comparable effort into a successful play, the team's spirit may rise.

The read may result from a teammate's intentional efforts, that is, from a designed signal.

Player X signals that she will not pass by stepping away from her position in the serve-receive formation. Player Y sees, or reads, this, and understands that she must pass (Section IV, Chapter 1).

The middle-front signals her setter, by vacating the area around the ball, that her team's second touch is free to be set. A player from the serve receive signals her setter, by moving toward a poor pass, that she intends to set it.

Other signals are not intentional. When the right-back player reads tip and releases to cover, middle-back senses this. She knows that the court behind her teammate, a line shot, is open; only she can cover (**219**). She must move before the shot has been made.

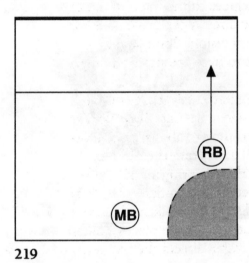

219

When a player chases the ball off the court, her teammates may wait on the court for the return. Their hopes are seldom realized.

The ball is usually top-spinning, which means that it jumps away from the court at contact. The chaser's momentum also moves away from the court. Her best play usually sends the ball straight up. By the time her teammates see, it is too late.

At least one of the chaser's teammates must respond by following her. Another needs to follow the follower, and perhaps another still.

The intelligent player connects her teammate's running off the court and the likely result. She follows.

220

Reading helps the hitter to anticipate the location of her teammate's set. The hitter first evaluates her setter. *Evaluate* means that the hitter considers the setter's skill. The twelve-year-old 85-pounder, for example, may deliver every set low and inside.

The world class setter, on the other hand, may deliver the ball on target, even though she is falling down (**220**).

When the setter is moving, the hitter expects the setter's momentum to influence the set. The setter running toward the hitter, for example, likely sends the ball farther than either of them would like. The hitter adjusts.

The setter who retreats from the hitter often delivers a short, weak set. The setter who takes the ball either low or without balance does the same.

A pass that forces the setter to deepen may result in a deep set, especially if the setter does not turn toward the hitter. A pass that forces the setter to move toward the net may lead to a tight set.

221

222

A back set requires more power than a front set because the setter cannot extend her body backward, toward the target (221). The hitter must expect a back set that is low and inside. The back-set may be tight since the setter often positions her back toward the net.

A jump set requires more power than a floor set. It tends to be low and inside, especially when the pass has forced the setter toward the net. The combination of a jump and a back set means a set that is neither long enough nor high enough.

A ball that is spinning when the setter touches it tends to jump away from the net. The hitter expects a set that is deeper than usual.

When the setter chases the ball and then sets it with a forearm pass over her head, she gains power from her back arch. She often sends the ball a great distance. She tends to fear an overset; she delivers the ball deep in the court.

The player who steps out of the serve-receive formation to set often delivers the ball high (222). There are two reasons for this: the distance is great and the player, facing the net, easily directs her momentum into the ball.

A teammate's rebound of the opponents' attack offers the most sophisticated form of reading one's teammates—and the most fun. Two defenders on the court offer the player the greatest opportunity to read and respond to a rebound. It also reveals the principles used in six-player volleyball.

One player responds in a specific manner to her teammate's being attacked. The player receiving the attack is Player X, the reader Player Y. X faces the net on the left, Y on the right (223).

In general, the reader covers the worst possibility, that is, the worst shot that her teammate may make. If the reader cannot control the worst possibility, she covers the second worst and so on.

Consider, for example, a hard spike to X. X reaches with one hand up and to her right. The worst possibility is a miss by Player X, in which case Player Y is out of luck. The second worst is a tick, with the same result for Player Y.

What if, however, Player X gets a piece of the ball? Player Y has a chance. Y knows that her teammate's hand on the ball will send it on an arc toward the back wall.

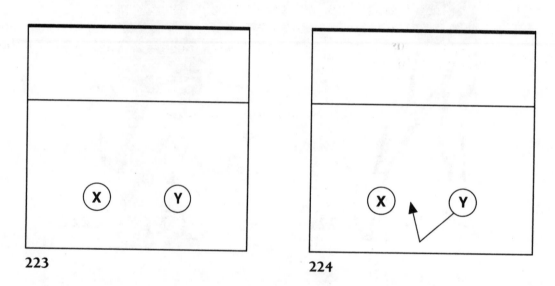

223   224

Here are the events: Player Y sees the spike and Player X's reach. Without knowing more, she heads at full speed toward the back wall.

The ball rebounds from X's arm. Y, who has started moving before the touch, makes a desperate swing and knocks the ball straight up. X, who has seen her teammate racing toward the ball, follows and sends the ball over her teammate and the net.

Players X and Y read well. They see and react before the eventuality.

What if Player X makes a better play? What if, for example, she digs the spike straight up? In this case, Player Y can reverse her direction from heading off-court (224). Her momentum, now heading toward the net, allows her to set her teammate.

There is a risk involved in reading. If Player X had somehow dug the ball with a perfect pass, Player Y would not have made the play. The chances of this happening in the circumstances, however, are infinitesimal.

In general, when Player Y, the reader, sees that the ball has been hit to Player X, she takes her first step toward Player X. If X deflects the ball downward, Y is heading toward that possibility. If X deflects the ball less directly to the floor, Y has a better chance.

The direction of Player X's reach makes a difference. If she reaches forward, Player Y starts forward. If she reaches to the side, Y starts in the same direction. If she reaches up, Y likely heads for the back wall.

If Player X runs to recover a ball that has hit the net, Player Y runs with her. X may only be able to deliver the ball a short distance.

Before the attack, Players X and Y tend to move together. If X moves left, Y likely moves left and vice versa. Why? The defenders see the attack in the same way.

For example, if Player X, in reading her opponent's spike, moves toward Player Y, Player Y senses this and moves in the same direction. By moving, X has taken responsibility for part of Y's area. Y adjusts.

The defenders don't always move in the same direction, however. If both players eliminate the area to their outside as an attack site, they may move toward each other. X and Y see an identical hit; they read the attack as arriving in the same place.

When the movement is either toward or away from the net, the defenders often move in the opposite directions. When Player X, for example, moves forward to cover a short shot, Y often moves behind her (**225**).

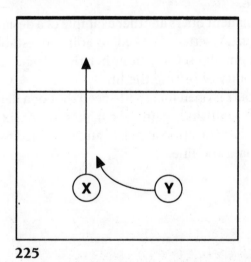

225

The defender's goal is to align herself exactly with the direction of the attack. She must temper this with an awareness of the position of her teammate and the court's boundaries.

When the defender makes an error in reading her opponents' attack, she prefers that the misread ball arrive toward the inside of the court. A desperate deflection in this case flies toward her teammate, rather than out of bounds. This is called playing the ball "outside-in."

With six players on the court, reading one's teammate becomes both easier and more complicated. It becomes easier because more players cover the court. It becomes more complicated because five teammates must be considered rather than one.

Specialized offensive responsibilities for the six players further complicate matters. The setter, for example, must consider her role on the team before she changes location.

The player's decision to react to a read depends on the coach. The coach often doesn't like the player to abandon her primary responsibility in the defense. The authoritarian coach, especially, may not see reading as increasing the team's defensive chances, but as symptomatic of the player's poor discipline.

Reacting to a read in these circumstances becomes even more difficult when some players cannot do it. Does the player who sees an event about to happen, and also sees that no teammate will cover, leave her position in an attempt to make the play?

Here is one high school middle-back's solution. She is positioned near the baseline, on the midline of the court. She senses that the attacker will tip on the sideline and that right-back, who has tip responsibility, has not moved.

Middle-back, without a second thought, abandons her position. She makes a rolling save of the tipped ball on the sideline about two meters from the net. The coach cannot decide whether to scold the player for leaving her deep responsibility or to praise her for making a spectacular save.

A recreational tournament offers another example of a designed responsibility inhibiting the perceptive player. A setter is asked to join an established team for one day. Throughout the tournament she senses, from her right-back position, that the spiker in front of her has no possibility of hitting the line.

The middle of the court is open for an off-speed shot or a deflection from the block, so the setter goes to this area again and again. She makes five or six saves in the middle of the court, never has her right-back position attacked and is warned twice by her teammates that her responsibility is to guard the line.

The Ball

The Net Rebound

Reading the ball's rebound from the net is similar to reading one's teammate: the player covers the worst possibility. A net with no spring offers the worst possibility. The ball falls straight down or, worse yet, heads toward the opponents' court.

The reader positions herself close to the ball, lowering herself and expecting the ball to go away from, rather than toward, her. If she has the time, she turns her side to the net. In this position, she can both reach toward her opponents and remove herself from the path to her teammates.

The Spinner

Reading the spin on the ball is useful, especially to the setter, who wants to counteract the spin.

Seeing and discerning whether the ball has topspin or underspin is impossible. Fortunately, the ball spinning on a horizontal axis, with a minor exception, always spins in one direction. It spins as if it were rolling from the center line to the baseline, comparable to a top-spin serve. The spin derives from three touches: the top-spin serve, the spike and the shanked pass or dig.

(The exception is a ball that is dug by the opponents and crosses the net without another touch: it spins in the opposite direction.)

The setter pushes the spinning ball toward the net, since it tends to jump in the opposite direction. On a forearm set, the ball jumps more sharply.

The backcourt player, in digging a hard spike, usually receives a ball with topspin. She occasionally digs a ball that is spinning on a vertical axis, however, as does the baseball pitcher's curve.

How does the digger anticipate the direction of the curve? By noting how the spiker swings at the ball.

The spiker who turns to the digger's right and hits across her body often spins the ball in the same direction. The digger expects a ball curving left-to-right.

The spiker who turns the ball to the digger's left often spins the ball left. The digger expects a ball curving from right-to left.

In general, the side-spinning ball tends to curve out of bounds. A ball near the left boundary curves left, a ball near the right, right.

The ball that spins from the side of the teammate-blocker's hand does so in a predictable manner. The ball that touches the outside of the blocker's left hand curves from left-to-right. The ball that touches the outside of the blocker's right hand curves from right-to-left.

SECTION IV: COACHING A TEAM

The idea of coaching a team, even a beginning one, can be disquieting. The prospective coach finds at the library a description of individual skills that are fine enough to be taught. He also finds analyses of offensive and defensive systems. What he cannot find, however, is a discussion of the relationship between the systems and the players' skills or a discussion of the relationships between the systems themselves.

Section IV is based on the following axiom: team systems must fit players' skills. There is no reason to use a back-row setter when the team cannot spike. Nor is there reason to double-block when the opposing attack consists of an underhand shot on the first or second touch.

If team systems fit players' skills, it follows that offenses and defenses correspond. A beginning offense corresponds with a beginning defense, an intermediate offense with an intermediate defense, and an advanced with an advanced.

Section IV discusses offensive and defensive systems. The levels of the players' skills provide the order: beginning, intermediate and advanced. Once a coach understands how offenses and defenses connect, he can design a complete system for his team. And once he understands how they evolve, he can lead his team to a more sophisticated system when the time is right.

An Introduction to the Lineup

The lineup is the order in which the players serve. It reflects the position each player starts on the court: the first server starts right-back, the second server right-front and so on (**227**). If the team receives serve, the first server is right-front, the second middle-front, et cetera (**228**).

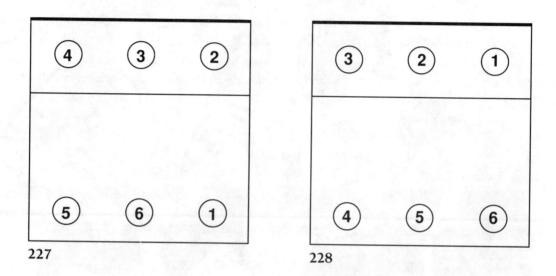

227

228

The lineup and the team's offense and defense interact. The coach arranges his lineup according to the strengths and weaknesses of his players and, also, the systems he plans to employ. He evaluates a beginning team, for example, by the performance of each player in attacking, setting, serving, passing and playing the backcourt.*

Here is a likely arrangement for the beginning team: the two best attackers are aligned opposite each other, meaning that one or the other is in the front row at all times. The two best setters are likewise opposite. The best attacker starts left-front so that her first three rotations are in the front row. The best setter starts middle-front so that she can set the best attacker on-hand. The best server starts right-back; the best passers or backcourt players start in the back row. If the best server is capable of dominating her opponents, the lineup can be rotated back one slot when the team receives serve at the start of the match.

*These considerations do not change with the level but others are added.

Determining a lineup is not this simple. What if the best setter is also the best passer? Or the best spiker the best server? Does the team rotate back to allow a strong server to serve first if this is the team's weakest rotation? Specialization, which means that players switch court positions during play, adds questions.

How does the coach decide? The answer is never scientific. The coach can see his choices by moving player-models—names on paper work fine—through the six rotations.

Some coaches recommend a pie chart divided into six sections. Revolving the pie changes the rotation. This is neater and more portable than the models. Switches, however, must be performed in the imagination. Holding switches in one's memory while trying to understand their implications is difficult. Evaluating both front- and back-row switches is particularly challenging.

*   *   *   *

The team now has a balanced lineup from which to implement its beginning offense. One of its two best attackers plays in the front row at all times, as does one of its two best setters. Its best server likely starts in, or rotates quickly into, the serving position.

CHAPTER 1:
BEGINNING OFFENSE

The term *offense* means mounting an attack with several or all team members working together. It starts with a team's receiving either a serve, an attack or a free ball.

Receiving serve is the most important offensive skill at the beginning level. A good serve-receive allows the setter to fulfill her role. And the attacker can send the ball into her opponents' court.

Receiving Serve

Beginning offense starts with a successful serve-receive formation, an arrangement of five passers in the backcourt and a setter near the net. The goal of the offense is to deliver a pass that can be set and then to deliver a set that can be attacked.

The W

The beginning serve-receive formation arranges its passers in a "W." The setter stays at the net (230). When players do not switch during play, middle-front is always the setter. Middle-back, in line with left-front and right-front, becomes the middle point of the W; left-front and right-front are the left and right points (231). Bunching the team in the backcourt allows the receivers to pass without moving far.

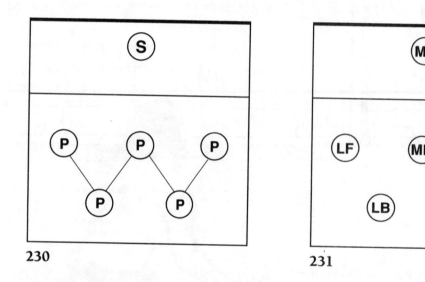

230   231

Beginning players are not comfortable positioning themselves close to each other in serve-receive. Sometimes left-front and right-front creep forward and wide, taking themselves out of position to pass all but misdirected serves. Middle-back likewise tends to stay deep. Players must be forced to position themselves near each other in the W.

S = SETTER	LB = LEFT-BACK	MH = MIDDLE-HITTER
P = PASSER	MB = MIDDLE-BACK	L = LEFT
LF = LEFT-FRONT	RB = RIGHT-BACK	M = MIDDLE
MF = MIDDLE-FRONT	B = BEST ATTACKER	O = OPPOSITE
RF = RIGHT-FRONT	LH = LEFT-HITTER	

Shifting the W

The serve begins its flight from the left one-third of the baseline as the receiving team faces it. Most serves also arrive on the left so the serve-receive formation shifts left (**232**).

The left point of the W positions herself less than a meter from the left sideline; the right point positions herself more than a meter from the right sideline. The middle point locates her right foot on the midline of the court so that she, too, is slightly left. The back-row receivers are in the seams, between the passers immediately in front, and about 1½ meters from the baseline. A serve arriving above their waists is out of bounds.

Shifting the serve-receive formation left covers the likely serves. The right sideline now becomes a tempting target for the server. It is difficult to hit, however, and usually results in a serve out of bounds. The rare crosscourt serve that arrives inbounds forces the passers to move farther than usual, but it is long and usually high. Right-front or right-back have time to move to it.

The Setter

The setter positions herself at the net 1-1½ meters to the right of the middle point of the W (**232**). She faces left. Why? The left-side receivers, nearest the server, usually pass. She keeps them in front of her.

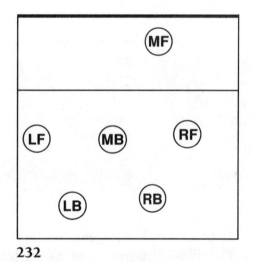

232

Facing left also allows her to see, and orient herself by, the net. Receiving the pass with her back to the net, in contrast, offers no such view or orientation.

Front-setting is easier than back. A front-set facing left means that the right-handed spiker hits on-hand, that is, with her hitting hand nearer the setter. Hitting on-hand allows the attacker to face the setter as she spikes. She can adjust to an inside set, the likely mistake, by running toward the setter and reaching with her hitting hand.

The off-hand hitter does not have the same benefits. In order to see the set, she must turn her back and look over her shoulder. An inside set forces her to move toward the setter and then turn away to spike. Her head is in the way of her hitting hand. She loses power.

The setter delivers the ball left, to her on-hand hitter, when either the left-front, left-back or middle-front receives the serve. By moving backward, she may also be able to set left on a pass from the right-back. This is a long set. The beginner may find turning 180 degrees and setting the off-hand hitter more effective.

233

The Receivers

The receivers hold themselves high, ready to move quickly (**233**). They watch the serve.

The roles of the front-row and the back-row players in the serve-receive differ. The backs prefer to pass, freeing the fronts to attack. The backs must call loudly for the serve—"ball" or "mine"—since the fronts, being closer to the server, tend to commit themselves early to pass. The back-row passers are obligated to call "out" or "good." This is a great benefit to a teammate-receiver who, concentrating on passing, cannot see the out of bounds line. The backs take no serves above their waists.

The front-row receivers, in contrast, avoid passing so that they can focus on the attack; the middle-front at the beginning level is the exception. The fronts pass when the ball arrives even with, or in front of, them. They move back no more than one-half step. The fronts' responsibility to remove themselves from the deep serve's path is greater than their responsibility to call.

Like the back-row receivers, the fronts do not pass a ball that arrives above their waists. They move away from the path of the serve and face the passer in the back row (234). The move is called *opening up* and serves three functions: (1) it signals the backs that the ball is their responsibility; (2) it removes the fronts from the backs' line-of-sight; and (3) it positions the fronts to help with a misdirected pass. Ducking a high serve is a mistake. A back-row passer finds it nearly impossible to concentrate on the ball with a teammate crouched in front of her.

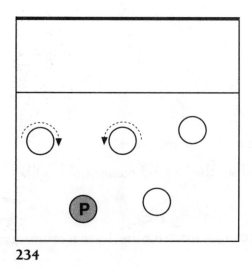

234

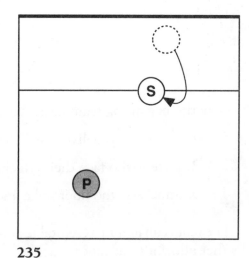

235

The Setter's Movements

As the ball flies toward her teammates, the setter sidesteps from the net toward her passer (235). She follows a soft curve (Section III, Chapter 1, Setting). Beyond passing well, the setter's curved path is the most important factor in a team's ability to use three touches in its attack.

Beginning passes often arrive two to three meters from the net, so the curved path positions the setter to handle most of them. For those too deep, she calls "help" and a teammate sets. For balls served behind her, that is, to right-front or right-back, the setter turns 180 degrees and sets forward to right-front.

The setter pushes the ball high—3–5 meters above the net—so that her spiker can move underneath it. She sets wide, giving her attacker a long crosscourt shot. For those who lack the strength or accuracy to set wide, facing the attacker and setting high is enough.

A note about the beginning setter: if she forearm passes the ball over her head into the opponents' court, she is either late moving from the net or failing to call for help. The problem is likely the former since leaving the net is not comfortable. Most setting practice takes place near the net and so do the best combinations of set-and-attack. The coach must force the setter to deepen.

The Beginning Shots

The floor spike is the first shot the attackers must learn. It is easier than a conventional spike, crisper than either an underhand or an overhand pass and can be performed from anywhere on the court. The attackers need to command the tip, the easiest skill in volleyball, for sets near the net. The attackers must know that, except for tips, the best attacks travel deep and to the corners. A deep shot forces the opposing team to make a long pass in order to start its attack. A corner shot forces an even longer pass.

* * * * *

Now the beginning team has:

1. passers who deliver the ball to the middle of the court,

2. setters who face their attackers and set the ball 3-5 meters high, and

3. attackers who floor-spike and tip.

The team can mount a creditable attack. It can also have fun and learn movements and skills that allow it to advance quickly.

To Specialize or Not

The discussion of the beginning serve-receive and attack does not designate certain players as setters and others as attackers. Whoever is middle-front sets; whoever is left-front and right-front attacks. No player is a specialist.

There are sound reasons to use this system, especially for young players:

1. It treats the team members alike. When handled well by the coach, the team can gain a sense that each team member contributes comparably. It also relieves the coach from the responsibility of determining how his players should specialize.

2. It gives each team member an opportunity to learn all parts of the game. This is an advantage to players who will both set and hit in the future.

Specializing, on the other hand, strengthens a team. It allows the best setters to set and the best attackers to attack. Even the youngest players are aware of this. When they see opposing teams switch positions, they want to do the same.

The decision to specialize means that the coach designates certain players as setters and others as attackers. *Designate* is too strong a word for the reality. Most players have a clear idea both of the positions they would like to play and the positions for which they are best suited.

The coach arranges his best setters opposite each other and does the same with his best attackers (page 226). This means that one of his best setters is always in the front along with one of his best attackers. Now the coach wants the two best setters, whoever is in the front, to set all the time. The other four team members attack all the time. This offense is called the "4-2": four attackers, two setters.

Switching

In two rotations the setter must switch into middle-front whenever she is left-front or right-front. The switch takes place during the flight of the serve.

The switch is easy during the switching team's serve, less so during its serve-receive. The problem is to arrange the players without violating the overlap rule. The overlap rule prohibits a player from being out of position in relation to the player immediately in front, in back or to the side. The players' locations on the court do not matter, only their locations in relation to their teammates.

The setter at left-front is an example. Middle-front can move back and to the left side of the court, becoming the left point of the W. The setter, however, must stay to her left; the middle point of the W, middle-back, must stay slightly behind her (236). When the setter is right-front, the formation flip-flops.

It is important to note that the setter and the left point of the W are less likely to overlap than the left and middle points. The team becomes comfortable in a symmetrical W, with its three points in line, and forgets that middle-back must be deeper than middle-front.

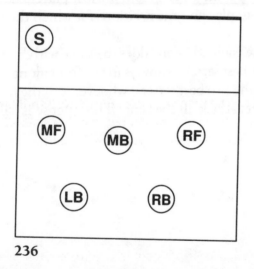

236

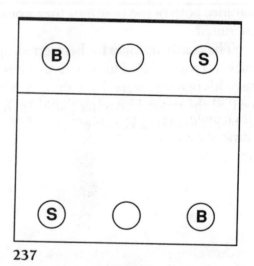

237

Keeping the Strong Hitter On-hand

The coach must decide whether he wants his strongest attacker to hit more often on the left, on-hand, than the right. If the answer is "yes," the coach arranges his line-up so that the best attackers serve immediately before the setters. This is called the attackers' leading the setters through the rotation.

If, for example, the coach wants his best attacker to start left-front, he locates his best setter left-back (237). Or if he wants his best setter to start left-front, he locates his best attacker middle-front.

The best attacker hits from the left-front four times out of six times with this arrangement: when she is left-front during both serve and serve-receive and when she is middle-front during both serve and serve-receive. She hits on the right when she is right-front both during serve and serve-receive.

Putting the best attacker ahead of the setter in the rotation is a natural way of positioning the best hitter on the left four times out of six. The players may see it as the obvious switch—setter to the middle—that happens to give the best attackers more opportunities to hit from the left than the other attackers.

The coach can offer his best attackers five opportunities to hit from the left, but at the expense of the natural switch. When his team serves, the coach switches his best attacker from right-front to left-front, leaving his setter in the middle. The best attackers gain their fifth opportunity on the left, but at a cost. The switch magnifies the disparity of opportunities among the attackers, increasing the possibility of social instability on, especially, a young team.

* * * * *

Once the setter has switched, she is free to stay in the middle and to move as described above. To set right-front, she turns to face her hitter; furthermore, her first set upon arriving from left-front may well be to right-front since her momentum is in that direction.

* * * * *

The specialist-setter has an influential role on the success of the team. She handles the ball virtually every time it is in her court. She chooses what attacker receives her set and, in advanced play, what kind of set her attacker receives. When she runs a 5-1, her role as the team leader is enhanced.

* * * * *

Switching can include back-row players. Like the front-row, the players must avoid overlapping. The likely switch for a beginning team is to move the quickest or most athletic player into the middle-back position, where many attacks arrive.

Planned Substitutions

The coach can make planned substitutions to increase the offensive and defensive strengths of his team. These typically involve front- and back-row specialists.

The small, quick player may be more effective in the back row than the tall, high-jumping attacker. The small player may pass and serve better; she may also react more quickly and aggressively on defense. Substituting her into the back row improves the team.

The planned substitution has an added benefit: it gives a seventh or eighth team member a consistent, first-team role. The presence of many active players increases the spirit of the team. If two players' abilities are comparable, the coach may substitute to distribute playing time evenly. A beginning or intermediate team may substitute twelve times, the legal limit at lower levels, among four players per game.

Every three rotations, the coach or the captain substitutes the front-row player for the back and vice versa. The team can consider the substitution as part of its lineup. Any player notifies the coach or the captain if, in the excitement of the match, the substitution is forgotten.

Sometimes the player to be replaced does not start left-front or right-back. This means that at the beginning of the game, she plays only one or two rotations before leaving. In these cases, starting the bench-sitting player, thus saving one substitution, may be beneficial.

Once the team has made ten or eleven substitutions, the coach must decide which of the substitutes stays in the game. He often chooses the front-row player, whose strength in the front may outweigh her counterpart's strength in the back.

Whichever player serves better usually serves. If the better server is the front-row player, the coach substitutes after her serve.

* * * * *

Planned substitutions can detract from the team's success. Each substitution stops play and, therefore, breaks the team's rhythm. Exchanging four players, furthermore, can add up to twelve substitutions per game, leaving no more for unplanned ones.

Players often have difficulty maintaining a high level of physical and mental readiness moving in and out of the lineup. Back-row players, especially, fight this. Sometimes they do not exert themselves enough to overcome cooling on the bench.

CHAPTER 2:
BEGINNING DEFENSE

Beginning defense is little different from beginning offense in the starting arrangement of its players. The W formation works as well during a rally as it does for serve-receive. During a rally, however, the team shifts its W formation to accord with the attack arriving from different points along the net.

The Shallow W

In beginning volleyball, the spike is rare. Virtually all attacks loop over the net. Blocking is of little value against this offense; in fact, it can limit the players' moving into position in the backcourt, where most balls arrive.

The players' starting positions against a no-hard-spike offense is a shallow version of the W (239). The points of the W, particularly left-front and right-front, position themselves near enough to the net to handle tips, fisted balls, oversets, and overpasses. The setter stays at the net and helps left-front and right-front with the shallow shots. Middle-back positions herself less deep than in the serve-receive formation; she is responsible for balls not taken by the setter. Left-back and right-back position themselves in nearly the same places as in serve-receive.

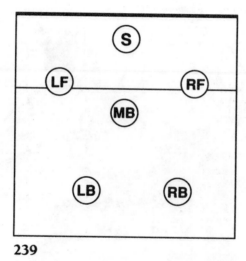

239

How deep should left-front and right-front position themselves at the start? Where should they go when the ball crosses into their opponents' court? The more shallow they can position themselves—and still retreat in time to play deep balls—the better. There is a reason for this. When the opponents' offense does include hard spikes, the team wants to block. This means that its front-row players stay at the net as their opponents attack.

A team whose front row has stayed deep during its opponents' attack finds it difficult to start at the net. Its players drop back from habit, rush to the net as they realize their mistake and arrive in time to see a free ball arcing over their heads.

The solution is for the team to position its front row so that it must deepen when a free ball becomes clear (239). The team has a shallow-deep-shallow rhythm that accords with a more sophisticated defense.

Shifts

The next step for the beginning defense is to shift its coverage into the area of the court most likely to be attacked. In general, this is toward the attacker.

An attack taking place near the right-front defender, for example, is likely to travel from right-to-left into the center of the court (**240**). This means that line shots are unlikely as are shots angled sharply crosscourt. Right-front and right-back move toward the net; left-front deepens; left-back aligns herself with the point of attack and the corner; middle-back shifts right (**240**).

In left-side attacks, the team shifts to the left in a mirror image of the right shift.

In middle attacks, severe angle shots are unlikely. The outside defenders in the front row, left-front and right-front, shift inward (**241**).

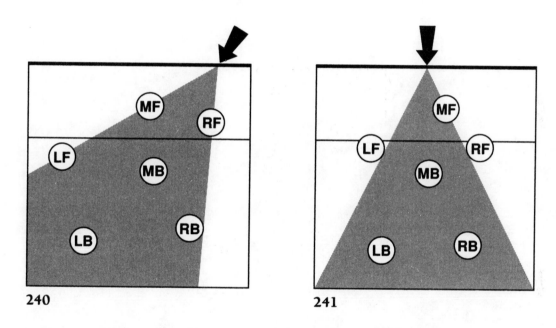

240   241

Now the team moves shallow-deep-shallow and shifts toward the ball, which increase its chances of fielding the attack. From these movements it learns to read its opponents, a valuable skill for the future.

The shallow W is the team's starting position; shift-right, shift-left and shift-center are its final defensive positions. Both the starting position and the shift are common to all defenses.

CHAPTER 3: INTERMEDIATE OFFENSE

Intermediate offense exhibits greater precision than the beginning in all aspects of the attack. Passes near the net mean accurate sets which, in turn, mean spikes with an approach and a jump.

In the intermediate stage, the team evolves from positioning its setter in the middle of the net to positioning her on the right. With this arrangement a formidable attacker can dominate the center of the net (where much of the action in volleyball takes place). The center-attacker prepares the team to run a three-hitter attack.

The intermediate team quickens its attack. On free balls, and perhaps at other times, the team sets lower both to the middle and to the outside.

The Setter-Middle

The intermediate team continues its setter-middle offense. The movements of its players, however, are tighter. Improvements in passing make three offensive touches the norm.

The setter deepens less during serve-receive. She receives the ball closer to the net. Her sets have less angle, that is, they travel more nearly parallel to the net. She can deliver the ball near the net without trapping her hitter or, worse, setting to her opponents.

At this level, the setter pushes her sets, meaning that she increases their length. A set near the sideline gives the attacker an opportunity to hit a long, almost 13-meter, crosscourt shot. This decreases the chance of an out-of-bounds attack. The extra length liberates, especially, low-jumping attackers. The net is high in relation to their stature so they cannot spike the ball sharply downward.

Setting the ball wide does not prevent the spiker from attacking straight ahead, or hitting the line. A wide set, however, means that she has less margin for error because of her proximity to the sideline. When the opponents employ a middle-front who blocks all along the net, a wide set allows the attacker to avoid her more easily.

Setter/Spiker Communication

As the setter's accuracy increases, the need for communication between the setter and the spiker grows. The ideal distance on the set, as shown by the spiker's location after the attack, is the main topic of discussion.

The ideal distance on the set leaves the hitter's feet on the sideline after the attack. Since this requires a long set, inexperienced setters often deliver the ball inside. The attacker starts her spike approach inside, giving the setter justification for her mistake. No sets go to the sideline.

The coach must make it clear that an inside set is the setter's mistake. He must make it equally clear that the spiker's responsibility is to start her approach outside, even though the sets tend to pull her inside. The coach also must explain that the hitter's error—positioning herself inside on an outside set—is more serious. It implies a lack of confidence that the attack can unfold as planned.

The Angle vs. the Line

The attacker usually directs her shot crosscourt, called the angle, since it offers the greatest possibility of hitting inbounds. If her spike includes an approach and a jump, she starts her approach outside the court and directs it toward her opponents' opposite corner. Her jump and the ball meet on the sideline, as mentioned.

For a left attacker, an approach on the angle is preferred at all levels of play. It allows an easy crosscourt shot. It also allows a natural body turn, from right to left, for hitting the line. The spiker may choose to attack the line without turning her body. This increases her deception at the expense of power.

The right attacker takes a straighter approach, that is, more nearly parallel to the sideline (**243**). This allows her both to hit the line and to turn her body right-to-left to hit the angle. Both left and right attackers generally avoid turning their bodies in the opposite direction, that is, left-to-right, which reduces power.

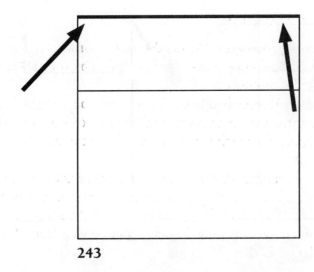

243

The intermediate setter, in directing the ball to her right hitter, likely continues to face her. She can see where she sets and develops more power with a front-set.

The setter who back sets usually finds that her sets are both low and inside. The back set generates less power than the front. The setter needs to sense that she is setting the ball twice as high and twice as far as she would for a front-set.

A short and inside set to the right attacker is worse than a comparable one to the left. The right cannot reach for the ball because her head is in the way. Furthermore, the attack requires the left-to-right body turn, away from the attacker's momentum, that results in a loss of power.

Covering the Hitter

Balls attacked near or above the net invite blockers. The attacking team arranges itself to recover a blocked ball. This is called covering its hitter, a misleading term. The covering players arrange themselves near the blockers, from whose hands the ball rebounds.

The goal is to have two lines of coverage, a shallow and a deep, made up of all five non-attacking team members. The lines are arranged either with three players shallow and two deep or vice versa (**244**). Since more balls fall shallow, the former is more common.

The shallow line of coverage includes the setter; left-back for a left-side attack and right-back for a right; and middle-back, who plays shallow in both the beginning defense and the intermediate (to be discussed). The two remaining team members position themselves in the deep line. They shift toward the attack.

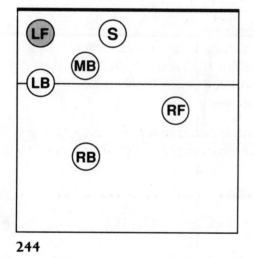

244

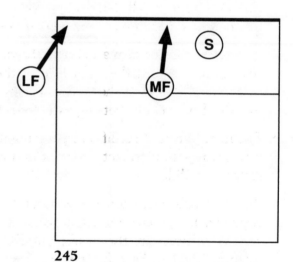

245

The Setter-Right

The Benefits

In the next step of the offense's evolution, the setter positions herself on the right rather than the middle. (245). This is begun either as an offensive or a defensive improvement, but the result is the same: more action in the middle of the net.

The offense initiates the setter-right for two reasons: (1) to match a tall attacker against a short defender in the middle-front and (2) to take greater advantage of its second hitter, formerly right-front.

The right setter has both hitters in front of her. She sets the middle hitter without pushing the ball far; she sets the left as before. She distributes her sets more evenly although the left still receives the majority of the sets.

The Difficulties

1. The ball must be passed accurately. The setter positions herself to the right of center; she no longer chases balls left or right with equal ease. Passing is more difficult, particularly for the left-side receiver. She must make a long, angled pass.

2. The setter cannot turn and set to the right since no attacker is stationed there. A pass that travels toward the right side of the net (behind the setter) leaves two difficult options. The setter either moves backwards or turns 180 degrees and back-sets to the middle. Both require setting away from her momentum.

3. The middle-hitter has difficulty leaving the net when it is time to attack. She gets in the way of the setter. In fact, it is not unusual for an inexperienced middle-hitter and the setter to collide.

4. The free-ball formation is less natural. Right-back becomes the right point of the W which, in the setter-middle offense, is taken by a front-row player (246). When the right-back forgets to move forward, the right point is left open. Middle-back cannot move right because right-back is in her way. Left-back cannot move right either because middle-back is in her way.

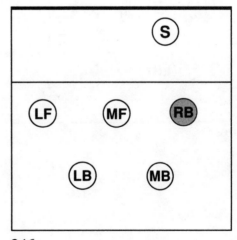

246

Receiving Serve with the Setter-Right

The serve-receive formation for the setter-right offense presents greater problems than the setter-middle, especially when the setter is left-front. She starts near the left sideline, dashes across the court and turns 180 degrees to set (247). Or she turns 180 degrees about halfway across and backs the rest of the way. Either move is difficult for an intermediate player.

There is an easier way. The team runs a setter-middle attack in this rotation. Or it runs the setter-middle on the first attack and thereafter—during play—switches the setter to the right-front. When the right-front attacks, the switch is easy. The setter first covers the attacker and then they switch. The setter whose rotation is middle-front starts left of the middle point of the W, faces the left sideline and backs into position. The team can also run one wide attack (setter-middle) and then make the middle-front/right-front switch mentioned above. An occasional right-side attack offers variety to the setter-right offense.

When the setter's rotation is middle-front, the team must make another switch. The designated middle-attacker and the designated left-side attacker are in each other's positions (248). They switch after the attack.

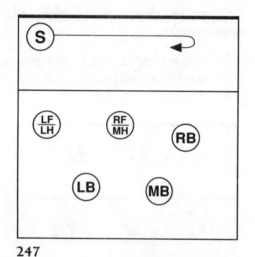

247

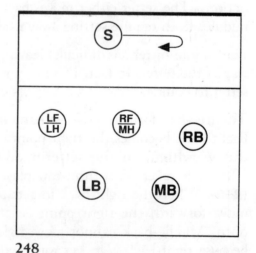

248

248

* * * * *

The setter-right offense allows the setter to back-set. On a left-of-center pass, she crosses the path of her middle hitter and, at her discretion, sets back.

* * * * *

When the attack takes place on the left side, the formation for covering the hitter is comparable to the setter-middle: a "3-2," including the left-back, middle-hitter and the setter in the shallow line (249). A middle-attack brings the middle-back into the shallow line along with left-front and the setter (250).

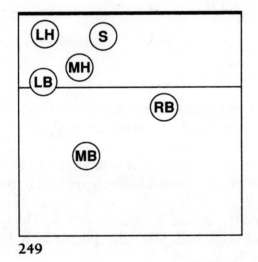

249

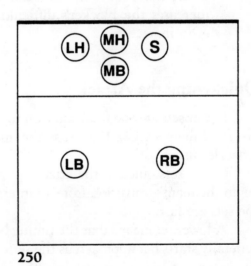

250

The Middle-Hitter's Approach

In the setter-right offense, the middle-hitter starts her approach to the left of the court's midline. She angles her approach to the net (251).

An angled approach has two benefits:

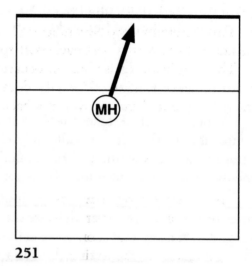

1. It maximizes the attacker's range, which is her capacity to hit both left and right. She either hits in line with her approach (right) or turns right-to-left and hits left—exactly as do the outside attackers.

2. It helps the left-side attacker avoid the opposing middle-blocker, who must position herself right to defend against the middle-attacker. Combining an angled approach by the middle-attacker with a lower set to the left attacker increases the blocker's difficulties even more.

251

Quickening the Attack

Lower sets are the final addition to the intermediate team's setter-right offense. These are 1½-2 meters above the net to the middle hitter and 2-2½ meters above the net to the left-side hitter.

Lower sets quicken the attack, preventing the defense from composing itself. They begin the team's transition from an intermediate to an advanced offense, in which most of the sets are fast.

A lower set means that the timing between the set and the spike is tighter. The spiker generally starts her approach as the setter touches the ball. Since the spiker does not have much time to adjust her position, the set must be accurate.

To set lower, the team needs passes near the net. This is especially true for sets to the middle-attacker, who must look backward, away from her target, in order to watch a set coming from deep in the court. There is an easy way to implement the lower set. The coach limits the use of this attack to free balls, which are passed overhand to the setter. This increases the likelihood of a good pass and gives the team time to get ready.

The setter and the hitters must learn the best heights for sets delivered from different places in the court. When the pass forces the setter to move away from the net, for example, she must set the ball high once again. Back-row players, in general, set high.

The Single Setter

There is a third intermediate system that employs one setter only. It is technically a 5-1, that is, five hitters and a setter who takes the second touch regardless of her rotation. The actions of the setter, however, bring it closer to a 4-2.

The single setter always acts as a front-row player. She positions herself near the net and sets as usual. In order to do this from the back row, she switches with the player opposite her in the line-up, who now plays in the backcourt throughout the rally. The setter cannot block when she has switched from the back row. She covers tips.

This system has two advantages: (1) the team's best setter performs her role all of the time and (2) the team's best backcourt specialist does the same.

The disadvantage is that on occasion the setter is called upon to deliver the ball directly to her opponents. When she does so, she may touch the ball above the plane of the net, which is a foul for a player in a back-row rotation.

* * * * *

The intermediate team has evolved from a tight setter-middle offense to an even tighter setter-right. Its setter delivers the ball nearly vertical to her middle-hitter, pushes long sets to her left-hitter on the sideline and sets back. She sets lower, quickening the team's attack, without forcing her attackers into mistakes. The attackers make crisp, jumping spikes, usually inbounds. The team is ready for the advanced offense.

CHAPTER 4:
INTERMEDIATE DEFENSE

The intermediate team faces a mixed attack: occasional hard, jumping spikes on one hand and tips, off-speed shots and free balls on the other.

It employs a single blocker—in either of two patterns—to defend against the spikes and a shallow, backcourt rover to cover everything else.

Blocking Pattern 1: The 3 x 1

The easiest of the two blocking patterns is the 3 x 1, which includes the three front-row players singly.

Each 3 x 1 player blocks the attacker in front of her. Left-front blocks the attacker on the left-side of the net, middle-front blocks the attacker in the middle of the net and right-front the right (**253, 254, 255**).

The 3 x 1 system does not require the blocker to move far. She faces the net and adjusts her location with side steps (page 113).

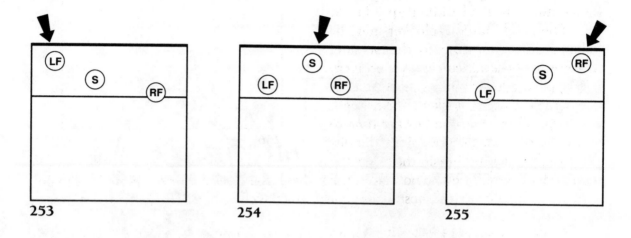

253   254   255

The blocker positions herself as do blockers at all levels:

1. She aligns herself initially with the most likely attack. For the outside blocker, this is a crosscourt spike. For the middle-blocker, this is a shot angling to the blocker's left.

2. She adjusts her position according to the spiker's approach.

3. She blocks in the direction of the spiker's arm and hand motion.

When the set is near or over the net, the 3 x 1 blocker jumps at the same time as the spiker. When the set is a meter from the net, the blocker jumps later than the spiker. She does not jump on sets that are deep. *Deep* may be only 1½ meters from the net. The blocker's decision is based on the skill of the attacker.

The 3 x 1 block fits with either the setter-middle or the setter-right offense. It is more likely to be used with the setter-middle, whose attackers block the opponents' outside hitters.

Blocking Pattern 2: The Single Middle

The single middle-block allows one player to block the entire length of the net (256). It is the logical system to be used with the setter-right offense.

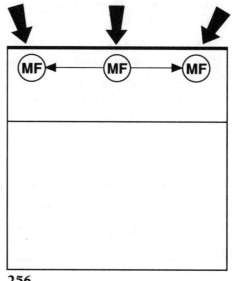

256

The setter-right puts a tall, formidable attacker in the middle. The attacker is often an effective blocker as well. Since she blocks the length of the net, the opponents always face an intimidating block.

The single middle-blocker must be able to move. Getting to the outside, however, is not as difficult as it seems. First, the opposing team, if its skill level is comparable to the blocker's—uses high, slow sets. These give the blocker time to reach the outside. Second, since the distance to the sideline is great, the sets of the intermediate setter often do not make it. For these, the blocker does not move far. Finally, the blocker lines up for the most likely attack, which is crosscourt. This lessens the distance she must travel.

The single middle-block, like the 3 x 1, results in few blocked balls. It represents a transition to the double-block. During this transition, the team (1) intimidates the opposing attackers with its tallest and most effective blocker, (2) trains its middle-blocker to move and (3) reduces blocking errors.

The latter point is important. Blocks at all levels result in more errors than points. The problem, according to one international coach, is that "the team has to block."

"Having to block" is a reality at high levels of play, where most attacks are hard spikes. It is not true at low levels. Beginning teams that block, for example, gain little and lose points to easy attacks. Its players cannot move quickly enough from blocking to the W, which is the formation for receiving the beginning team's frequent free balls.

Intermediate teams spike frequently enough to justify blocking. The majority of the intermediate team's shots, however, are slow. These are easily handled by the backcourt, except when they are deflected from the blocker's hands.

A second blocker means another pair of hands from which off-speed shots can be deflected. It also means one less player in the backcourt.

The single blocker must be judicious in her decision to block or not to block. Unnecessary blocking results in points lost on attacks that could be handled by the backcourt defenders.

The Backcourt Pattern: The Middle-Up

At intermediate levels, many balls fall into the center of the court. These result from tips, off-speed shots, misses, backcourt attacks, blocks, deflections and overpasses. Assigning a player to cover these balls leads to the middle-up backcourt pattern.

The middle refers to the middle-back player, who plays shallow or *up*. She is a rover. From about the depth of the three-meter line, she faces the attack regardless of where it takes place at the net (**257, 258, 259**). She covers tips and other balls that fall behind her team's block. She avoids taking spikes above her waist.

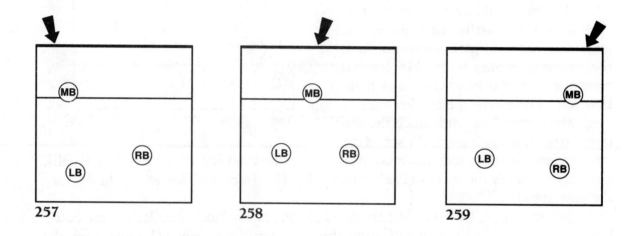

257   258   259

The middle-up occasionally finds herself face-to-face with a strong spiker uninhibited by a block. In these cases, she must protect her face with an overhand dig.

The middle-up defense has one disadvantage: only two players, left-back and right-back, cover the backcourt on good-set, hard-spike attacks (**257, 258, 259**). On free balls, the team shifts into its W as usual.

The middle-up defense fits any of the intermediate offenses. There is one shift that is unusual. The up-player must move to the right on a free ball when her team is using the setter-right. She assumes the right point of the W; middle-front assumes the middle point.

* * * * *

The combination of the single-block and the middle-up results in all six defensive players aligned against the most likely attack. The pattern is 1-2-2-1 (**260**). The formation does not change. The players in each location, however, move from different starting positions depending on the blocking scheme and, in one case, the offense.

One example is the right-front player defending against an attack from the right. She blocks if her team uses the 3 x 1 blocking scheme (**261**) but drops away from the net to cover tips if it uses the single middle-block (**262**).

This principle applies to all the players in the formation except for right-back and left-back. They play the same positions regardless of the team's blocking scheme or its offense.

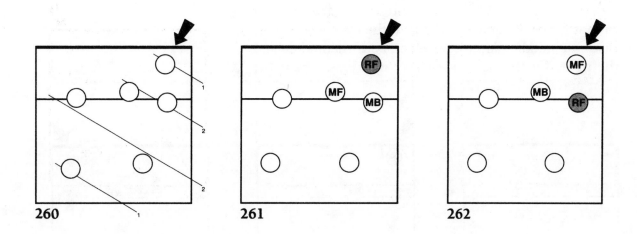

260   261   262

Middle-back is another example. She defends, with a teammate, in the second line. But sometimes she positions herself near the sideline, sometimes near the middle of the court. If her team uses a 3 x 1 block, she positions herself near the sideline (**263**); if her team uses a single-middle block, her teammate does so (**264**). If her team uses a single-setter offense—and her setter is a back-row player positioned right-front—middle-back locates herself near the sideline on an attack from the left, near the middle on an attack from the right (**265, 266**).

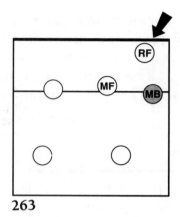

263

The single setter offense is unusual because its setter cannot legally block when she is in the back row. In this case, the middle-player must block both the middle and the right. Or the right-side player must block both the right and the middle (**266**).

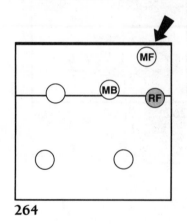

264

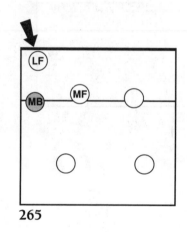

265

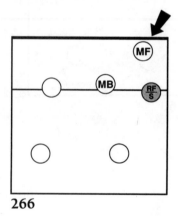

266

* * * * *

The intermediate team's defense has trained all its players to block. Each player watches the approach of, moves to and blocks the attacker directly across the net. The middle moves left and right as if she were forming a double-block. All players decide when to block and when not to.

The backcourt players position themselves in relation to the attack, a single blocker and their backcourt teammates. They see and react to spikes from the left, middle and right, and move into unusual free ball formations. The team has acquired the skills for advanced offense.

CHAPTER 5: ADVANCED OFFENSE

The intermediate team passes the ball to the right-front position most of the time.

Its setter moves well on the court. She knows how and when to deepen, to cross in front of her middle-hitter and to wait at the net—all before the ball has been passed. She faces her hitters during her set and delivers the ball from the middle of the court to the sideline. She sets back.

The attackers move well enough to hit medium-height, vertical sets in the middle and lobs on the outside. All of the players move smoothly from offense to defense to offense again.

The team is ready for the setter-back, or 5-1, offense. This system requires the setter to defend from the backcourt and then to penetrate—move to the net—in order to set (**268**). The backcourt setter improves the team's attack in two ways: (1) it allows the best setter to perform her task in all rotations and (2) it allows a multiple attack, in which three, four or five spikers attack in different places at different times.

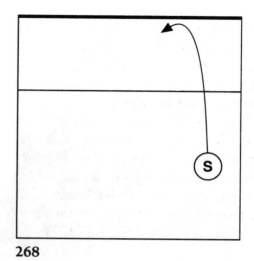

268

The Setter

Advanced setting requires greater movement than intermediate. The setter crosses the court almost every time her team changes from offense to defense and vice versa.

The setter penetrates, in general, from right-back. When her team is serving, she switches easily into this position. When her team is receiving, she starts behind one of the points of the W. If she is right-back, she starts behind the right point; if she is middle-back, the middle point; and left-back, the left point. She advances to the net on the right of each of these players (**269, 270, 271**).

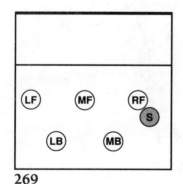

269

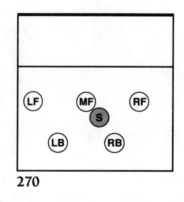

270

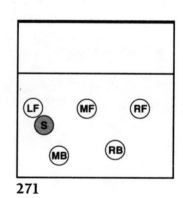

271

The setter exhibits an up-and-back rhythm on the court. She starts from the backcourt, moves to her setting position at the net, sets, covers her hitter and returns to the backcourt to defend.

There is only one difference in the setter-back for the players in the front row: the right-front is now an attacker. She must be aware, as she retreats to attack, of her setter's advance from the backcourt. The setter moves to the net between the right-front and middle-front players (272).

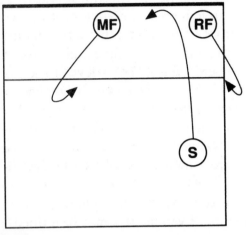

272

The team that chooses to use one setter in all rotations, that is, to run the 5-1 offense, has three front-row attackers half the time—when the setter is in the back row. When the setter is in the front row, the team runs what is, in effect, the setter-right offense.

The team that has two accomplished setters, both of whom can attack, may choose to use the back-row setter in all rotations. This offense is called the 6-2.*

In the 6-2 system, the two setters start opposite each other in the lineup. The back-row player sets; the front-row attacks. The team has three front row attackers in all rotations.

International teams use the 5-1 more than the 6-2 for three reasons:

1. Accurate setting is an extreme benefit to the team.

2. The 5-1's greatest disadvantage—two front-row hitters half of the time— has been made less so by the addition of the back-row attacker. (It is not unusual for international teams to have four attackers when the setter is in the front row and four or even five when she is in the back.)

3. Setters have a rhythm with which they deliver the ball. The attackers find it easier to time their movements with one setter than with two.

---

* Volleyball's rule-makers chose the designation 6-2, with its mathematical anomaly (6 + 2 = 8 players?), over 6-0. The latter was considered less descriptive.

The Sets

Once the advanced team has added the back-row setter, it quickens its attack again. It adds four sets: a low, quick set near the middle of the net, delivered to its middle attacker in front of, or behind the setter, traditionally numbered *one* (273); a low, quick set halfway between the left sideline and the setter, also delivered to its middle attacker, traditionally numbered *three* (274); a low, fast set to the left sideline, delivered to its left-front attacker, *four* (275); and a medium-height back-set near the right sideline, delivered to its right-front attacker, *five* (276).*

The team also retains the high set that it used at lower levels.

What happened to the *two*? The team uses the set at the intermediate level: the lowered, medium-height set to the middle-hitter is a two (277).

The advanced team uses the *two* for combinations; it becomes the play set. Its definition expands to include all medium-height sets except for those on or near the left sideline. Even the five may be termed "a back two on the right sideline" (although the five is often higher).

Now the team's numbered sets are one, two, three, four and five.

273

274

* Some teams define the *four* as the medium-height outside set. The definition of the four as a low, fast set follows Beal ("Offensive Combinations," The AVCA Handbook, page 143).

275

276

277

The Rhythm of the Attack

The advanced team's sets can be classified by their height: low, medium or high. The team associates a set-to-spike rhythm with each height.

The low sets include the one, the back one, the three and the four. They evolve quickly, that is, they have a fast rhythm, requiring exact synchrony between the setter and the spiker.

The one, the back one and the three play a different role from the four in the team's offense, however. They form the basis for the combination attack. They are termed quick; the four is not.

The quicks are different from the four in other ways, although these differences are not pivotal in the definition of the term *quick*:

1. The quick attacker approaches closer to the the setter. On the one and the back one, the spiker approaches no more than a step from the setter; on the three, she approaches about two meters from the setter. On the four, in contrast, the spiker approaches five–six meters from the setter.

2. Because of the shorter distance between the setter and the spiker on the quick, the time from the set to the spike is also shorter than on the four.

3. The quick attacker jumps when the ball is set; the four-attacker jumps after the ball has been set.

4. The middle-hitter, a specialist, usually attacks the quick set; the left always attacks the four.

5. The defense accords the quick set special consideration; blocking schemes are defined by their treatment of the one, the back one and the three.

The medium-height sets exhibit a slower rhythm than the low sets, and the high sets exhibit a slower rhythm still. Less setter/spiker synchrony is required.

The different heights of the sets are associated with an attack point on the net. A set near the center of the net, for example, may be high, that is, slow, as it would be performed by the beginning team. It may be medium-height, that is, medium-speed, as it would be performed by the intermediate team (a two). Or it may be low, that is, fast, as it would be performed by the advanced team (a one).

A set to the left sideline likewise may be delivered high and slow (a regular), medium-height and medium-speed (a hut), or low and fast (a shoot). A set to any location on the court can be classified in this way.

Are there not more than three rhythms on the court? Yes. But further division is of little use in describing the team's plays. Further division benefits the players, whose on-court discussions can be summarized in four words: higher, lower, faster and slower.

It is useful to equate the high-apex set with a slow rhythm and the low-apex set with a fast rhythm. The rule, however, does not always apply. An exception is the one delivered by a tall setter to an equally tall spiker. The set is high but quick. A short setter delivering a low-apex set to a short attacker may result in a slower attack.

The One

The *one* provides the key to the quick attack. It forces the middle-blocker to wait and, perhaps, jump before moving to block near the sideline.

The middle-blocker confronts a dilemma. The attacker opposite her is jumping to spike. If she does not wait and at least raise her hands, the attacker hits an unobstructed one.

If she waits too long and the set goes elsewhere, she may be too late to help her teammate block. The attacker has the one-on-one match-up she ought to win.

In a second offensive pattern, a timing combination, the quick hitter jumps near the opposing middle-blocker. If the blocker jumps with the quick hitter, a second player attacks over or near her as the blocker returns to the floor.

These combinations occur again and again in advanced volleyball. Each begins with a quick set, usually the one.

The one is the quickest set of all. The setter touches the ball and the spiker attacks it a fraction of a second later.

The one is the easiest set to hit. On a well-set ball, the spiker does not have to worry about the path of the one. The ball ascends to the perfect spot.

The spiker with a good setter can hit the one blindfolded.

There are two main considerations in setting and spiking the one: the location of the spiker's jump and the timing of the set and spike.

1. **Position.** The attacker jumps close to the setter. When the setter is facing left, the spiker's feet at take-off are, in general, less than one-half meter to the left of the setter's, but deeper in the court.

As the setter moves left or right along the net to receive the pass, so does the spiker. If the setter receives the ball in the center of the net, the attacker approaches to the immediate left of her; this is slightly to the left of the court's midline (**279**).

If the setter receives the ball to the right of the midline, the spiker again approaches to her immediate left (**280**).

If the setter receives the ball farther right, the spiker approaches in the same manner (**281**).

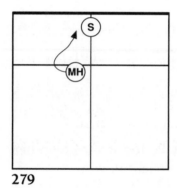 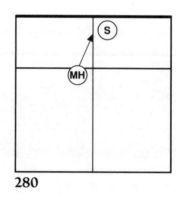 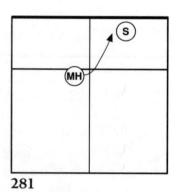

279 280 281

The exception is a pass that brings the setter to the left. In this case, the attacker must approach to the right of the setter (**282**). If she stays to the left, the opposing middle-blocker moves to the left, too. The middle-blocker approaches her blocker-teammate on the left. In the likely event of a left set, a double-block is assured.

When the pass brings the setter away from the net, the spiker moves left. This allows both the setter and the spiker a better view of the other. In general, the spiker moves to the left about the same distance as the setter has moved away from the net (**283**).

Why does the spiker move left? If she stays in a left-to-right line with the setter, she's forced to look back to watch the set. This reduces both her power and her vision.

When the setter is deep, the attacker does not jump deep with her; she adjusts her approach so that she attacks near the net (**283**). She must delay her jump to allow for the set's extra distance.

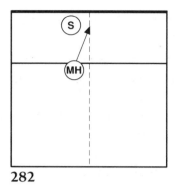

282

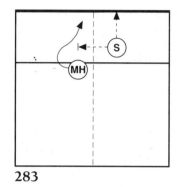

283

2. **Timing.** The spiker must jump on time. The fastest *one* requires that she peak as the setter touches the ball. The slowest requires that she jump as the setter touches the ball.

The ultimate responsibility for timing is the setter's. She adjusts the height and speed of the set depending on three factors: the reach of the spiker, the timing of the spiker's jump and the height at which she receives the ball.

An extreme is the short, late-jumping spiker. She receives a slow set that goes slightly higher than her reach. The ball is falling when it is attacked. Another extreme is the tall, early-jumping spiker. She receives a fast set that continues upward if it is missed.

In general, the one is delivered fast when the setter receives the ball low, slow when she receives it high.

* * * * *

1. The inexperienced one attacker jumps late.

2. The inexperienced one attacker jumps too shallow, that is, too close to the net. She traps herself.

3. It is easy for the attacker to watch a pass on her right. Both the ball and the setter are in view. When the ball is passed from her left, she has no choice but to watch over her left shoulder. This takes the setter out-of-view.

4. Jumping is a benefit to the 5-1 setter whose offense includes the one. Jumping gives her the chance to tip or spike the second touch when she is in the front row. It also creates doubt in the minds of her opponents about her attacking the second touch when she is in the back row. (Most international setters jump for every quick and medium-height set.)

5. Passers must deliver the ball high to tall, high-jumping one-setters.

The Three

The *three*, or inside shoot, is a quick set, usually directed to the middle-front attacker. Like the one, it functions both to score points and to draw blockers from other attackers.

At its height the three reaches less than a meter above the net. It moves fast, meeting the hitter about halfway between the setter and the left sideline. The spiker attempts to arrive before both the middle- and the left-blocker.

The middle-blocker usually moves to the left to stop the three. Now the right opens, freeing the right spiker to attack a back-set near the sideline. The left-front spiker is less likely to be free because the middle-blocker has moved closer to her.

Middle-front is not the only candidate for the three. As the team grows in experience, it directs the set to its left-front player. When left-front hits a three, both middle- and right-front have the opportunity to hit back-sets.

The international team expands its use of the inside shoot to include the right hitter, who crosses two-thirds of the court to make the attack. When the right hits a three, the middle often attacks a back-set.

To time the fastest three, the spiker must jump as the setter touches the ball. To time the slowest, she must have planted to jump as the setter touches the ball.

Inexperienced quick-attack teams usually run a slow three to reduce errors in timing. Experienced and international-level teams run a fast three to force the defenders to react quickly.

The setter who delivers the ball from a high position, as at the peak of a jump, increases the speed of the three.

The Four

The *four*, or outside shoot, is a low, fast set that is directed to the left-front attacker.

At its height the four reaches 1-1½ meters above the net, an increase over the three. The greater distance between the setter and the spiker makes the difference. The outside shoot moves faster, and is more difficult to time, than any other set.

The spiker meets the four on the left sideline. She wants to attack before the middle-blocker moves to join her left-blocker teammate.

The four arrives a second or less after it leaves the setter's hands. When the middle-blocker is delayed, even slightly, she is too late to block. Even the left-blocker, if she has located herself away from the sideline, may be late.

Why, then, isn't the four used all of the time? The speed of the ball brings difficulties for the attacker in both timing and range:

1. Timing. The spiker does not always hit the ball squarely. Occasionally she misses it. She may be forced to tip.

2. Range. The spiker cannot always angle her shots in the direction she would like. She is especially limited when the set arrives close to the net. The spiker is easily trapped by a four.

The solution is to slow the speed of the four, increasing both the spiker's power and her range. A higher four gives the blockers more time to position themselves. The middle-blocker still has a great distance to travel in a short time.

To time the fastest four, the spiker takes her last step before jumping as the setter touches the ball. To time the slowest, she begins her approach when the ball has traveled about halfway to the left sideline.

The play that complements the four directs the middle- and right-front attackers to the right, that is, behind the setter.

The Two

The *two* is a medium-height set that can be directed to any player on the court, including those in the back row. When the intermediate team quickens its middle-attack (page 250), the unnamed set is a two. The advanced team quickens its right-side attack with a long, back two.

The two, often called the *play set* or *combination set,* is the workhorse of the multiple attack. When a blocker jumps with a quick attacker, the second attacker hits a two.

The setter uses the two as an alternative to a quick set when the pass is deep or the hitter is late.

The two rises about 1½ meters above the net and arrives at any location on the court. In combination with a quick attack, it is often directed slightly away from the net. A depth of 1-1½ meters keeps one of the hitters from inhibiting the other.

Unlike a quick set, the height of the two is influenced by the other attacker in the combination. When the quick-hitter is late, for example, the two must be higher to allow for the blocker's delayed jump.

The spiker of the two takes her last step before jumping as the setter touches the ball. She jumps as the set peaks.

The two is many spikers' ideal. It is quicker than a high set, and yet it moves more slowly than either a high set or a shoot. It offers the attacker a view of the blockers that is unavailable to the quick attacker.

The two that is directed away from the net allows a full range of shots. The spiker cannot be trapped.

The two lends itself to all approaches, including straight, angled, veered, slide, back-row and pump.

The Hitters

The advanced team, like the intermediate, designates its setter and its two middle-hitter/blockers. It also designates its two left hitters. The sixth player is designated *opposite*, which describes her position in relation to the setter.

What are the characteristics of the designated attackers?

The middle-hitter is generally tall and has long arms. Her height and reach allow her to block first-tempo sets without jumping high, after which she can move quickly to block with a teammate.

The middle can read the opposing setter and react to the read. She is fast, especially laterally.

The middle has stamina. She blocks every hard attack, regardless of its location, and jumps on almost every offensive play.

The middle can time her approach for quick sets, especially ones and threes. Consistent timing means that she hits the ball high on these attacks.

The designated left usually hits harder than any other team member. She attacks with great left-to-right range. She commands at least one and perhaps two or three off-speed shots.

The left caroms her shots from both the top and the sides of the blockers' hands. She hits off the block in two instances: when she confronts a tight double- or triple-block and when she is trapped by a set close to the net. The left hits any set, from a fast shoot to a high and angled set. She hits from deep in the court.

The designated opposite performs all of the skills well. She is mobile. She hits the two from anywhere in the court and does so after a fast and often curved approach. She hits equally well on the right or the left side. She can attack from the back row.

The Four-passer Serve Receive

The advanced team usually wants its designated hitters to attack in their positions all of the time. This is especially important for the middle-hitter, whose role is more specialized than either the left or the opposite.

The problem is in receiving serve. How does the middle-hitter position herself for the first set when she is left- or right-front (288)?

The solution is for the middle-hitter to position herself near the net during serve-receive. From here, she can retreat to attack in the center of the court (289).

When the middle-hitter is at the net, the serve-receive formation has only four passers. They arrange themselves in a U (289).

Receiving serve without the middle point of the W is not difficult for the advanced team. All of its players are skilled passers and move quickly to the ball.

The emphasis on positioning the middle-hitters means that in some rotations, the outside hitters attack out of position: the opposite attacks on the left and the designated left on the right (290). The disparity must be tolerated in these rotations or corrected with a left-front/right-front switch after the first attack.

The left and the right wings in the U formation are responsible for short serves in the center of the court. The back receivers have no responsibility in this regard.

Most serves fly to the left- and right-back receivers. This is especially true when the server delivers the ball from well beyond the baseline, a common serve for advanced teams. In this case, serving the ball shallow is difficult.

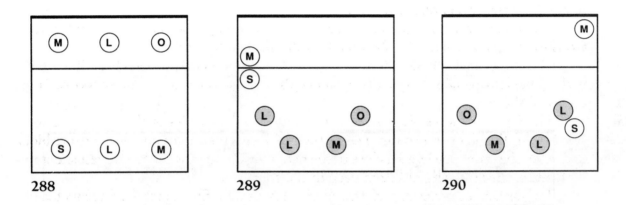

288   289   290

The 5-1 team arranges its lineup in one of two ways. The setter either leads or follows the middle-hitter through the team's rotations. Leading means that she serves before the middle-hitter; following means that the middle-hitter serves before she does.

The team bases its lineup on three considerations. The first is the number of rotations in which the serve-receive contains five, rather than four, passers. Five cover the court better than four. The five-receiver formation positions the designated middle at middle-front. The four-receiver formation positions her to the side.

The second consideration is the number of rotations in which the opposite, rather than the designated right, attacks left-front. The fewer the better.

The third consideration is the number of awkward formations. Awkward means that the players find it difficult to move into position without inhibiting each other. One formation (292, the second rotation) offers the setter two difficult possibilities: looping to the right or heading straight toward the net. If she loops, she crosses the ball's path to both the right-back and right-front receivers. If she moves straight, she intersects the middle getting into position to attack.

The team usually arranges itself according to Lineup 1, in which the setter leads the middle-hitter (291). Lineup 1 contains three five-passer formations, two formations in which the opposite hits left and no awkward formations. Lineup 2 contains two five-passer formations, one in which the opposite hits left and one awkward.

FOUR PASSER SERVE RECEIVE
Setter Leads

ROTATION

O L M
M L S

	M
THREE HITTERS	

O   **L** S

M   L

Double Cross

M O L
L S M

M	
THREE HITTERS	

O   **L**

S

L   M

Double Cross

L M O
S M L

	M
THREE HITTERS	

L S   **O**

M   L

S L M
M L O

S M	
	TWO HITTERS

L   O

M   L

M S L
L O M

M S	
	TWO HITTERS

L   M

L   O

L M S
O M L

	S
TWO HITTERS	

L   **M**   L

O   M

291

FOUR PASSER SERVE RECEIVE
Setter Follows

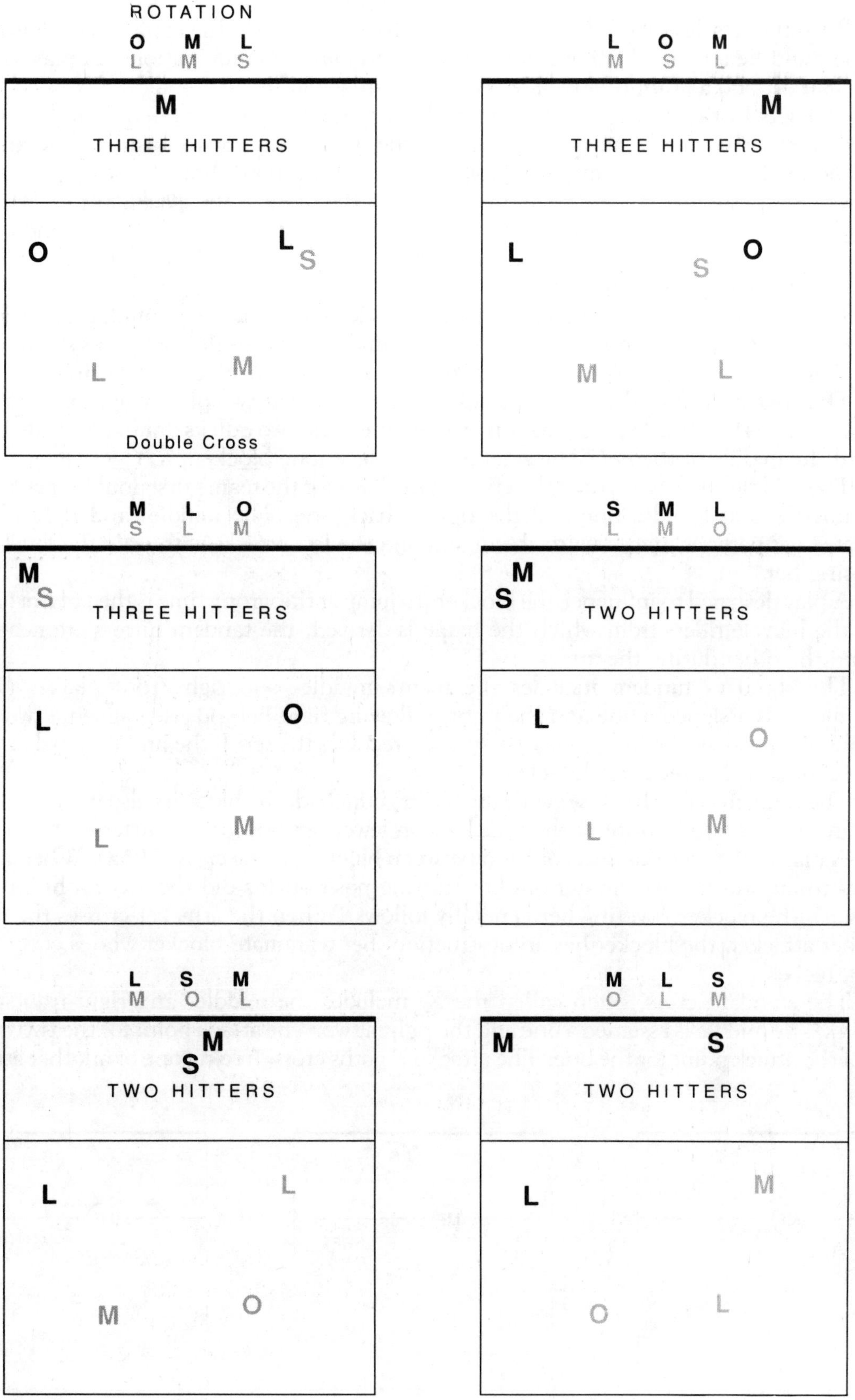

ROTATION

O M L
L M S

| M |
| THREE HITTERS |

O   **L** S

L   M

Double Cross

L O M
M S L

| M |
| THREE HITTERS |

L   S   **O**

M   L

M L O
S L M

M S

THREE HITTERS

L   **O**

L   M

S M L
L M O

M S

TWO HITTERS

L   O

L   M

L S M
M O L

S M

TWO HITTERS

L   L

M   O

M L S
O L M

M   **S**

TWO HITTERS

L   M

O   L

292

The Multiple Attack

With the sets described above—one, two, three, and four—the team has the foundation for the multiple attack. It combines these sets into plays or combinations. A play assigns a particular set and a point of attack for each front-row player.

The sets in the play are not random. They are designed to influence the blockers to spread themselves along the net, to jump at the wrong time or to obstruct one another's movements. Many plays attempt to manipulate the block in all three ways.

The best example of a play designed to spread the block is the *quick/shoot* (**293**). In the quick/shoot, a front-row player attacks a quick set near the center of the net and another attacks a shoot on the sideline. The speed of the attack and the spikers' locations make it difficult for the opponents to form a double-block.

The team's first quick/shoot likely includes its left- and middle-front players (**293**). The middle is assigned a one and the left a four. The middle-blocker hesitates—as she must—to defend against the one, and the left attacks with only the left-blocker opposing her.

The *double-quick* works like the quick/shoot except that two players approach to attack quick sets (**294**). A third approaches on the sideline. The two quicks draw an outside blocker toward the middle of the net. The sideline hitter faces one blocker.

The middle- and right-front players form the basis for the team's first double-quick (**294**). The middle is assigned a one and the right a back one. The middle- and right-blockers hesitate—or perhaps jump—with the quicks and the left attacks with only the left-blocker opposing her.

A play designed to influence the blockers to jump at the wrong time is the *tandem* (**295b**). Like the bicycle riders from which the name is derived, the tandem hitters are nearly one behind the other during the attack.

The standard tandem includes the team's middle- and right-front players (**295b**). The middle is assigned a one and the right, following right behind, is assigned a two. If the middle-blocker does not jump, the first attacker receives the set. If the middle-blocker jumps, the second attacker receives the set.

The tandem is rare because, with the hitters bunched, the blockers also bunch. Blockers that are side-by-side in front of the attack mean fewer options for the hitters.

A play designed to cause a collision between blockers is the *cross* (**295a**). When a spiker moves to an attack point away from her starting position (as did the second hitter in the tandem), the blocker covering her generally follows. When the attacker crosses the path of another attacker, the blocker has an obstruction: her teammate-blocker who is covering the first attacker.

The standard cross, often called the X, includes the middle- and right-front players (**295a**). The middle is assigned a one and the right a two. The attack point for the two is to the left of the attack point for the one. The attackers' paths cross, freeing one or another attacker.

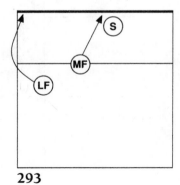

293

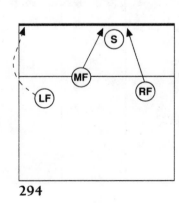

294

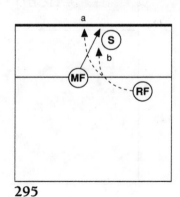

295

276

All of the team's combination plays can be considered variations of the quick/shoot, the double-quick, the tandem and the cross. These include the double-cross, in which the path of one spiker crosses those of two others; the slide, in which an attacker approaches at one point on the net and then slides to another; the pump, in which a single attacker fakes a quick and then hits a two; and the back-row attack, in which back-row players are part of the combination.

The Spiker's Approaches

The ideal approach to spike consists of: (1) a straight line for balance; (2) four steps, for a combination of control and speed; and (3) a good angle to the net for range.

The multiple offense occasionally allows the spiker to make the ideal approach. The left-front who attacks a medium-height or a high set on the sideline, for example, has time to move outside the court and approach with control toward the opponents' right corner (296a). The left may be able to do likewise on a two near the center of the net (296c), or on a three (296b).

These opportunities are exceptional. The multiple offense requires the spiker to move quickly and far. The ideal approach changes, sometimes dramatically.

The spiker makes nine variations on the ideal approach: the loop, the short pattern, the glide, the veer, the quick slide, the one-footed slide, the pump, the broad-jump and the creep.

1. The Loop. The most common change is for the spiker to follow a looped path toward the attack point. When the left-front attacks immediately to the left of the setter, for example, she must curve from right to left (297). The curve gives her range, that is, the opportunity to attack both left and right.

2. The Short Pattern. The spiker may change the steps of the four-step approach. The middle, for example, usually hits quick. She starts closer to the net than the outside hitters and eliminates one or two steps of the four-step approach (298).

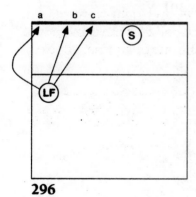

296

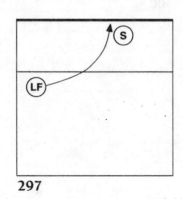

297

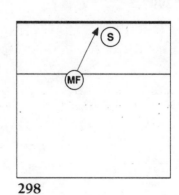

298

3. The Glide. The hitter who travels a great distance changes her steps in a different way. The left-front, for example, often hits on the right sideline (**299**). She glides into her final approach. Her first two steps are longer and faster than the ideal. They are indistinguishable, in fact, from the other steps in her lope or run to the ball.

4. The Veer. The fake cross, an adjunct to the cross, requires a dramatic change in direction. The right-front, for example, may attack either a cross or a fake cross in combination with the middle-front's attack of the one. In order to fake the cross, the right starts toward the center of the net and then, at what is called the break-point, veers to the right of the setter (**300**). The faker pivots on her left foot at the break-point and changes direction sharply.

5. The Quick Slide. The quick slide is one of three plays in which a single attacker both fakes and attacks in short succession. It is a favorite of men's teams.

   The attacker nears one point on the net and then moves sideways— slides—to another. The middle-front, for example, approaches as if she intended to hit a back one. She plants her feet normally and then broad jumps to the right along the net. She receives a quick back-set that is nearer the sideline than the back one (**301**).

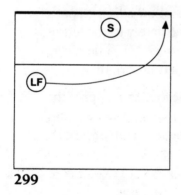

299

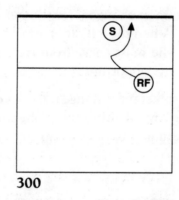

300

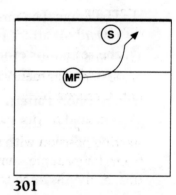

301

6. The One-footed Slide. The one-footed differs from the quick in that the attacker fakes a quick and then attacks a play set. It functions as a one-hitter combination and is a favorite of women's teams.

   The middle-front, for example, approaches the net as if she had been assigned a three (302). She turns sharply to the right, moves down the net with a long left-step, jumps from her left foot and hits a medium-height set to the left of, but deeper than, the setter. Jumping from one foot allows the attacker to travel a greater distance along the net than the two-footed jump of the quick slide. It also makes the one-footed slide different from any other approach.

   The one-footed slider works either to the left or to the right of the setter. To the left, the slide is called a step-in, that is, toward the setter; to the right, it is called either a step-around, that is, around the setter; or step-out, that is, away from the setter.

   A right-hander is limited to one-footed sliding from left to right because of the approach's take-off.

7. The Pump. The pump is the most rarely used single-attacker play. In the pump, the attacker fakes a jump, hesitates and then jumps to attack a play set. The middle-front usually performs the attack, aiming it at the middle-blocker who jumps high to stop the one.

   In order to fool the blocker, the attacker must time her approach as if she were attacking a quick set. She plants, swings her arms forward as far as her hips, rises slightly and then lowers herself again to jump for the attack.

8. The Broad-jump. The attacker often jumps both high and forward. Quick sliders broad-jump, as mentioned. So do back-row players, who like to attack close to the net. Crossing hitters broad-jump when their break-point is far from the attack.

9. The Creep. In the final variation on the ideal approach, the spiker adjusts her starting position with short steps, often to the side, as she watches the ball. Right-front, for example, may creep left before she attacks the three (303). The combination of the distance to the attack point and the quickness of the set prevents her from starting in her usual position. The hitter disguises her creeping.

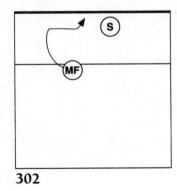

302

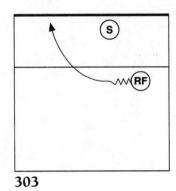

303

Each position on the court requires a variety of approaches. The left-front's possibilities differ from the middle-front's, the middle-front's from the right-front's and so on.

The discussion of each position does not address which designated player is in that position. The left-front, for example, may be a designated middle-hitter, an opposite or a left.

The term setter in the discussion indicates the ideal position on the court from which to set, not the actual location of the setter. "The spiker creeps toward the setter," for example, means that the spiker creeps toward the setting spot, whether the setter is there or not.

* * * * *

The left-front, who attacks from sideline to sideline, starts one-half to one meter inside the court and deeper than the three-meter line (**304**). The majority of her attacks are medium-height or high sets on the left sideline.

The left makes five approaches to attack low, fast sets; all but the *four* are quick.

1. The Four. The left usually attacks the four with a straighter approach than she does to attack slower sets in the same location. She does not have time either to position herself outside the court or to follow a wide loop, especially if she receives the serve. If she does not pass, she creeps or sidesteps left to increase her angle. The left uses a four-step approach in the direction of the angle (**304a**).

2. The Three. In attacking the three, the left uses a straight, four-step approach. The attack allows both balance and the best angle of arrival (**304b**).

3. The One. The attacker loops from right to left and glides into the final approach. The angle of attack on arrival is ideal (**304c**).

4. The Back One. The attacker loops wider than she does in hitting the one. Her final approach is straight, at the ideal angle (**304d**).

5. The Back Slide. The attacker plants in the same spot as she does in attacking the back one but broad-jumps to the right. She hits the ball about halfway between the setter and the sideline (**304e**).

QUICK AND SHOOT APPROACHES
LEFT-FRONT

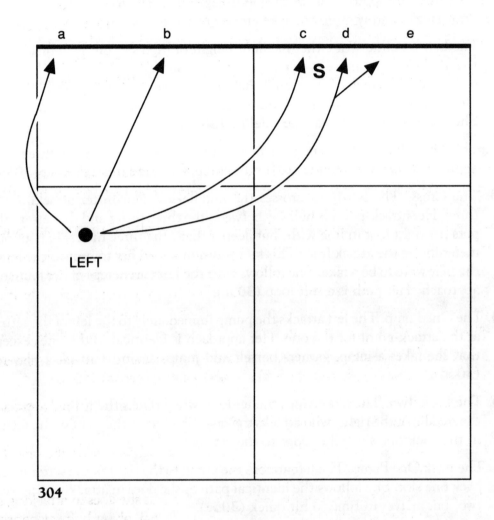

304

The left uses sixteen approaches to attack medium-height sets. They can be divided into three categories: continuous, fake cross and slide.

The continuous approaches, with one exception, curve to the attack point (305). They do not break sharply as do the fake crosses or the slides.

1. The Left Sideline. For either medium-height or high sets on the left sideline, the attacker's first move is to position herself outside the court. On her exit, she can either creep or sidestep if she has the time; otherwise she must lope. Her final approach consists of four steps toward the opponents' right corner. She contacts the ball near the sideline (305a).

2. The Three Pump. The left hits a pump at the attack point for the three. She approaches as if she intended to hit the three, fakes and hits a play set (305b).

3. The Cross. The left-front crosses the middle- or right-hitter attacking the three. Her attack-point is halfway between the three hitter and the setter. She puts her right foot in line with, but deeper than, the three hitter—about one meter inside the attack line. This foot position allows her to veer to the left if the play were to be a fake. She follows with the last three steps of her four-step approach. Her path is a soft loop (305c).

4. The One Pump. The left attacks the pump immediately to the left of the setter, at the attack-point for the one. Her approach is identical to the one, except that she fakes a jump, gathers herself and jumps again to attack a play set (305d).

5. The Back Two. The left crosses the middle, who attacks the three, or crosses the middle or the right, who attacks the one. She hits to the right of the setter, in the back one slot. She loops to the attack (305e).

6. The Back One Pump. The left attacks the pump to the right of the setter in the back one slot. She follows the identical path as she does in attacking the back two, but arrives in time to hit quick (305e).

7. The Pushed-Back Two. The left crosses with the middle or the right, who attack the back one. She follows a path that is nearly identical to the back two, except that it is to the right of the back one slot (305f).

8. The Right Sideline. The left-front makes a looping attack on the right sideline. She crosses the middle, who hits the three, or crosses the middle or the right, who hits the one. Her last few steps carry her nearly parallel to the sideline. She glides into her final approach (305g).

PLAY SET APPROACHES
LEFT-FRONT

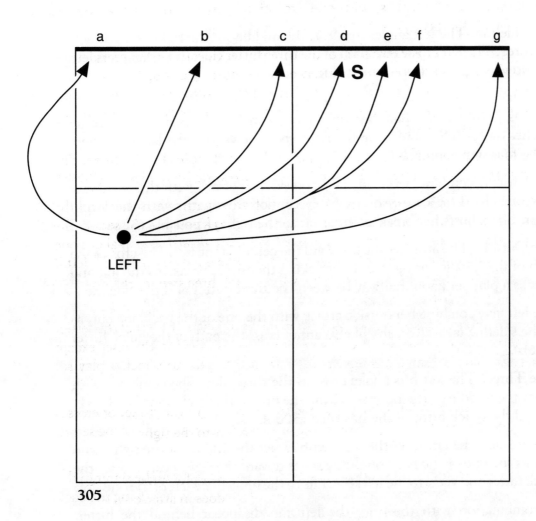

305

The left attacks four fake crosses. Her goal is to *disappear,* that is, to move behind the quick attacker, screening the blockers' view. The blocker must ask herself: will she cross or fake?

9. The Sideline. The left angles inside as the middle- or the right-front attacks the three. The left crosses the path of the three hitter (ideally), then veers left. She attacks a play set on the left sideline.

   The left's break point is about one meter inside the attack line and as far to the right as possible. She puts her right foot on the break point as the setter touches the ball. She pivots on her right and follows with the last three steps of the four-step approach.

   The left may combine her inside fake and sideline attack with the one or the back one. In these cases, she probably cannot cross paths with the quick-hitter. She adjusts her break-point as far to the right as possible (306a).

10. The Outside. The attacker starts toward the center of the net. She crosses the path of the middle- or right-front attacking the three, breaks to the left and attacks a play set about halfway between the three-hitter and the sideline.

    The left may combine her outside attack with the one or the back one but, as in the sideline fake-cross, she likely cannot cross the path of the quick hitter (306b).

11. The Three. The left hits a fake cross in the three slot. She combines with either the middle or the right attacking the one or the back one. She breaks behind the quick hitter if she has time (306c).

12. The Inside. The left fakes the cross with either the middle or the right, who attacks the one or the back one. She starts toward the right post, crosses the quick hitter and veers to the left. She hits to the immediate left of the one slot.

    In combination with the one, the left can disappear behind the hitter. In combination with the back one, which is farther from the attack point, she may not. As in all fake crosses, the hitter moves as far to the right as she can (306d).

PLAY SET APPROACHES
LEFT-FRONT

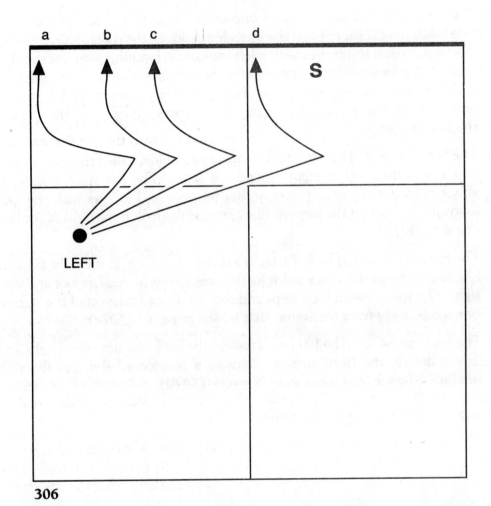

306

The left attacks four one-footed slides. She moves toward, around and away from the setter.

13. **The Step-In.** The left attacks a one-footed slide to the left of the setter. She heads toward the net as if she intended to attack the three. She adjusts her footwork so that she arrives with a left step at the jumping point for the three and on time for a quick set. She pivots on her left foot, takes a short, quick step with her right, crosses with her left and jumps from her left foot. The attacker moves toward the setter, stepping in, and contacts the ball near the center of the net (**307a**).

14. **The Step-Around.** The left attacks a one-footed slide, called the step-around, that moves from left to right around the setter. The left starts toward the attack point for the one, pivots on her left foot and follows with the same footwork she uses for the step-in. She contacts the ball to the right of the back one slot (**307b**).

15. **The Front Step-Out.** The left attacks a one-footed slide on the right sideline. She starts toward the attack point for the one, pivots on her left foot and veers right. She follows with long steps and the one-footed take-off of the step-in. She moves away from the setter, that is, she steps out (**307c**).

16. **The Back Step-Out.** The left heads toward the back one slot, veers right and, as she did on the front step-out, attacks a one-footed slide on the right sideline. She uses her usual slide footwork (**307d**).

PLAY SET APPROACHES
LEFT-FRONT

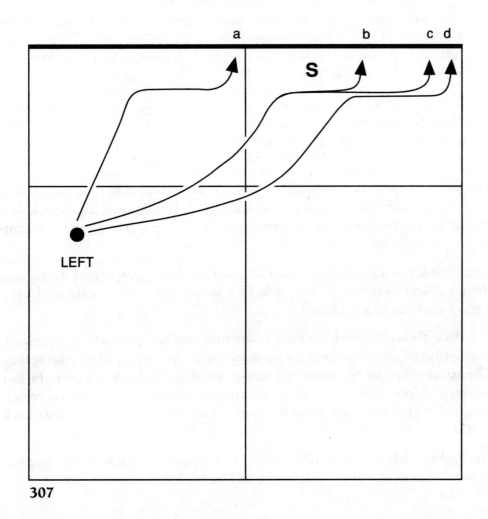

307

The middle starts closer to the net than the other hitters—on or slightly deeper than the three-meter line (308). She positions herself to the left of the setter, about halfway between the points of attack for the one and the three (308).

The middle uses a two- or three-step approach for most of her attacks, which are quick. At other times the middle attacks at a distance from her starting position; she ranges from about one and one-half meters inside the left sideline all the way to the right sideline.

The middle attacks five low, fast sets; all but the *Sideline* are quick.

1. The Three. The middle cannot approach straight for the three as the left can. She must loop from left to right in order to attack to the right with power. She likely creeps left to increase her angle but tries to do so without telegraphing the attack. This is creeping at its most delicate (308a).

2. The One. The middle's starting position allows a straight, balanced approach for the one. She attacks at the ideal angle. It is not unusual for the middle, particularly one who is tall, to move from her starting position to her jump in two steps (308b).

3. The Back One. The back one requires an initial loop from right to left and then a straight approach. The spiker's last two steps are straight and offer a good angle of attack (308c).

4. The Back Slide. The middle's most frequently used isolation attack is the back slide, which, like the back one, takes place to the right of the setter. The attacker follows the same path as she would for the back one until the last two steps. Upon planting to jump, she turns her body to the right and broad-jumps along the net, away from the setter. The setter pushes a quick set back (308d).

5. The Right Sideline. The middle attacks a shoot on the right sideline. Because of the distance, she must creep right and loop (308e).

QUICK AND SHOOT APPROACHES
MIDDLE-FRONT

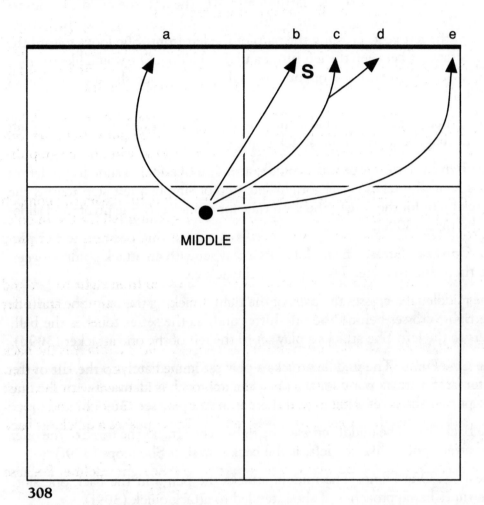

308

The middle uses fifteen patterns to attack play sets.

1. The Left-Three Cross. In her farthest attack to the left, the middle combines with the left attacking the three. She takes one right step and then heads toward the left post, crossing the path of the left front. She loops toward the net, attacking between the left hitter and the sideline. She would like to angle her approach toward the opponents' right corner, but she usually cannot (309a).

2. The Three Pump. The middle hits the three-pump exactly as does the left except that she loops to the attack point (309b).

3. The Step-In. Like the left, the middle attacks a one-footed slide to the left of the setter. She takes either a right-left step or simply a left step toward the attack point for the three. She is on time for a quick set. She pivots and slides to the right (309c).

4. The One Fake-Cross. The middle hits a play set with an attack point between the three and the one. The set is the classic two.

   The middle fake-crosses the path of the right attacking the one. She starts to the right, crosses behind the one-hitter and, as the setter touches the ball, veers to the left. She attacks a play set to the left of the one attacker (309d).

5. The One Pump. The middle attacks a play set immediately to the left of the setter, at the attack point for the one. Her approach is identical with the one except that she fakes a jump, and then attacks a play set (309e).

6. The Back Two. The middle crosses the right, who attacks the three or the one. Her attack point, like the left, is the back one slot. She loops (309f).

7. The Back One Pump. The middle attacks the pump in the back one slot. She times her approach as if she intended to attack quick (309f).

8. The Back Step-Out. Because the middle is a frequent attacker of the back one, she is a good choice to attack the step-out. She heads toward the back one slot, veers right and attacks near the right sideline (309g).

PLAY SET APPROACHES
MIDDLE-FRONT

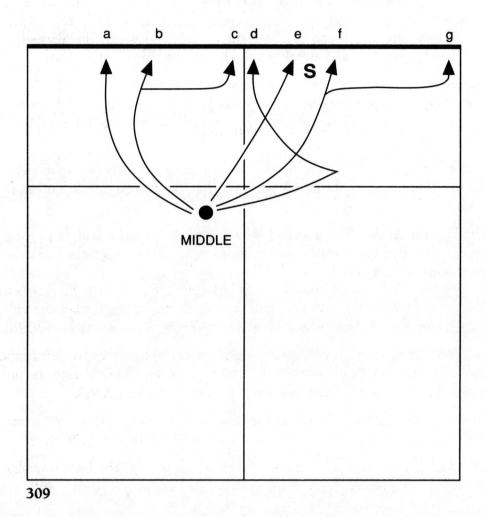

309

9. The Right-Three Fake. The middle both crosses and fake-crosses the right, who attacks the three. She first creeps toward the baseline, that is, she deepens, in order to give the three hitter the space to move. As she deepens, she also creeps left so that she can align herself with the three hitter's attack point. From here she disappears from the blockers' view. She breaks as the setter touches the ball and attacks to the left of the three hitter (310a).

10. The Right-Three Cross. The middle crosses the right, who attacks the three. She deepens, aligns herself with the three slot and breaks to the right of the three hitter. Her attack point is halfway between the the three hitter and the setter (310b).

11. The Step-around. The middle attacks the step-around exactly as does the left. Her position nearer to the attack point for the one, however, makes it easier (310c).

12. The Front Step-out. The middle heads toward the one slot and, with long steps and a flying one-footed take-off, slides right. She contacts the ball near the sideline (310d).

PLAY SET APPROACHES
MIDDLE-FRONT

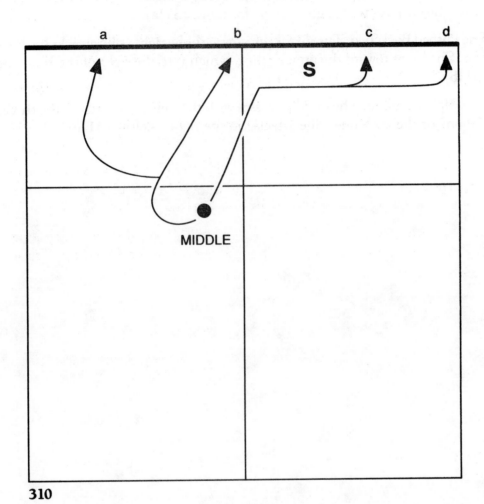

310

13. The Left-Three Fake Cross. The middle fake-crosses the left, who attacks the three. She starts toward the left post, plants her left foot as the setter touches the ball and veers right. She attacks a play set between the three hitter and the setter. She arrives with a good angle for range (311a).

14. The Pushed Back Two. The middle crosses with the right, who attacks the back one. She loops toward the attack point, which is to the right of the back one (311b).

15. The Right Sideline. The middle crosses with the right, who attacks the three, the one or the back one. She attacks on the right sideline (311c).

PLAY SET APPROACHES
MIDDLE-FRONT

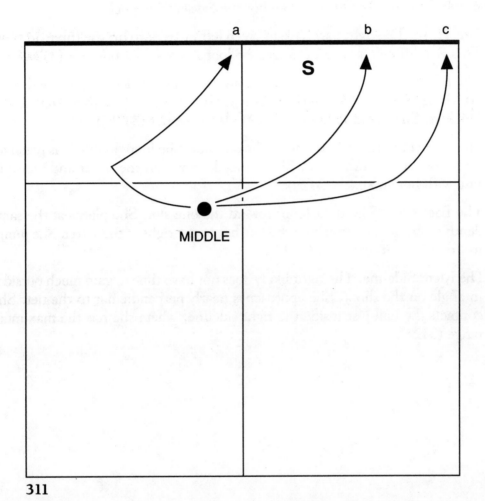

311

The right starts deeper than the attack line and one to one and one half meters from the sideline (312). She attacks along the net from about one and one-half meters inside the left-sideline all the way to the right sideline.

The right hits five low, fast sets; all but the *Sideline* are quick.

1. The Three. The right may have to creep left in order to hit the three on time. This is a difficult attack for range; she loops as much as possible (312a).

2. The Front Slide. The right heads toward the one slot, looping as she does in attacking the one. She plants deeper than the setter. She shows *one* to the blockers. She broad-jumps to the left along the net (312b).

3. The One. The right heads toward the one slot. She loops as much as possible, allowing her to attack right. She plants deeper than the setter and jumps in line with her approach (312c).

4. The Back One. The right loops toward the one slot. She plants at the same depth as she does in attacking the one but to the right of the setter. She jumps in line with her approach (312d).

5. The Right Sideline. The right likely does not have time to gain much outside-in angle on the shoot. She approaches nearly perpendicular to the net. She contacts the ball just inside the right sideline, where she has the maximum range (312e).

QUICK AND SHOOT APPROACHES
RIGHT-FRONT

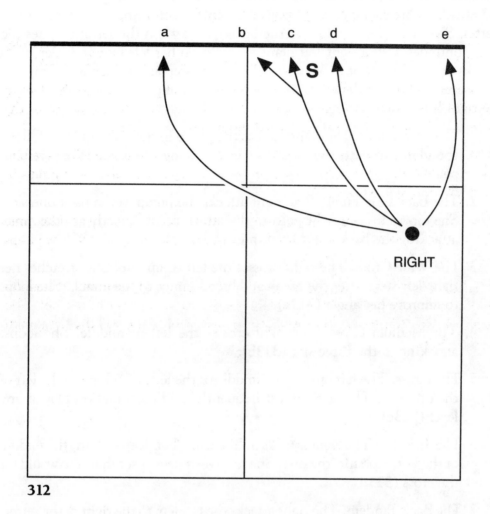

The right, in contrast to the left and middle, starts every play set approach in one direction (**313**). She takes her first two steps toward the center of the net. She goes as far to the left as she can. The left shows *cross* to the opposing blockers.

The attacker's break-point is in front of the three-meter line and slightly to the left of the setter. She plants her left foot at the break-point when the setter touches the ball. She either continues with a right-left plant or pivots on her left foot and veers right.

Attacks on the far left or right mean a long right step and subsequent jump. Attacks nearer the setter reduce the length of the step and the jump.

The right hits nine play sets.

1. The One Pump. The right attacks the pump in the one slot. She follows the identical path that she does in attacking the one (**312c**, previous page).

2. The Back One Pump. The right attacks the pump in the back one slot. She moves in a straight path to the attack point, exactly as if she were attacking the back one (**312d**, previous page).

3. The Wide Cross. The right crosses the left or middle. She stretches her right-left steps after the break and broad-jumps to the attack. She loops to improve her angle (**313a**).

4. The Medium Cross. The right crosses the left or middle. She loops, attacking in the three slot (**313b**).

5. The Cross. The left crosses the middle or the left, attacking to the left of the one slot. This is the most frequently used combination play at any level (**313c**).

6. The Tandem. The right attacks in line with, but deeper than, the middle or the left, who hits the one. She receives a deeper set than she would for the cross (**313d**).

7. The Back Tandem. The right attacks the tandem to the right of the setter. She follows either the middle or the left (**313e**).

8. The Fake Cross. The right starts toward the center of the net and then veers to attack in the back one slot (**313f**).

9. The Flair. The right starts toward the center of the net and then veers toward the right sideline. She stretches her right-left steps and then broad-jumps to the attack (**313g**).

PLAY SET APPROACHES
RIGHT-FRONT

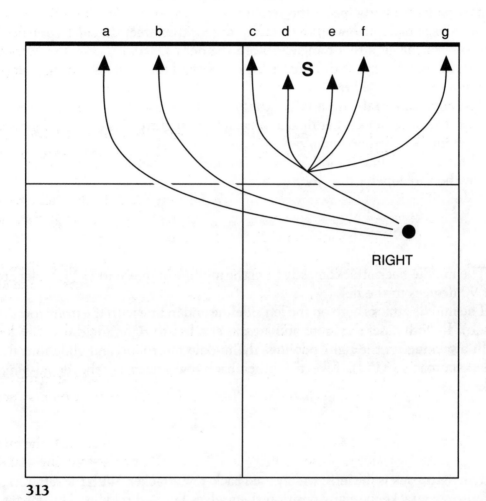

313

The left-back's sideline approach echoes the path of the left-front in attacking a medium-height or high set on the sideline (**314a**). She does not have to move as far outside the court, however; she starts near the sideline and angles less sharply to the right. She contacts the ball slightly inside the sideline.

In order to hit in line with the attack point for the three, she sidesteps left. From here she heads straight, at a slight angle, toward the net (**314b**).

For the middle attack, the left-back loops toward the midline and then approaches at 90 degrees to the net (**314c**).

The approach on the right sideline attack requires a long, deep loop (**314d**). Like the left-front, the hitter makes her final approach from slightly outside the sideline to slightly inside, giving her the maximum range.

The left-back, like the other back-row hitters, broad-jumps. She contacts the ball between the three-meter line and the net.

* * * * *

The middle-back attacks mostly from the midline of the court (**315c**). Her approach is about 90 degrees to the net.

The middle attacks both on the left sideline and in line with the front-row three hitter (**315a,b**). In both cases she loops and attacks at a left-to-right angle.

In attacking on the right sideline, the middle must loop and glide into the slightly angular approach (**315d**). Like the other back-row attackers, she broad-jumps on all attacks.

* * * * *

The right-back is the most widely used back-row attacker. With the setter in the front, the front-row attackers usually position themselves left and middle. This means that the setter, in order to spread the attack along the net, delivers the ball to the right-back.

The right attacks mostly on the right, using the slightly outside-in approach (**316b**). She also loops left, attacking in the middle (**316a**). Like the other back-row players, she approaches 90 degrees to the net.

The right-back combines with the left or middle-front in attacking the cross (**317**). The quick-hitter attacks the one, the back one or the sideline; the right-back crosses the quick's path and attacks to the left of the setter. The right receives a play set that is both slightly higher and deeper than the standard.

BACK ROW APPROACHES

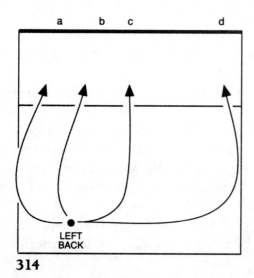

314

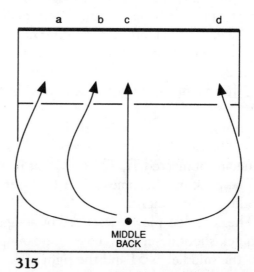

315

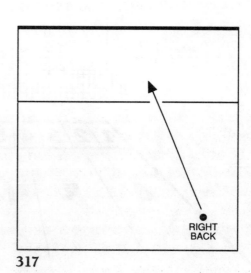

316

317

301

Numbering the Plays

Advanced teams have many plays. In order to be specific about the sets in each play, the team describes them by their location on the net and their height.

Regarding the set's location, the advanced team divides the net into nine attack zones (318). Each zone is about one meter wide and has a number associated with it. The standard system numbers the zones *one* through *nine*, from the left sideline to the right. The far left is *one*, the far right is *nine* and the setter is located in zone *six*.

The advanced team adds another number for the type of set. Some use the set's exact height, in feet, above the net. The number *1* represents a set one foot above the net, the number *2* represents a set two feet above the net and so on.

Other teams simplify the sets into three heights only. That is the system used here (318).

The *one* now becomes *51*, that is, a low set in zone 5. The *three* becomes *31*, a low set in zone 3. The *two* in the cross becomes *42*, a medium-height set in zone 4. Sets to the left sideline are numbered *11*, *12* or *13*, that is, in zone 1, low, medium-height or high.

The back one becomes *71*. A back-set on the sideline becomes either *91*, *92* or *93*, depending on its height.

The complete play is described by assigning each front-row player a two-digit number. The quick/shoot described above, for example, becomes *11-51-92*. The left hitter's set is an *11*, the middle's is *51* and the right's *92*.

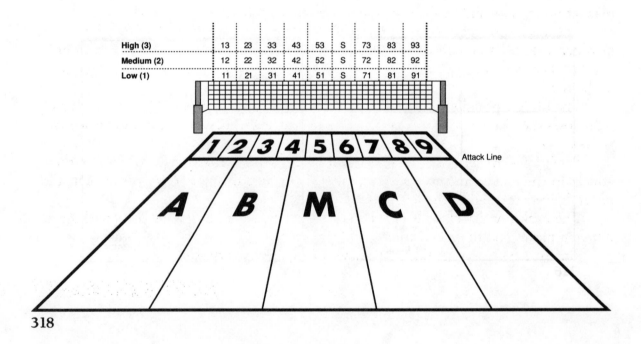

318

302

The system is accurate. A prominent member of the U.S. Volleyball Association's technique commission says, "Using this system, you can talk about volleyball with anyone in the world."

The numbers give equal importance to each of the three front-row hitters. The combination, however, usually includes two. The third hitter can be considered the *release*, or the setter's outlet, when the combination goes awry. Designating her as such makes the system simpler. The quick/shoot becomes *11-51-R*.

Now it is immediately apparent whether the combination is a left-side, as in the team's first quick/shoot (left- and middle-front), a right-side (right- and middle-front) or a left-right.

The R could be any height. It works as a constant, showing the position in the lineup of the third, non-combination hitter.

Using the R, the designation for the cross becomes *R-51-42*. The fake cross becomes *R-51-72*.

The system must describe three more attack patterns to be complete: the slide, the pump and the back-row.

The slide attacker approaches one point on the net and then moves sideways, or slides, to another. She is assigned a number for the approach point and a number for the attack point. The numbers are separated by a slash. *71/81* means a quick slide from zone 1 to zone 8. *71/92* means an approach in zone 7 and a play-set attack in zone 9.

The pump is indicated with a P, preceded by the number of the zone where the attack takes place. A pump in zone 5 is designated *5P*. The P includes both the quick fake and the play-set jump. The middle-front performs the standard: *R-5P-92*.

The advanced team uses the back-row attack for several reasons, the most important of which is to fill an empty attack lane. This occurs when the front row consists of only two hitters or when the play directs all three of its front-row hitters away from one zone at the net.

The fill is especially important on a bad pass. The setter drawn deep into the court often loses the chance to set one or more of her front-row attackers. In this case, a deep set is easy.

Sometimes the setter has no choice but to set the back-row attacker. If the front row attacks in the middle and on the right, for example, and the pass arrives on the left, the setter delivers the ball to the left-back.

The back-row attack adds diversity to the offense. Four or five players attacking at different places and times can confuse an opponent.

Finally, a back-row set takes advantage of an effective attacker.

The back row is divided into five attack zones, whose designations from left-to-right echo in letters the primary attack zones at the net. The five back-row zones are, from the left-side of the court to the right: A, B, M, C and D (318, previous page). The M zone in the center of the court is often referred to as a "pipe," as in "right down the pipe." In absolute time, it is the fastest back-row attack.

Each back-row player can be assigned an attack zone, although one or two attackers are standard. The height of the set does not need to be designated; the setter and the attacker settle this on the court. The setter delivers the ball inside the three-meter line, allowing the attacker to broad-jump toward the net.

A typical play, including both a front- and back-row attack, is written:

11-0-71;
0-M-D.

The first line—three numbers separated by hyphens—indicates the assignments of the players in the front row, left to right. The second line indicates the assignments of the back-row players.

In the play above, the *11* assigns the left-front a shoot set on the left sideline. The zero shows that there is no middle-front. The *71* assigns the right-front a quick set immediately behind the setter (**319**).

The zero indicates that left-back does not have a hitting assignment. The M assigns the middle-back an attack in zone M, that is, on the midline of the court. The D assigns the right-back an attack in zone D, near the right sideline (**319**).

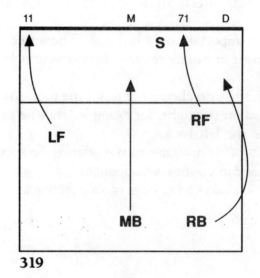

319

The players do not base their court patterns on the net's imaginary zones, but on their relationship to the ball, their teammates and the net. The setter, for example, positions herself inside, but at the extreme right of, the imaginary zone 6 (320). The hitter assigned to attack in the theoretical zone 5 attacks in the middle of zone 6 (320).

The cross or X hitter, assigned to attack in zone 4, attacks in zone 5 (320). The left who crosses the three hitter is also assigned to attack in the theoretical zone 4; like the right, she attacks in zone 5 (321).

The attack-points become even more difficult to identify when the ball is passed either to the left or right of the setter's ideal spot. When the setter receives the pass to the left, for example, zone 5 moves left with her. In this case, the right hitting the standard cross must adjust her attack left into zone 4.

Many of the real attacks, however, correspond with their theoretical counterparts. The three is attacked in the middle of the imaginary zone 3 (321). The zone 1 and zone 7 hitters attack according to theory (322). So does the zone 9 hitter (323). The zone 8 hitter divides the theoretical zones 7 and 8 (323).

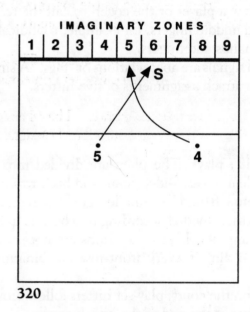

320

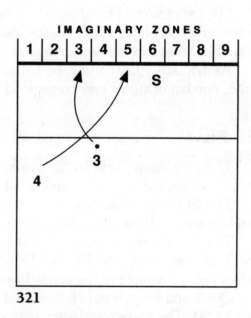

321

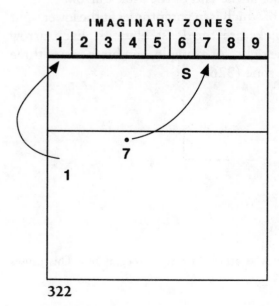

322

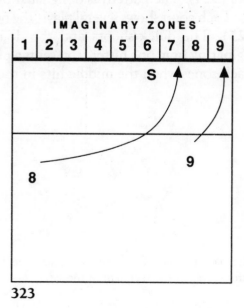

323

Names, Signals

The team names its plays. The name does not describe each player's assignment although most correspond to an attack pattern.

The play gains its identity from a characteristic of the play itself. The possible characteristics include a general location at the net, a point of attack, one or more hitters' lines of approach or the length of one of the sets.

Examples of names based on general locations include "inside," "outside," "front," "back," "wide," "left," "right," "on-side" and "off-side." Names based on a hitter's line of approach include quick/shoot, double-quick, cross, X, fake, slide, reverse, pump, and flair.

It is not necessary that play names be either reasonable or communicable to anyone outside the team. They only need to be identifiable to team members.

* * * * *

Plays are assigned hand signals. These allow a player or the coach to call the team's plays silently. A player may cross her index and middle fingers, for example, to indicate a cross. The team can use any configuration of hands and fingers.

As in football play-calling, both names and signals are abbreviations or "tags." A single name, number or signal may correspond to the attack assignments of five hitters.

The Plays

The play chart includes 50 courts and 134 plays. The plays are divided into six categories: quick/shoot and double-quick, tandem, cross, slide, pump and back-row.

The crosses and fake crosses are divided into left/middle, middle/right, left/right and double-cross combinations; each of these is further divided according to who hits quick.

The chart is not inclusive. Possible, but improbable, combinations are not shown. The back-row attack, which can be added to almost every front-row combination,* includes only a sample of the possibilities.

Quick and shoot hitters follow solid lines on the court; play-set hitters follow broken lines (324). The pattern is designated by number at the end of the attack arrow.

Each court shows several plays, the number of which is in parentheses at the lower right (325). The quick/shoots and the double-quicks are the least obvious. Each arrow originating from one hitter represents a play. The right, for example, can hit in any of three attack-zones when the middle hits in the three zone (326).

---

*The back-row attacker must not follow the front-row who attacks a medium-height set. This causes confusion about the recipient of the set.

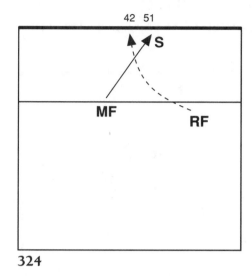

324

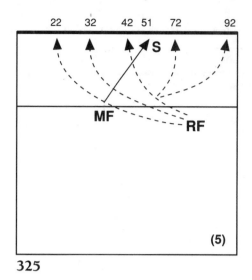

(5)

325

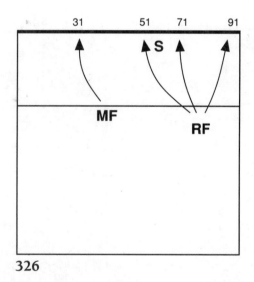

326

Most of the plays are two-hitter combinations. A third hitter, not part of the combination, can be added on each court, but the attack-zone must be vacant. Left/right combinations consist of two hitters, by definition; double-cross combinations consist of three hitters, by definition. Slide and pump consist of one hitter.

Quick sets immediately to the left and to the right of the setter can be converted with a broad-jump into quick slides. The other front-row hitter or hitters, in this, case, must attack near the sideline. Quick slides cannot be combined with the cross on most teams. The slider jumps into the crosser and likely brings a blocker with her.

The team can run one-footed slides from right to left if the hitter is left-handed. The patterns are mirror images of those for right-handed hitters.

QUICK/SHOOT, DOUBLE-QUICK

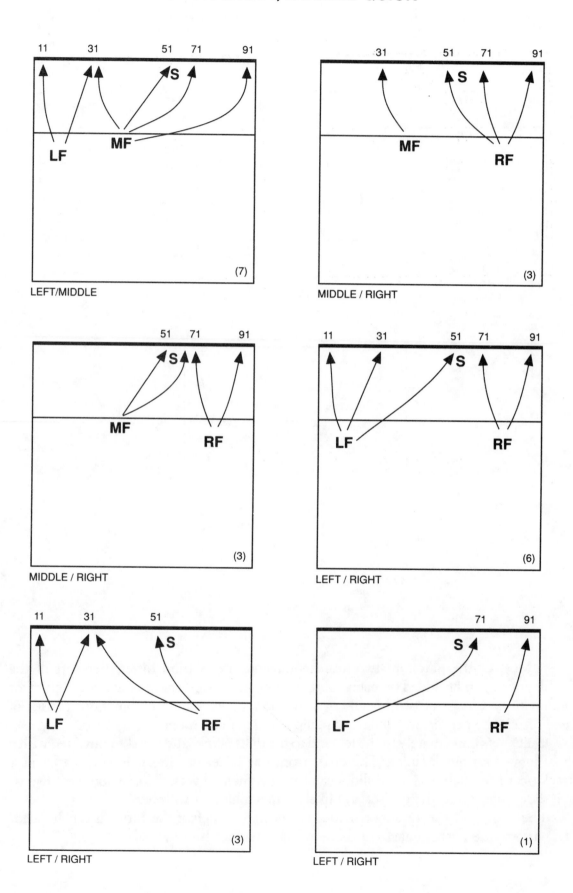

TANDEM

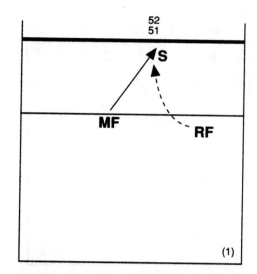

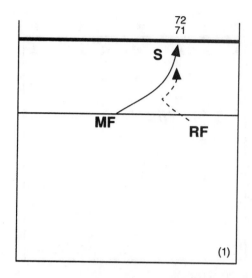

LEFT/MIDDLE CROSS

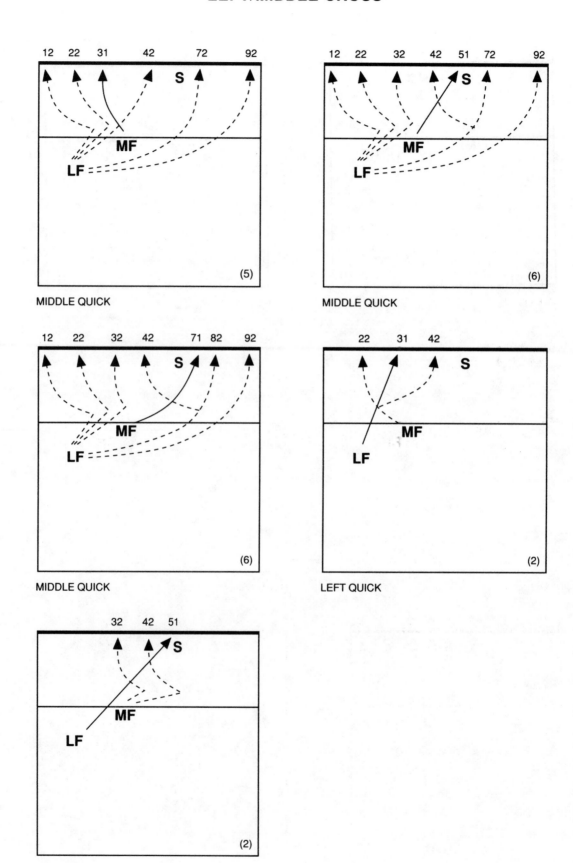

MIDDLE QUICK (5)

MIDDLE QUICK (6)

MIDDLE QUICK (6)

LEFT QUICK (2)

LEFT QUICK (2)

MIDDLE/RIGHT CROSS

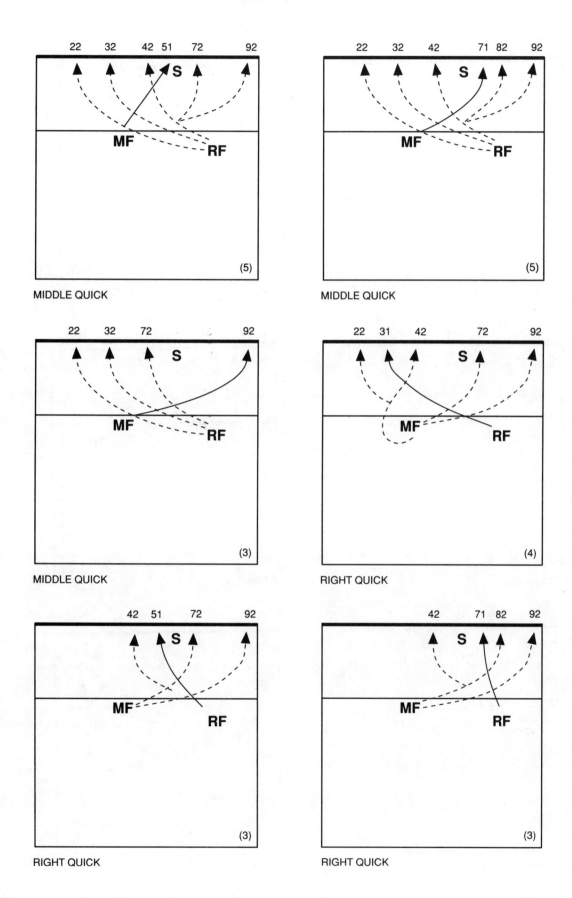

MIDDLE QUICK

MIDDLE QUICK

MIDDLE QUICK

RIGHT QUICK

RIGHT QUICK

RIGHT QUICK

LEFT/RIGHT CROSS

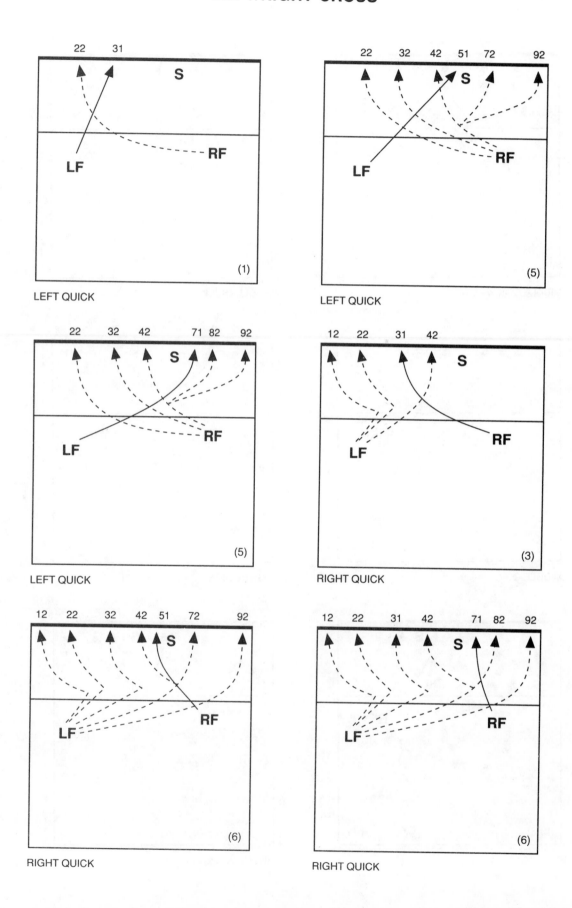

LEFT QUICK (1)

LEFT QUICK (5)

LEFT QUICK (5)

RIGHT QUICK (3)

RIGHT QUICK (6)

RIGHT QUICK (6)

DOUBLE CROSS

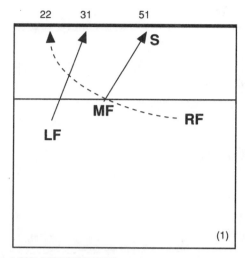

LEFT, MIDDLE QUICK

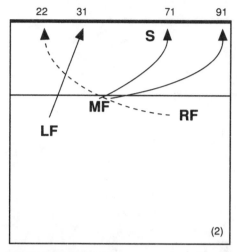

LEFT, MIDDLE QUICK

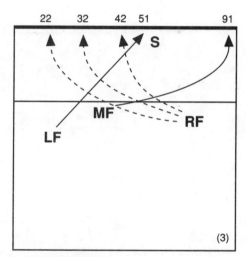

LEFT, MIDDLE QUICK

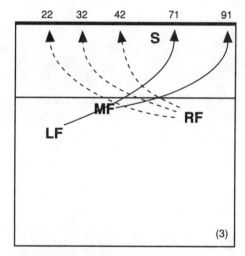

LEFT, MIDDLE QUICK

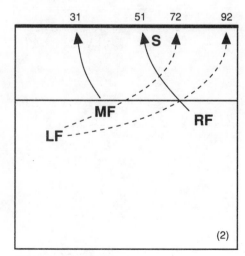

MIDDLE, RIGHT QUICK

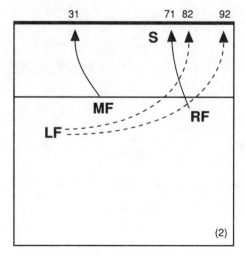

MIDDLE, RIGHT QUICK

SLIDE

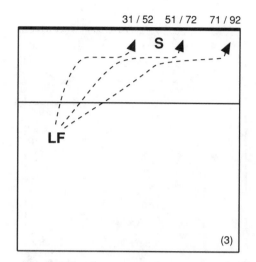

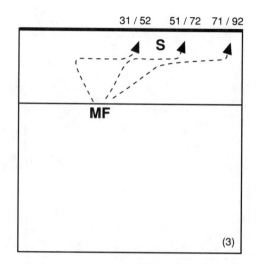

PUMP

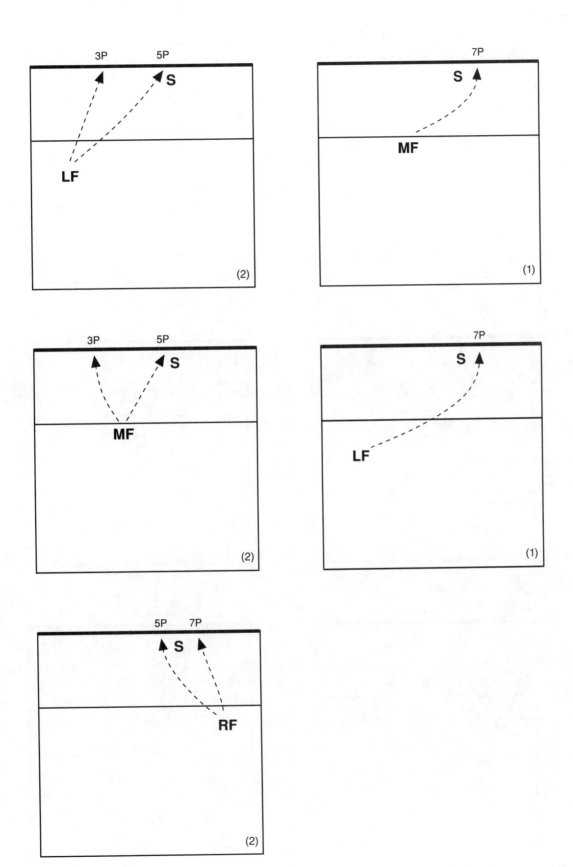

FRONT/BACK COMBINATION

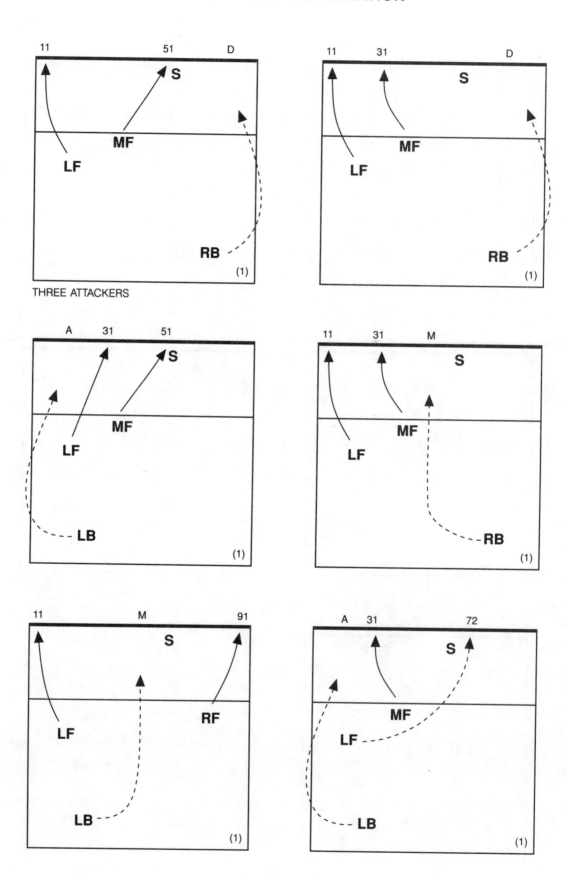

THREE ATTACKERS

FRONT/BACK COMBINATION

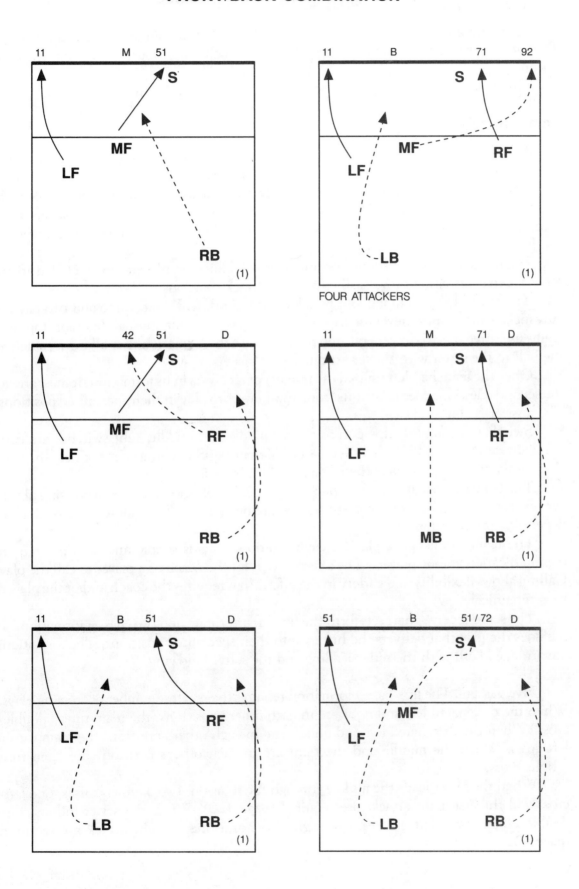

FOUR ATTACKERS

Organizing the Offense

Organizing the offense means deciding which plays to run and when to run them. Team communication is important in this regard; each player must know what the other is doing.

The team divides its organization into serve-receive and transition.

Serve-Receive

In organizing its serve-receive, the team answers two questions: (1) how many passers does it need? and (2) does it want its players in their specialized, front-row positions?

The proficiency of the team's passing likely determines how many passers it uses in the serve-receive. The team with good passers reduces their number. Fewer passers allow specialization. In the two-passer formation, for example, only the two best passers receive the ball.

Having fewer passers simplifies the offense. Front-row players not included in the serve-receive formation move easily into their attack positions.

The team chooses among four possible formations: five, four, three and two passers. Advanced teams almost never use five. Using four passers is not unusual, but most top-level teams use three or two. In general, the team chooses the formation that allows it to deliver the ball to the setter with the fewest number of passers.

Once the team has determined the number of receivers in its formation, it must answer the second question: does it want its front-row players to play in their specialized positions? The answer is almost always "yes."

Switches accomplish this purpose. Left/middle and middle/right switches are easy; left/right switches can be both difficult and disorienting. Switching does not help the team that wants its players to make their first attacks in position.

The team that always wants its players to attack in position must use a crossing play in certain rotations. The exact pattern varies among left/middle, middle/right or double, depending on the rotation.

The team can assign a play for each rotation. This is simple and does not require communication among players. The alternative is for the coach or a player to call the play. Calling allows flexibility and variety in the offense but requires the coach and/or the players to communicate.

The serve-receive chart sets forth the five-, four-, three- and two- passer formations. It includes the play that delivers the hitters into their specialized positions. The formations are arranged both with the setter leading and the setter following.

Five passers. The five-passer formation requires the greatest number of crossing plays. When the designated left and right are in each other's positions, the team runs a double-cross. When the designated left and middle are in each other's position, the team runs a left-cross. When the middle and the right are in each other's position, the team runs a right-cross.

When the setter leads the middle through the rotation, two double-crosses, one left-cross and three straight attacks are required (**page 320**). When the setter follows, one double-cross, three left-crosses, one right-cross and one straight attack are required (**page 321**).

Four Passers. Like the five-passer formation, the four-passer, or U, requires double-crosses when the designated left and right are in each other's position. Because the designated middle is in position to move to the center of the court during the serve, the four-passer requires no left/middle or middle/right crosses.

The setter-leading requires two double-crosses and four straight attacks (**page 322**). The setter-following requires one double-cross and five straight attacks (**page 323**).

Three Passers. Like the five- and four-passer formations, the three-passer or tri-line requires double-cross plays. It also occasionally requires its front-row passer to make a deep swing from receiving on one side of the formation to attacking on the other. This is the basis for the term "swing-hitter."

The setter-leading requires two double-crosses, one swing and three straight attacks (**page 324**). The setter-following requires one double-cross, three swings and two straight attacks (**page 325**).

Two Passers. The team using two passers does not need to position its players by using crossing plays. Two of its front-row players are near the net in all rotations; only one front-row player passes. This player, however, may make long swings.

The team can avoid long swings by positioning its front-row passer on the side of her attack in every rotation. This means that each passer positions herself half on the left—when she is in the front row—and half on the right. The front-row passer usually takes the left position so that she can attack left, where the sets are higher.

The team may position one player on either the left or the right all the time. This means, for example, that Player A always passes on the left and Player B always passes on the right. In this arrangement, long swings are required by one player half the time.

The setter leading the middle requires three swings and three straight attacks (**page 326**). The setter following requires the same number of each (**page 327**).

* * * * *

The team does not need to restrict itself to one or the other of the four serve-receive formations; it can use a different formation in each rotation. This means, for example, that the team receives serve with four passers part of the time and with three passers the rest of the time.

FIVE PASSER—SETTER LEADS

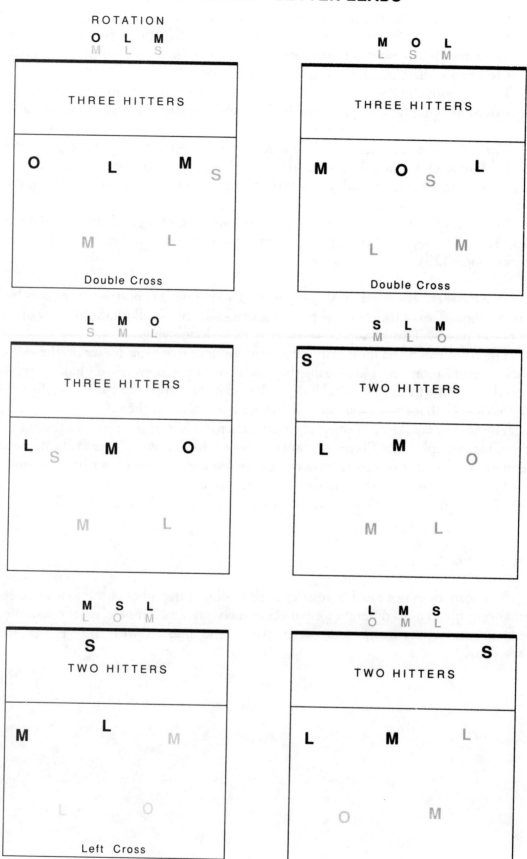

ROTATION

FIVE PASSER—SETTER FOLLOWS

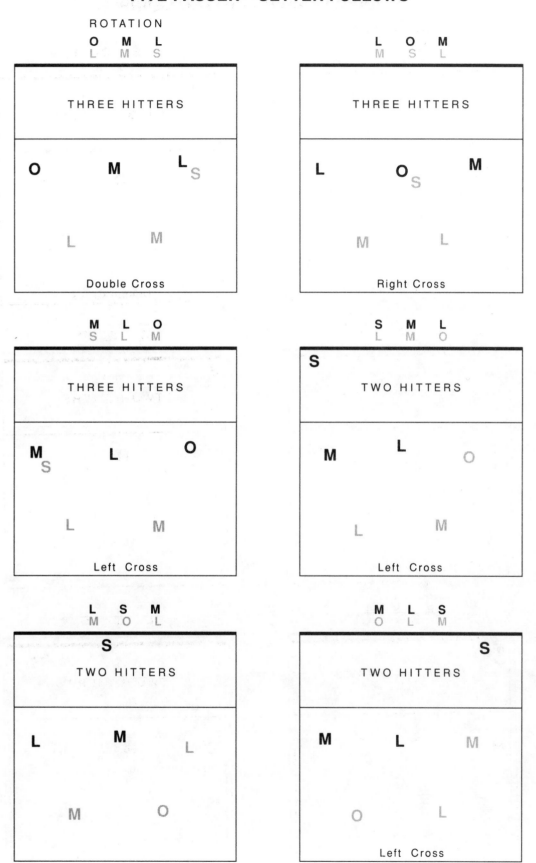

ROTATION

Double Cross · **Right Cross** · **Left Cross** · **Left Cross** · **Left Cross**

THREE HITTERS · TWO HITTERS

FOUR PASSER—SETTER LEADS

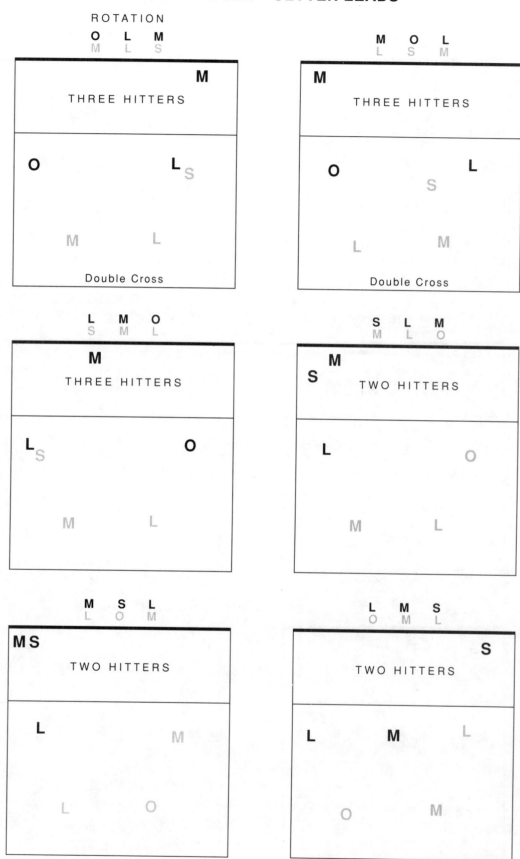

ROTATION

FOUR PASSER—SETTER FOLLOWS

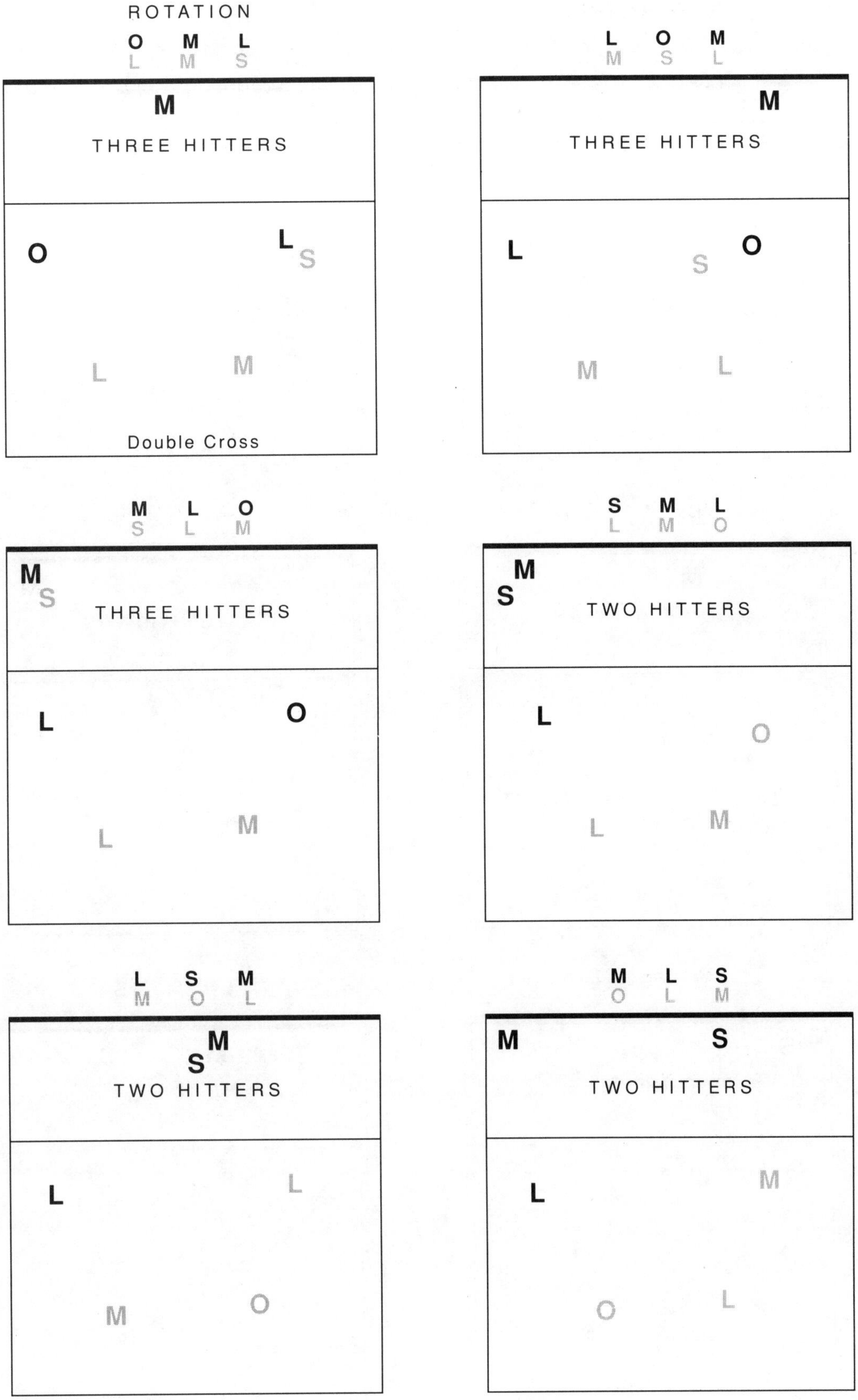

ROTATION

O M L
L M S

M
THREE HITTERS

O L S

L M

Double Cross

L O M
M S L

M
THREE HITTERS

L O
S

M L

M L O
S L M

M
S
THREE HITTERS

L O

L M

S M L
L M O

M
S
TWO HITTERS

L O

L M

L S M
M O L

M
S
TWO HITTERS

L L

M O

M L S
O L M

M S
TWO HITTERS

L M

O L

THREE PASSER—SETTER LEADS

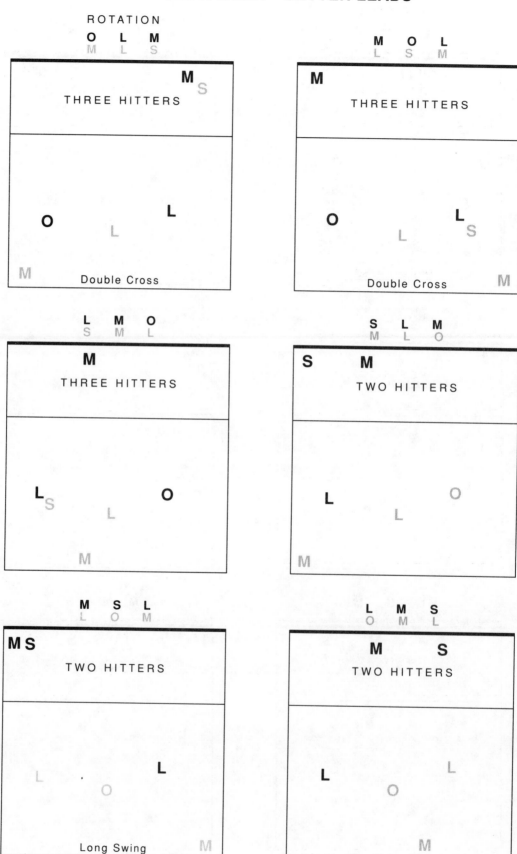

ROTATION

THREE PASSER—SETTER FOLLOWS

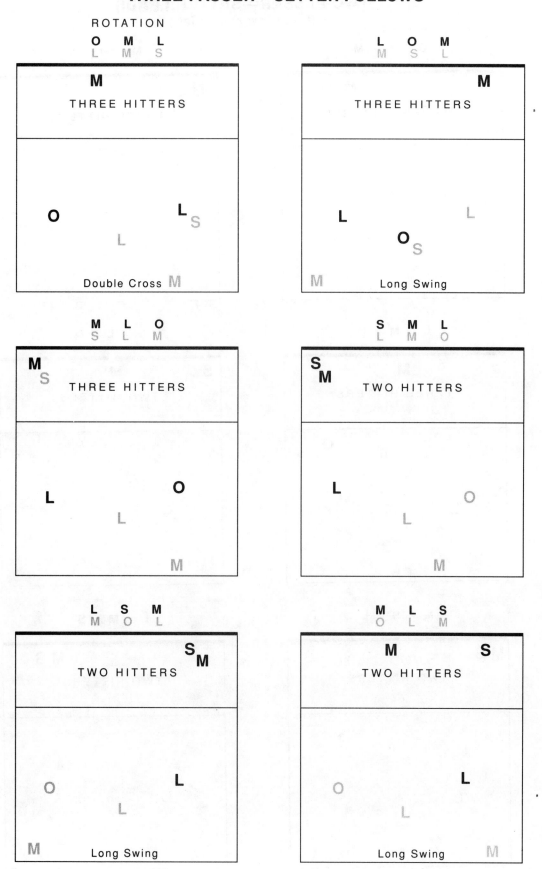

TWO PASSER—SETTER LEADS
(Front-row passer left)

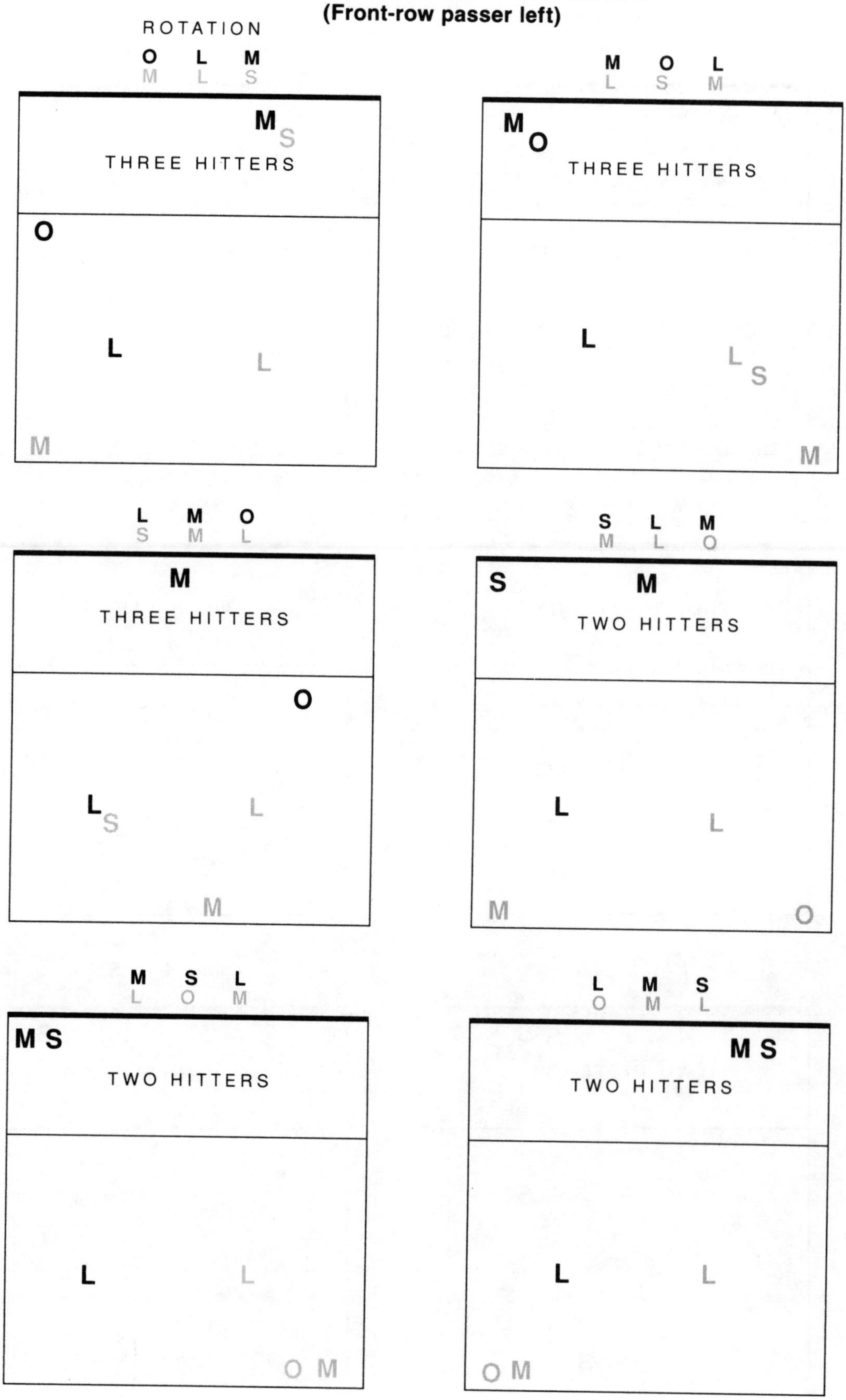

ROTATION

O   L   M
M   L   S

M S

THREE HITTERS

O

L   L

M

M   O   L
L   S   M

M O

THREE HITTERS

L

L S

M

L   M   O
S   M   L

M

THREE HITTERS

O

L S   L

M

S   L   M
M   L   O

S   **M**

TWO HITTERS

L   L

M   O

M   S   L
L   O   M

M S

TWO HITTERS

L   L

O M

L   M   S
O   M   L

M S

TWO HITTERS

L   L

O M

TWO PASSER—SETTER FOLLOWS
(Front-row passer left)

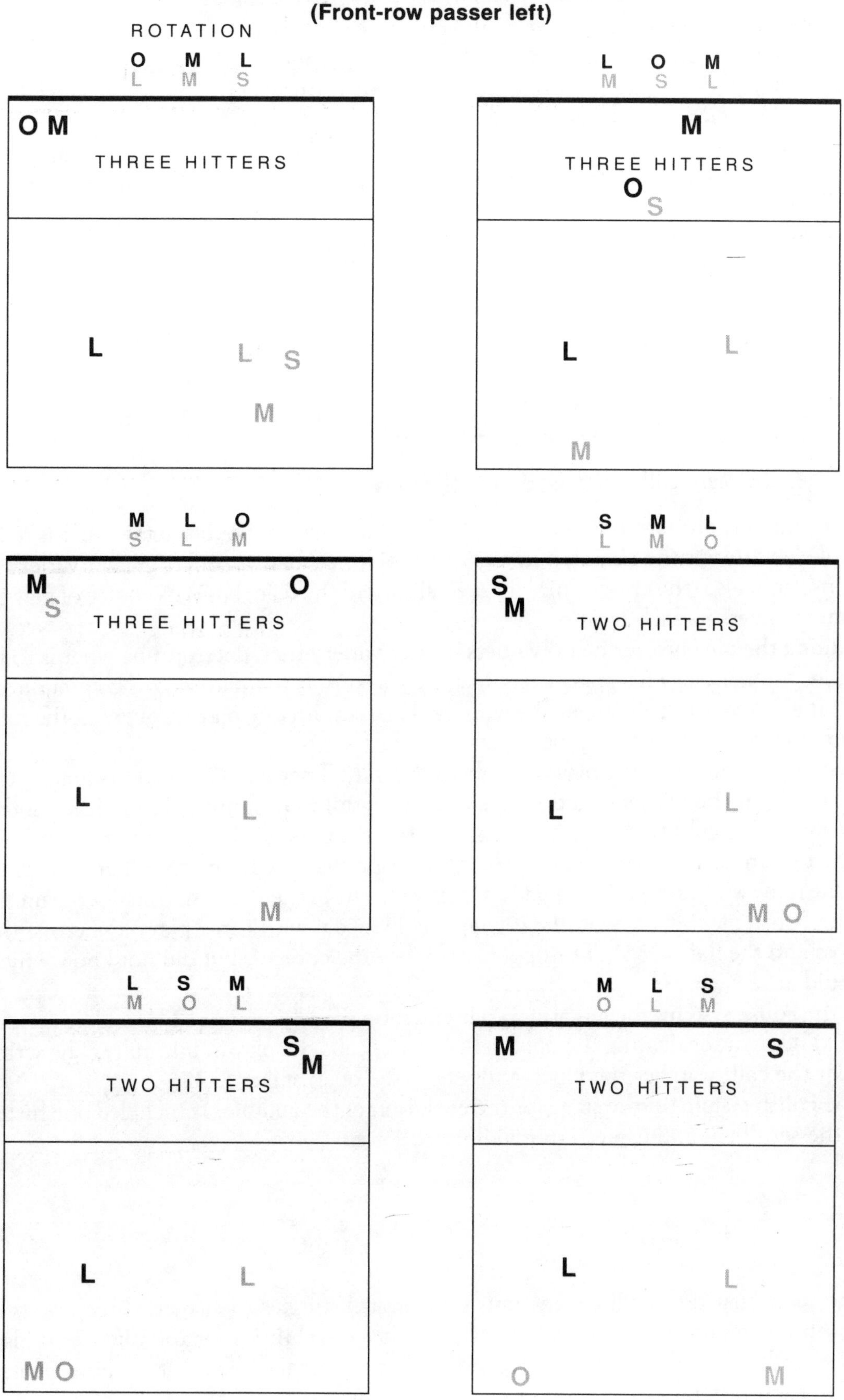

ROTATION

O M L
L M S

O M	
THREE HITTERS	

L L S

M

L O M
M S L

	M
THREE HITTERS	O S

L   L

M

M L O
S L M

M S	O
S	THREE HITTERS

L L

M

S M L
L M O

S M	
	TWO HITTERS

L L

M O

L S M
M O L

	S M
TWO HITTERS	

L L

M O

M L S
O L M

M	S
TWO HITTERS	

L L

O   M

Transition

Before the opponents serve, the team knows the play it will run from its serve-receive formation. The coach or a player has called the play before the serve, or the coach has assigned a play to the rotation. What if the team's serve-receive play is not successful and the opponents attack? What play will the team run if it digs the ball?

The term *transition* refers to the change from defense back to offense. A free ball allows a smooth transition. A hard attack often does not. The advanced team prepares itself to run a play from a successful dig.

Running a transition play means that the team must be organized during the rally. Each player must know what the other is doing. There are four ways to organize the transition attack, listed by increasing degree of difficulty:

1. the team runs one play all of the time;

2. the team runs one play per rotation;

3. the team calls the play before the rally;

4. the team calls the play during the rally.

Running one play all the time is simple. The team has no doubts about what is to be run; it likely performs the chosen play well. One play per rotation offers greater variety in the offense and, also, the opportunity for specialization: the team bases its choice of play on the team members in each rotation.

Calling the play before the rally offers greater variety than determining what is to be run before the match. This system requires signals so that the players can communicate silently. It also requires team members who can both sustain one play throughout the rally and then change to another without mistakes.

Systems 1, 2 and 3 fix the play throughout the rally. They provide certainty among the players, but limit the team's selection. As one successful international-level player notes, "The team is restricted to one or, perhaps, two transition plays throughout the rally."

The best international teams call their transition play according to system 4, that is, during the rally. Mid-rally calls, or *audibles*, originated from the Polish national program. In 1976, the Polish men's team won the Olympic gold medal with three plays: the cross, the fake-cross and the flair (335). The opponents knew the choices, but did not know which play would arise.

In the Polish system, the left attacks a high set on the left sideline. The middle attacks the one. The right, evaluating the opponents' block, calls the play in mid-rally. The setter listens for the call, watches the block and sets to the open spiker (335).

The Polish system set the stage for the evolution of the audible. It included one hitter calling the set. Two- and three-hitter audibles followed.

* * * * *

The team that uses audibles in transition must distinguish between three and two front-row-hitter rotations. Three hitters offer greater possibilities for the offense; it also restricts each hitter, whose patterns depend on her teammates. Two hitters give greater latitude to each hitter.

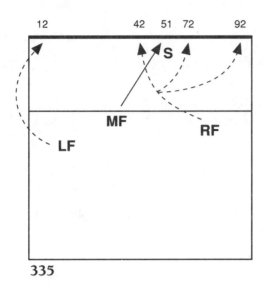

335

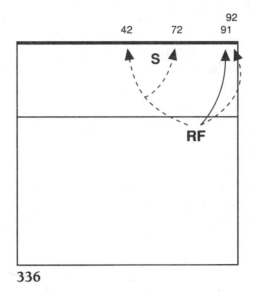

336

Three Hitters. The team's first audibles arise before it has determined to use them. A hitter (usually the left), calls the height of her set. She calls "higher" when she cannot arrive in time for the agreed-upon set. She may also call "shoot," "go" or "yes" to speed the tempo.

The team that systematically uses audibles starts as the Polish team did, that is, with the combination hitter calling her set. The increased time in attacking the play set benefits both the setter and the spiker; the team makes fewer mistakes.

The right hits the three sets mentioned above, often called the X series: the X (the standard two set), the fake X (the back two) and the flair (the sideline two). She also hits a release set on the sideline. She may hit a back shoot (**336**). She bases her call on the position of the blockers and her readiness to attack.

At the beginning, the middle restricts her attack to the one. She adds, as the team's transition attack evolves, the back one, the three, the front slide and the back slide. Her first addition is the back one.

The middle who hits either a front or back one in transition calls "front" or "back" during the rally. This specifies where she is attacking, a benefit to the setter and to the right.*

With the addition of the middle's call, the team has two hitters calling their sets in mid-rally: the middle and the right. They do so serially, that is, the middle calls first and the right calls second. This accords with the rhythm of their sets: the middle attacks the quick, the right the combination.

---

*The middle's call in mid-rally is not necessary, especially if the middle is restricted to the front or back one. The setter usually senses where the middle intends to attack. The setter's clues include the middle's location, the middle's preferences, the location of the pass and the game plan.

Serial calling allows the setter to absorb the attackers' patterns. The middle, especially, must call on time. A late call by the middle not only removes her as a possible attacker but may also disrupt the combination.

The middle's front- and back-one patterns can be characterized as *staying close* to the setter. When the middle stays close, the right can choose from her full range of attacks: the X, the fake X or the right shoot. She may also attack the five if she needs time (337). She watches the block and calls.

The right adjusts her pattern to accord with the middle's change from one to back one and vice versa. When the middle attacks the back one and the right hits the fake X, for example, the right adjusts her attack-point right, allowing room for the middle (337).

* * * * *

The middle adds the three. The right's possibilities decrease. Her best option is to attack on the sideline, either the flair or the shoot (338). The opposing middle likely moves left to cover the quick hitter. Hitting on the sideline distances the middle and the right hitters and creates the chance of a split block.

The right avoids the standard two, associated with the X, when the middle attacks the three (339). The two guides her to the middle blocker. The play also allows the right blocker unobstructed movement to the combination hitter's attack. The back two, associated with the fake X, is more difficult for the blockers. It does not spread them, however, as does a set on the sideline.

* * * * *

The middle adds the front and back slide (340b, 341a). The right must know where the middle starts her attack. The middle approaching from the right of the setter means a front slide, from the left a back slide.

The right avoids the standard two when the middle attacks the front slide (340a) and the back two when the middle attacks the back slide (341b). In both of these plays, the middle slides toward the combination hitter. Two things can go wrong: the blocker, in following the slide, positions herself in line with the combination or, worse, the quick hitter gets in the way of her teammate.

The best teams run these slide combinations. One world-class middle-hitter says, "We get away with it all the time; I just land and get out of the play-set hitter's way."

* * * * *

With three hitters in the front, the left confines her attacks to the sideline (342). She calls only the height of the set. The standard is medium-height. The left calls a shoot if she can arrive in time to attack it. The shoot becomes beneficial when the left blocker has positioned herself to the right.

If the left digs the ball and cannot arrive in time for the standard set, she calls "high."

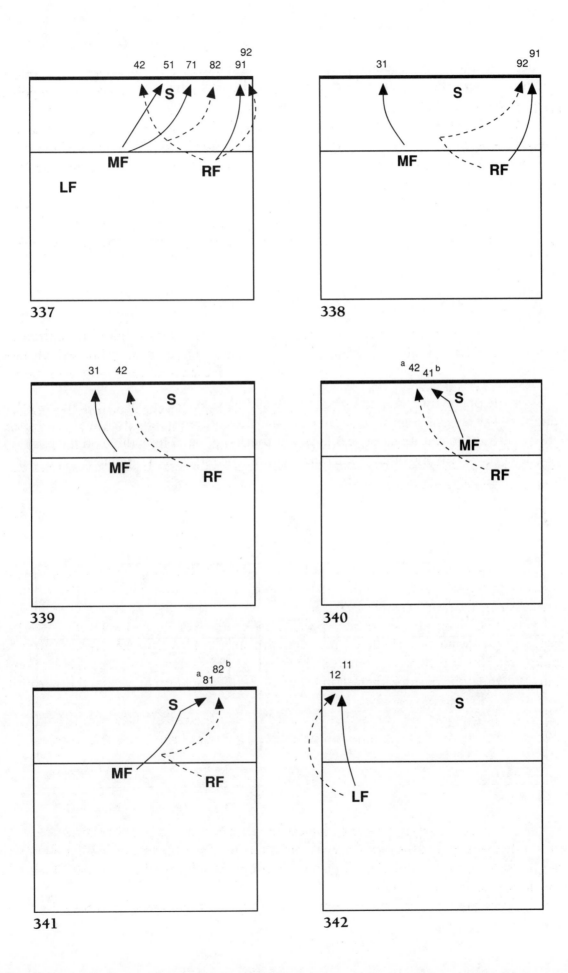

337

338

339

340

341

342

Two Hitters. When the team has a left and a middle in the front row, the left can communicate with the setter in mid-rally. The middle attacking the three allows the left to attack the X or the fake X (**343**). She calls her set.

The front and back slides, run by the middle, hold no risk when the team has two hitters in the front row. The medium-height or high set hitter stays on the sideline, away from the quick hitter's broad jump (**344**).

* * * * *

In general, the words used for the team's audibles must be discrete both in reference and in sound. The left may call "go" (shoot), "hut" (medium-height), or "high." The middle may call "three," "one," "back," or "slide." The right may call "two" (X), "four" (fake X), "red" (sideline shoot), or "five."

* * * * *

Does the opponent listen and react to the audibles? Perhaps. But the offensive team initiates; the defensive team reacts. By the time the call registers with the defense, the offense is already on the attack. The offense, furthermore, bases its audible on the position of the defense. When the offense calls well, the defense starts at a disadvantage.

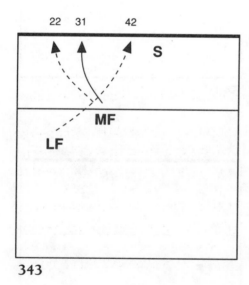

343

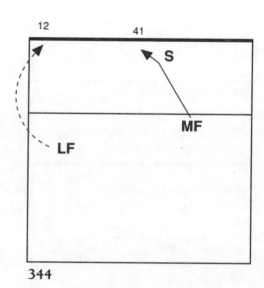

344

332

Offensive Strategy

Offensive strategy asks the questions "what plays?" "who runs them?" and "when are they run?" It implies a chain of command, an overall plan for the team's offense and plans for each opponent. Strategy influences, and is influenced by, the team's practices and its personality.

Which comes first, the plays or the players? For most coaches, the answer is the players: their strengths and weaknesses determine what plays the team runs. This accords with the axiom expressed in Section IV: team systems must fit players' skills.

* * * * *

One player determines what the team does in an immediate way. She calls the plays.

The coach appoints the play-caller. In doing so, he establishes the team's chain of command, which becomes part of the team's offensive strategy.

The coach can call the plays from the bench. He usually does not. He cannot communicate with the players as well as the players can communicate among themselves. When the coach calls, the captain or the setter must relay the play to the rest of the team. This takes time, offers more possibility for misunderstanding and reduces accountability. It also distracts at least one of the players, who must turn her attention from the court to the bench before each play.

The Chain of Command

The coach appoints either a setter or a hitter to call the team's plays. Two players may share the responsibility.

The most common play-caller is the setter. Appointing her rather than the hitter offers several advantages.

The setter is disinterested in which play is called. She does not gain personally; she can consider the success of the team above all else.

Because she is outside of the attack, the setter has a better perspective than a hitter. The setter can be compared to callers in other sports. The baseball catcher calls the pitches even though the pitcher throws the ball. The football quarterback calls the pass patterns even though the receivers run them.

Setting requires a control of the body and the emotions that may be absent among the hitters. The setter moves smoothly about the court and delivers the ball with precision. She does not participate directly in most of the dramatic, terminal plays—kills and stuffs—that take place at the net.

The 5-1 team benefits the most from the setter calling the plays. She consolidates the control of the team. She determines both who hits, through her choice of set, and which patterns are run, through her choice of play, in all rotations.

When the team uses the 6-2 offense, it loses the advantage of consolidating control. The other advantages stand.

The coach may appoint an attacker to call the plays. He usually does so when he wants his most effective hitter to determine her role in the offense.

The hitter can call the offensive patterns as does the setter, that is, for the entire team. This offers the psychological advantage of placing the responsibility for the success of the play on the attacker.

More commonly, the most effective hitter calls her own set. A second hitter calls a complementary set, meaning that the sets work together. In three-hitter rotations, the third hitter acts as a release.

The complementary-set system, by allowing two hitters to choose their attack pattern, increases the hitters' investment in the play.

The system has disadvantages. It does not allow complexity in the serve-receive offense. The complementary-set system's patterns, except for reverses, are limited to those called in transition. A double-cross, for example, is impossible to call. The absence of double-crossing plays means that the team may not be able to deliver its serve-receivers into their specialized attack positions.

Transition reveals a further disadvantage. In the complementary-set system, the most effective hitter calls first. This means that in transition she must hit quick; she must play the middle.

The team that wants its most effective attacker to play the middle can use the complementary-set system to advantage. The team that wants its most effective hitter to play elsewhere cannot.

One Setter Versus Two

The coach must determine whether his preferred system includes one setter or two. The main advantage of one setter is that the team's best can play her role all the time. The main advantage of two is that the team can attack with three front-row hitters in all rotations.

The decision to use one setter or two is not independent of other considerations. The coach must weigh the make-up of the players and his preferred chain of command.

Most international teams choose one setter. They want their best to touch the ball on each attack; they also want their setter to call the plays and control the team. The back-row attack reduces the adverse impact of the two-hitter rotations.

The two-setter attack, however, offers one great benefit over the single setter. Injury does not affect the team's fortunes as much as it does the single setter's. The 6-2 team that loses a starting setter can either continue its 6-2 with a third setter or switch to the 5-1.

Sometimes the team's best hitter is also its best setter. In this case, the 6-2 is the natural choice.

The Evolution of the Offense

Players improve; so does their teamwork. The team benefits by increasing the sophistication of its offense as its players improve their skills.

As the team develops, it both quickens its attack and adds deceptive patterns. The first quickening occurs when the team is in its intermediate stage; it lowers its sets (page 250). At the advanced level, the team incorporates the one set, giving it a true quick attack.

The team further increases the speed of its attack by adding a shoot. The left attacks the four. The middle attacks the one and the right attacks the five, a high set on the right sideline. The "4-1-5" lends itself both to serve-receive and transition; it is the simplest quick/shoot.*

---

* The team may define the four as a medium-height set; if so, the "4-1-5" cannot be considered a quick/shoot.

The team adds the three, or inside shoot, and quickens its set to the right sideline.

The team incorporates *series* plays, that is, crosses and their fakes. The X series includes the fake X and the flair (**345**). The middle initiates the attack with either the one or the back one.

The 31X series follows. The middle attacks the three (31) and the left attacks the X, the fake X or the left flair (**346**).

The reversed X series exchanges the roles of the quick and the combination hitters. The right approaches to hit the one or the back one as the middle usually does; the middle crosses or fake-crosses as the right usually does (**347**).

The reversed 31X series exchanges the roles of the left and the middle hitters. The left approaches to hit the three and the middle runs the cross or the fake, complementing the left (**348**).

The team adds the quick slide, usually performed by the middle; the one-footed slide; the tandem; the pump; the back-row attack. The coach adjusts the order of the plays' or series' introduction by the skills of the players and the weaknesses of the opponents.

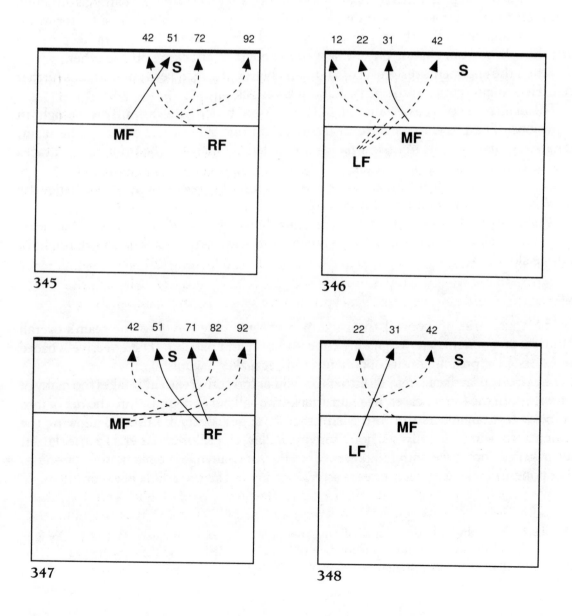

345

346

347

348

The team's serve-receive formation evolves with the increasing sophistication of its attack. When it advances from a slow to a quick attack, it changes from a five- to a four-passer formation. It wants its quick attacker/middle blocker in position.

When the team incorporates reversed plays, positioning the attackers by their specialties becomes less important. Any can hit quick and any can hit the play set.

At this stage, or before, the team may reduce the number of its passers from four to three or two. This allows the best passers to receive all of the time. It also increases the flexibility of the offense by freeing most of the attackers from passing duties. These non-passers can begin their attack from anywhere in the court.

The team is not obligated to choose one serve-receive formation and to continue it through all rotations. It may change its formation from rotation to rotation. The team may also rotate the personnel who pass. The team that uses the two-passer formation in all rotations, for example, may change its designated passers from one rotation to the next.

The designated passer in a two-passer formation, after receiving the ball, has difficulty arriving on time to attack. Weakening legs may be a greater problem. The passer works while her teammates rest; she approaches to attack almost every time from deep in the court; she swings from passing on one side of the court to attacking on the other.

When the opponents serve every ball to one player, the receiver's endurance is further tested. Her counterpart, on the other hand, can attack any set.

The team using two passers may align Passer A on the left and Passer B on the right in all rotations. The passers specialize in receiving on one side or the other.* The team, alternatively, may align its front-row passer on the left. From here, the front passer attacks on the left, where she has more time.

The team is not obligated to use only one two-passer arrangement; it can exchange the passers' positions from rotation to rotation.

When fatigue is a consideration, the team limits the range of its passers' attacks. The team excludes, for example, the left receiver from attacking quick sets to the right of the three slot.

Pace

The coach tries to control the pace of his team. Pace refers to the team's overall rhythm; its components are judgment, concentration and passion. The effectively paced team exerts great pressure on its opponents and yet makes few mistakes.

The poorly paced team may be either too wild or too conservative. It takes too many or too few risks. In the former case, the team attacks the ball out of bounds, into the net or into the block. Team members run into each other. The quick attack misfires, allowing the opponents to win the rally without moving. Players touch the net. In the latter, the attackers do not spike with full power. They do not challenge the block; they often tip. The opponents make easy recoveries. Passers hesitate as the serve falls between them.

---

* When the setter is right-back, the team usually does not position its back-row passer on the left. Doing so means that the middle-front and the right-front are near the right sideline and the opposite near the left sideline. Attacking from these locations is awkward.

The team's number of unforced errors best indicates its pace. The coach wants the team to limit, but not to eliminate, its unforced errors. Why not eliminate? Because the team that makes no unforced errors does not know, or test, its limits. Its pace is too slow; perhaps it could exert greater pressure on its opponents without significantly increasing its errors.

The coach takes special note when the team or a player both hits the ball out of bounds and is never stuffed. The aversion to being blocked may be so great that the spiker prefers to hit the ball out. Challenging the block sometimes succeeds; hitting out never does.

The coach can influence the pace of the team by exhorting it or calming it; also, by adjusting the degree of difficulty—quickness and deception—of its attack.

The quicker and more deceptive the attack, the more pressure is exerted on the opponents. The team pays for this pressure with an increase in errors.

The team's ideal pace may change from match to match. It may change within one match.

Does the ideal pace change when the team switches from point-making to siding-out? No. The team that takes fewer risks because its opponents have served decreases the pressure on its opponents. It thereby gives the opponents a greater chance of winning the rally.

The team may adjust its ideal pace between serve-receive and transition. It mounts a sophisticated and vigorous attack when it receives serve and a simple, low-risk attack in transition.

In the case of serve-receive, the team's chances of delivering a perfect pass with its attackers in position and in repose are good. In the case of transition, the chances of the team being in a comparably fine position are not good. Whether the team is point-making or siding-out is unimportant.

Fakes

The team's attack becomes more deceptive as it increases the sophistication of its offense. Almost every attack includes a fake, from the team's mixed-speed combinations to the individual disguises of its setters and hitters.

The effectiveness of the team's fakes must be considered from the viewpoint of the defender, who tries to read the fakes (Section III, Chapter 2, The Opponents). A good reader sees small changes. The player who makes an exaggerated fake may fool the reader once or, perhaps, twice. After that, the reader discerns the fake.

An example is the player who spikes with a conventional rhythm several times and then, after an aggressive approach, tips. The discerning reader expects the tip on the attacker's next aggressive approach.

So what's the best disguise? The most effective faker moves the same way every time, regardless of what she intends to do. In effect, she does not fake.

The hitter, for example, approaches on the same line with the same degree of passion every time. No part of her lead-in varies. Unavoidable differences, occasioned by the shot, occur as late as possible.

The setter assumes one body position. She receives the ball in one place. To the extent that the pass allows her, she jumps, or does not, every time.

Moving one way is more difficult than faking. The player must vary the effect of her motion without showing. She must have a broad range.

The reader gains no clues from watching these players. She must respect every possibility.

Play Selection

The team, its setter and its play-caller observe certain guidelines in choosing its plays:

- Quick is better. The team runs its plays as fast as it can without mistakes. Speed increases the pressure on the defense. The team tries to attack with at least one quick hitter every time.

- The team benefits by running the play against the flow of the defense. Blockers tend to follow the pass; they move left if the pass is left and right if it is right. The uncovered hitter may be found on the opposite side of the court from the pass.

- The team matches its best hitter against the weakest blocker. If the best hitter can attack the opponents' weakness with her favorite set, this is ideal.

- The team uses, most of the time, the plays that it performs well. It complements these with other plays that offer a new look to the defense. The team tries to find the right mix between its staples and its non-staples.

- With only two front-row hitters, the team runs a pattern that splits the hitters most of the time. Or, it directs the two front hitters to the left side of the court and adds a complementary right-back attack.

- The team runs a sophisticated play from its serve-receive formation. The pass is likely to be good, most of the attackers are in position and the team members understand their roles and those of their teammates.

- The team runs a sophisticated play on its first transition, that is, after it serves. The team is more composed after having been attacked only once than after having been attacked several times. The play usually includes a release.

- The team runs a sophisticated play from its serve-receive, another after having been attacked once and then either continues with the latter play or audibles throughout the rest of the rally.

- The team runs a sophisticated play from a free ball.

- The team runs a play that eases the duties of its auxiliary setter when its setter digs. The auxiliary does not set as well as the designated; she also sets with a different rhythm. The middle, for example, may swing right to attack a high set on the sideline. This distracts the defense with movement and relieves the auxiliary from setting quick.

* * * * *

The scouting report on the opponents determines, to a great extent, the team's play selection. The report contains the opponents' blocking and backcourt schemes and also the strengths and weaknesses of its players. It is organized by rotation.

The first consideration is the opponents' blocking scheme. Do they read or commit (Chapter 6)? Do their outside blockers start near the sideline or near the center of the court?

In facing read-blockers, the team sets quick: the one, the back one or the three. In facing commit-blockers, it sets combination plays, particularly those in which the play-set hitter approaches on the outside. The pump, also, creates difficulties for the commit-blocker.

In facing teams whose left blocker positions herself inside, the team shoots to the sideline. When the left blocker's primary responsibility is stopping the sideline attack, the team sets the three, the one and inside combinations. The team may fix its right hitter to the sideline and allow its left to call 31X audibles against the sideline blocker.

The opponents' personnel influences the team's play selection. The main consideration is the height and mobility of the opponents' middle blockers. The team attacks the small, fast middle with the one, the tandem and inside crosses. The team attacks the tall, slow middle with the three and the quick slide. Quick/shoots and double-quicks are also effective.

The opponents' backcourt scheme influences the team's shot selection more than its play selection. The team uses the tip as its change of pace when its faces a perimeter defense. It uses the deep, off-speed spike as its change of pace when it faces the middle-up, rotating or counter-rotating defense.

Serving

The team would like each of its servers to perfect, at least, one serve. It would also like a variety of serving styles among its players. One player, for example, perfects the jump; another perfects the flat floater delivered from the baseline; another the high floater served from beyond the baseline. A mix forces the opponents to handle balls of different rhythms.

The team also benefits from its players having perfected more than one serve. When the team confronts an opponent who has difficulty with a particular serve, it can use the serve in most, or all, rotations.

In general, the team serves to the weakest passer. The server may target the passer's nose, forcing the passer to reach back. Or, the server targets an area away from the passer, but not so far away that the ball is taken by another. A sideline is a good choice. So is a corner. The seam-side of the weak passer creates doubt about who will pass. A shallow serve forces the passer to move forward and, perhaps, pass on the run.

Sometimes it is not clear which passer is weak. In this case, the server targets the tall or awkward-appearing receiver. Or she serves to the front-row, especially the quick, hitter; to the substitute; into the path of the setter; to the left sideline, which means that the ball is passed from behind the setter; or into a seam, which may result in two players colliding, stepping aside or both.

The team may determine that one player deserves to receive every serve. This is usually the player who loses her composure or tires after passing again and again.

CHAPTER 6: ADVANCED DEFENSE

The advanced team faces a fast, multi-dimensional attack. Hard spikes arrive from almost anywhere, at almost anytime. The opposing players' movements obstruct the defense's view; their shouts disrupt its concentration.

The attack can be likened to a battery of guns arranged along the net. The primary battery is supported by several guns in the rear. Screens move in and out among the guns, which fire with little warning.

How can the defense stop such an attack? Most of the time it cannot. The advanced offense is not random, however. It develops in patterns. The defense must position itself for the most likely attack, recognize the offensive pattern as it develops and react quickly. The will of the defense, furthermore, is hardened by the knowledge that success usually means a point.

In advanced defense, as in the intermediate, the blockers can be arranged independently from the backcourt. The coach usually addresses the team's blocking scheme first.

The Block

Numbers show the difficulty of stopping the attack at the net. The net spans nine meters in-bounds. A blocker eliminates, with perfectly positioned hands, slightly more than one-half meter, or about 7% of the net. Two blockers eliminate from 1 to 1½ meters, about 17%, including the distance between them.

The perfect set arrives 1 to 1½ meters from the net. The blockers slide their hands across the net, that is, penetrate, a distance of one-half meter or less.

When the perfectly positioned double-block confronts the perfectly executed attack, the block can protect more than half of the court (**349, 350**). The problem is that the team forms its double-block no more than about 20% of the time. And when it succeeds in covering a portion of the court from left to right, the attacker may still spike over the block.

The depth of the set influences the area of the court that the blockers protect. A deep set means less protected area (**351, 352**). A set near the net gives the advantage to the blockers.

* * * * *

The offense is designed to prevent the opponents from forming a double-block. It often succeeds. Its main weapons are the quick/shoot, the double-quick and the cross.

The quick/shoot and the double-quick spread the blockers. The attackers arrive nearly at once; the blockers do not have time to help their teammates. They block one player versus one, a match-up that is difficult for them to win. The quick/shoot and the double-quick are the block's greatest challenge, regardless of its blocking scheme.

The cross tricks the blockers in two ways. The crossing hitter forces the blocker opposite her to move around, or change positions with, her blocking teammate; and by combining with a quick attacker, the crosser challenges the blockers to jump at the right time.

* * * * *

Advanced teams use two main blocking schemes: read and commit. In read-blocking, the blockers watch the hitters peripherally but focus on the setter. They read the setter to determine where the set will go. Then they react. Read-blocking is the most common system at all levels of play.

In commit-blocking, one blocker commits to stop, that is, attack-blocks, the quick hitter. With the commit-blocker in the air, the other two blockers form the double-block. They must follow the attacker, often crossing their commit-blocking teammate in the process. Commit-blocking is used at high levels of play and, on most teams, sparingly.

In deciding which blocking scheme to use, the coach first looks at his opponents' offense. How often and how well do the opponents set the quick-hitter? Use crossing plays? Double-quicks? The answers to these questions usually clarify the best system.

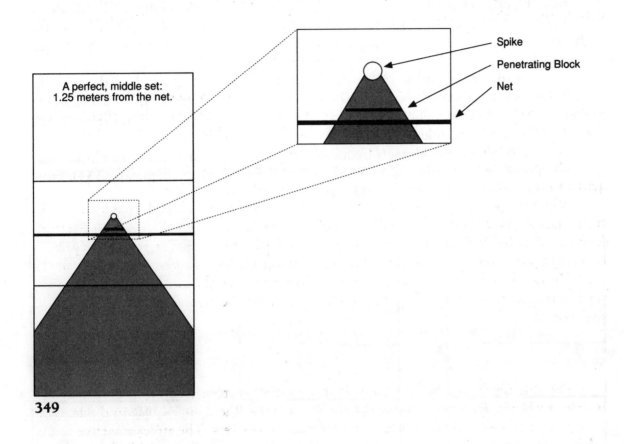

A perfect, middle set:
1.25 meters from the net.

Spike

Penetrating Block

Net

349

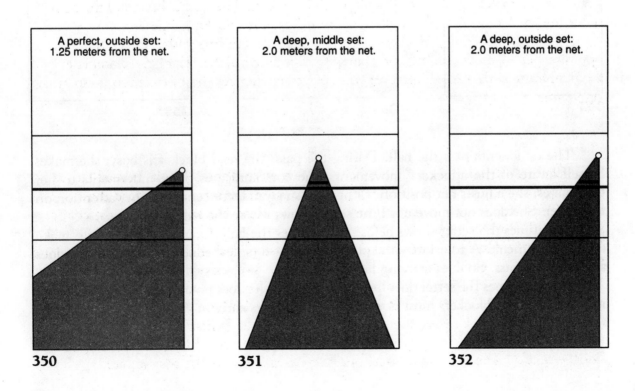

A perfect, outside set:
1.25 meters from the net.

350

A deep, middle set:
2.0 meters from the net.

351

A deep, outside set:
2.0 meters from the net.

352

Read-Blocking

Read-blockers align themselves near the middle half of the net as they await the attack (353). The left blocker starts about one-fourth of the distance from the left sideline, the right about one-fourth of the distance from the right sideline and the middle between the two.

A balanced starting position allows the blockers to cover any attack along the net. The middle moves left to cover the one or the back one, or right to cover the three. She moves to either sideline to form a double-block with a teammate. The left helps the middle with the one; the right helps the middle with the three.

Against an opponent who sets frequently to the right sideline, the right blocker may position herself farther to the right, as close to the sideline as 1 to 1½ meters (354). From here the distance is short to the outside attack.

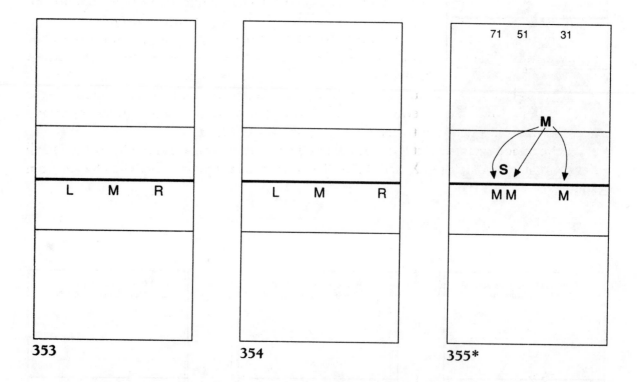

353   354   355*

The opponents pass the ball. During the pass, the read blocker is busy: she makes herself aware of the attackers' movements; she communicates these movements to her teammates; she adjusts her position. Otherwise she waits, concentrating her attention on the setter. She does not move until the setter shows where she will set.

Sometimes the setter shows before she touches the ball. Court conditions can make disguising difficult. A rotation with two hitters, for example, reduces her options. So does an imperfect pass. So does arriving late to set.

At other times the setter does not show at all, or she does not do so until the ball is on its way. The read-blockers must not commit themselves early.

The movements in read-blocking are simple. The blockers move left and right but stay in their relative positions. The left blocker stays on the left, the middle blocker stays in the middle and the right on the right. They move as if guided by the overlap rule: convergence at any point along the net is fine but crossing is not.

The Middle Blocker. The middle blocker's first responsibility is to protect against the quick attack. She guards the center of the net, fronting the opponents' one, back one and three.

The middle blocker covers the opposing middle (355)* unless the middle leaves the center-of-the-net zone and another quick attacker enters it (356).

If the middle blocker thinks the one (or the back one or the three) will be set, she jumps with the quick attacker and stuff-blocks. If she is uncertain, she jumps low and soft-blocks. If she sees little or no possibility for a quick attack and a great possibility for another, she abandons the quick and moves to double-block with a teammate (357).

The reading middle blocker follows the inside-to-outside pattern again and again. She guards against the quick and then moves left or right to double-block. Forming a timely, coherent block with her teammate is the middle's greatest challenge.

In read-blocking, the middle must insure that the X is double-blocked. She guards the quick hitter. When she determines that the X attacker will be set, she moves right and positions herself in front of the X. The left joins her (358).

The middle must not attack-block when the left-attacker may hit the X. Not only will she be unable to block the X herself, but her presence may prevent her left blocker from doing so.

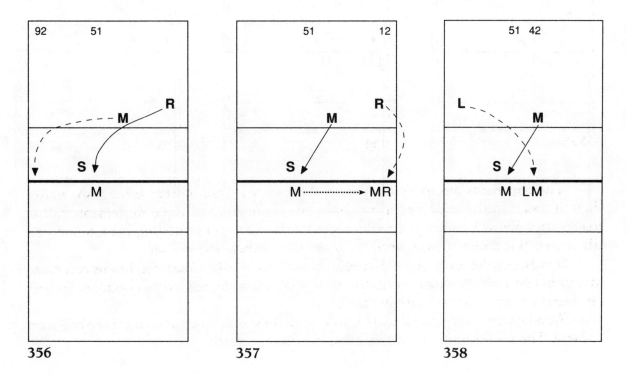

356   357   358

*The numbers below the opponent's baseline refer to the zone and height of the set.

The middle may abandon the quick when the opponents have two hitters in the front row (unless the opponents attack from the back). The opposing team usually positions its setter on the blocking team's left in these rotations; it attacks with two hitters on the right. The middle moves right before the ball has been set, giving herself time to form the double block. The left blocker slides right and covers the quick attacker (359).

If the opposing team attacks with one of its hitters to the left of the setter, the blockers read as usual (360). If both attackers approach on the left, the middle may abandon the quick to form a double-block on the left (361). The latter arrangement, with two hitters attacking to the left of the setter, is uncommon.

The blockers' early shift in confronting two attackers, called *release* blocking, is not spontaneous but part of the team's plan. All blockers must know when to release and when to remain. They do so in concert.

The middle has an added responsibility with two hitters in the opponents' front row. She must read the tip by the setter. She keeps her hands up, and may even jump, as the setter receives the ball. She forces the setter to tip upwards. Her teammates can recover a high tip more easily.

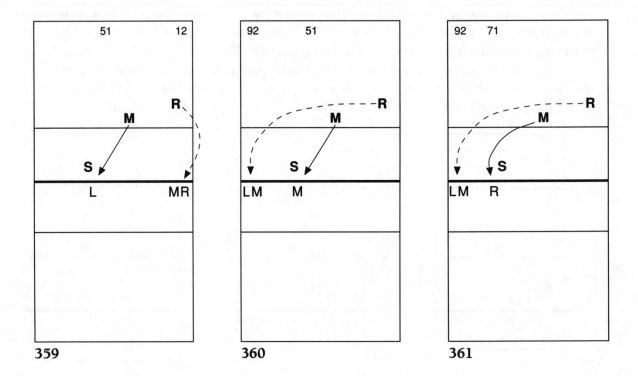

359   360   361

The middle covers the setter's tip, as a first responsibility, only when the quick hitter attacks to the left of the setter. The left guards the quick hitter (362).

If the opposing middle attacks the one, in contrast, the middle-blocker helps the left with the setter's tip, but her first responsibility is the quick (363). If the middle attacks the three, she does not guard the setter but moves right with the quick hitter.

The Left Blocker. The reading left blocker has responsibilities that, like the middle's, range the entire length of the net. Her first, but least exercised, responsibility is to retrieve the setter's tip. She readies herself to move away from the net, that is, toward the baseline (364).

The left helps the middle-blocker with both the back one and the one (362, 363). She may attack-block if she expects the quick; she may soft-block if she is unsure; she may remain on the floor with her hands high, making the setter aware of her presence and, perhaps, deflecting an attack.

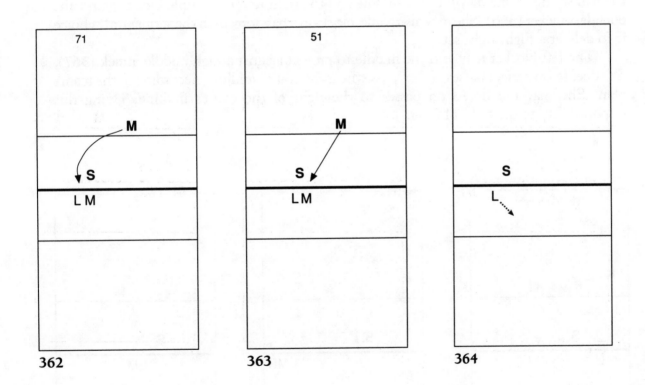

362   363   364

The left blocks all sets on the left side of the net, including shoots, flairs and back-row attacks. She double-blocks with the middle on these attacks, positioning herself in front of, or to the right of, the attacker, according to the team plan. If the middle cannot arrive, she likely positions herself right to protect against the cross-court attack.

The reading left's greatest challenge is blocking the X and the fake X. In blocking the X, she moves right, following the attacker. When the middle blocker moves right, she forms a double-block with the middle against the X attacker (365). When the middle commits by mistake, the left must cross behind the middle. She sees the middle jump and moves back and right.

Read-blocking does not include one blocker switching positions with another in mid-rally; the left resorts to this tactic, which is likely to fail, because she has no other choice.

In blocking the fake X or the flair, the left blocker follows the attacker, who breaks from right to left. Failure means that neither the left nor the middle can block. The left impedes the middle's movement.

The left blocker replaces the middle when the middle releases early to double-block. She covers the quick attacker, reading the setter as does the middle (366). When she sees the ball set right, she may join the middle and the right to form a triple block against the outside attacker (366). She may also triple-block on a pass for which the setter's only choice is to deliver a high, right set.

The left blocker may join the middle to protect against a high middle attack (367). She does so on perfect passes and on passes near the court's midline, according to the team's plan. She may not do so on passes to the right of the court's midline, giving this responsibility to the right blocker.

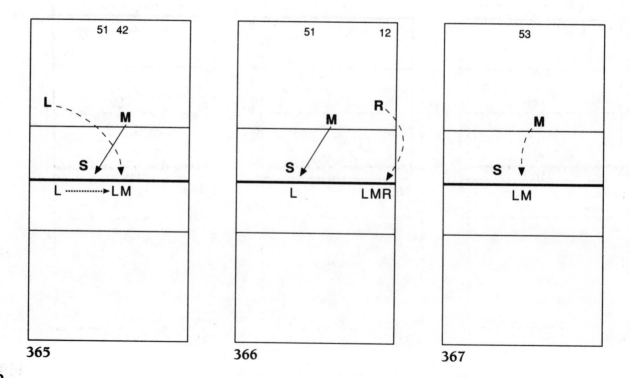

365   366   367

The Right Blocker. The reading right's first responsibility is to help the middle with the three. She positions herself directly in front of, or slightly to the right of, the attacker (**368**).

The right's primary responsibility is to block the set on the sideline. For the shoot, which is usually hit cross-court, she likely blocks the angle. For the high set, she positions herself according to the team's plan, either protecting the line, the angle or between.

The right responds to the right X, fake X and flair as the left does to the standard X and its complements. She moves left, joining the middle to double-block the X (**369**). She moves right to double-block the fake X and the flair, also with the middle. She moves behind and around the middle to block the X when the middle mistakenly commits to the three.

The right may block the left X, joining the left and the middle in a triple block, but this is difficult for her because of the distance (**370**). She has a better chance of success if the play set is higher than normal.

The right may join the middle in double-blocking a high set in the middle of the net (**371**). She often does so on a pass to the right of the court's midline. She may also join her teammates in a triple block on a high, middle set. She moves left to triple-block when the ball is passed on the court's midline.

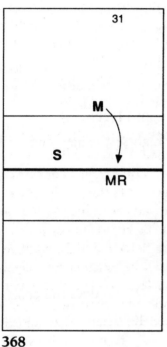

368

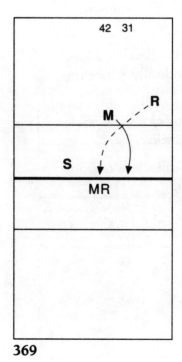

369

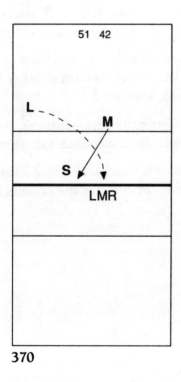

370

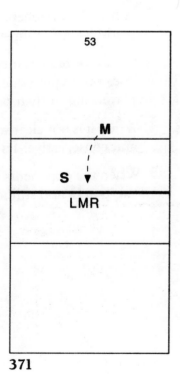

371

The quick/shoot and the double-quick represent the greatest challenge to any blocking scheme, as mentioned. In read-blocking, the blocker covers whichever attacker enters her zone (372). If the blocker is positioned outside, she attack-blocks the shoot, probably on the angle. If a combination attacker also enters her zone, she soft-blocks (372). Soft-blocking allows her to shift her coverage from the low- to the medium-set hitter.

The read blocker's zone is not fixed. It varies with the positions of the other blockers. The left's zone, for example, may include a narrow area bounded by the left sideline and the middle blocker, who has moved left. Or, if the middle blocker has moved to the right sideline to cover a high set, it may include the entire net.

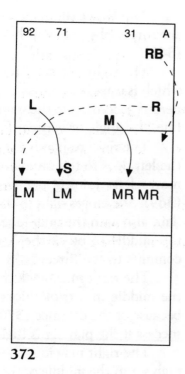

372

* * * * *

When does the coach choose read-blocking?

1. When the team is inexperienced. Read-blocking is simple, with well-defined responsibilities. Blockers do not question who blocks where.

2. When the opponents do not execute the quick attack well. The strength of read-blocking is in stopping the combination and the outside attacks.

3. When the team wants its specialized players in their positions. Read-blocking does not require one blocker to switch with another in mid-rally. Once the players are in their positions, they stay.

4. When it is not clear what offense the opponents use. Read-blocking is flexible and conservative. Its blockers have a chance to stop all attacks.

5. When the opponents run double-quicks. Reading allows the blockers to front two quicks and still assemble, in time, at the combination.

350

Commit-Blocking

Some teams hit quick sets high, well and often. They cannot be stopped with a read-blocking scheme, in which the middle, with responsibilities to block near each sideline, stuffs the quick only seldom.

In order to stop the quick-setting team, the middle blocker must commit to the quick. This means that whenever the one, the back one or the three is a possibility, she attack-blocks (373).

The commit-blocker, like the attacker opposite her, jumps high. After jumping she wants to reposition herself and block with a teammate. In most cases, she cannot. She does not have the time both to commit and then to double-block.

The two outside blockers form the double block (374). One or both follow the play-set hitters, covering the entire length of the net. In following the hitter, the outside blockers cross the commit-blocker, who is jumping with the quick. Crossing blockers are a characteristic of the commit scheme.

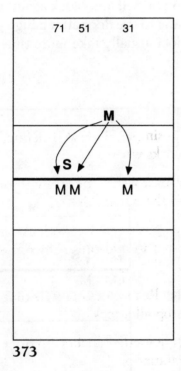

373

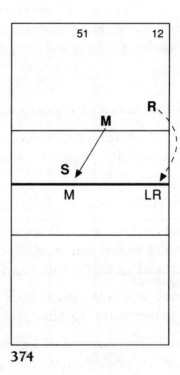

374

The Commit-Blocker. In commit-blocking, the middle starts in the same position as she does in read-blocking, that is, near the center of the net (**375**). The center-of-the-net location is about halfway between the attack points for the back one and the three, her most distant quick responsibilities; it is also near the attack point for the one, the most frequent quick set (**375**).

The middle blocker may adjust her starting position either left or right, depending on the location of the opposing middle and the tendencies of the opponents. Against a team that runs primarily the one attack, she starts left. Against a team that runs primarily the three, she starts right.

In general, the committing, middle blocker covers the opposing middle attacker (**373**, previous page). If the middle attacker leaves the zone bounded by the back one and the three attacks points, the middle blocker covers whichever attacker enters the zone (**376**). This mid-rally change in responsibility is the same as that required by read-blocking.

The middle moves to a position in front of the quick hitter as the opponents' attack unfolds. When the pass is good, she jumps high and stuff-blocks, as if she knows that the quick attacker will be set.

If the quick is not set, the middle wants to re-position herself and block again, as she does in read-blocking. Her chances are not good. Returning to the floor after a high jump, moving to another position and jumping for a second block usually take more time than she has.

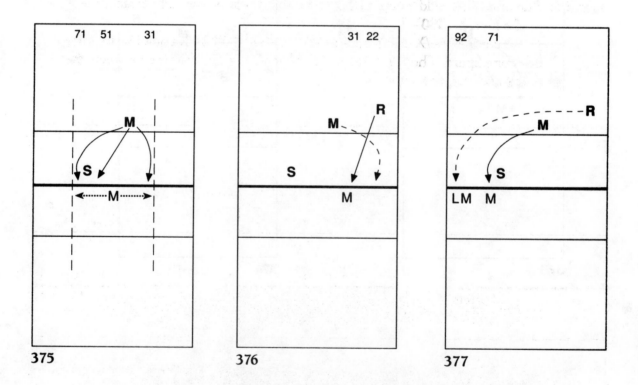

375   376   377

352

The commit-blocker may jump twice. In order for her to succeed, the play and the quick sets must be near each other; and the combination must be slow. Six combinations offer the middle blocker a realistic chance of jumping twice.

1. The opposing middle approaches to hit the back one and the set is delivered to the left sideline (377).

    The back-one/left-sideline combination offers the middle blocker her best chance. The attack points are only two zones apart and the back set is more likely to be high than a front set of comparable distance.

2. The opposing middle approaches to hit the three and the set is delivered to the right sideline (378).

    As in the back one/left combination, the attack points in the three/right combination are two zones apart. The latter is generally more difficult, however, because the play set can be quicker.

3. and 4. The opposing middle approaches to hit the one and the left attacks the standard X or the fake X (379).

    The attack points on both the X and the fake X are only one zone apart. They are difficult combinations for which to jump twice; the timing between the quick and the play set is tight.

5. and 6. The opposing middle approaches to hit the three and the right attacks the X or the fake X (380).

    Like the one/X combination, the three/X and fake X combinations are one zone apart. They are also difficult because of tight timing between the quick and the play sets.

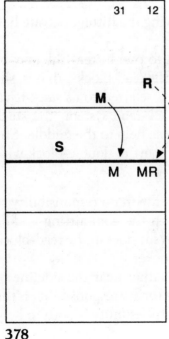

378

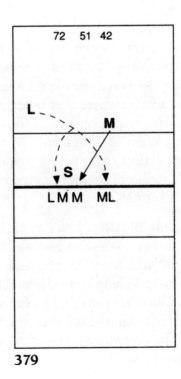

379

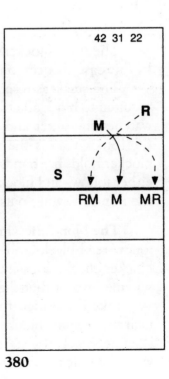

380

The Following, Outside Blocker. At least one of the outside blockers in the commit scheme is assigned to follow the hitter opposite her. Wherever the hitter goes, she goes.

When the outside's responsibility is to follow the hitter, she often crosses the middle blocker, who is fixed on the quick attacker. In order to cross quickly, the follower starts near and slightly behind the commit-blocker (**381**). She *stacks* behind the commit-blocker; she is referred to as the stack-blocker.

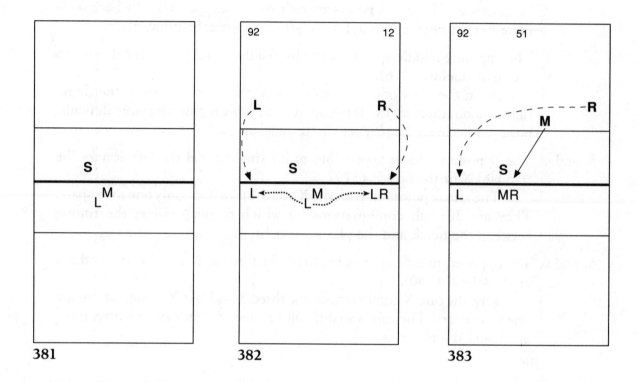

381   382   383

The stack-blocker's responsibility may be limited to following the hitter opposite her. In this case, her responsibility is referred to as *stack-man*.

The stacker's responsibility, however, may not be limited to one hitter. She may be required to block all attacks, no matter where they take place. She read-blocks, that is, she watches the setter and reacts. Her responsibility in this case is referred to as *stack-read*.

Stack-read is the most common arrangement. In the stack-read system, the stack blocker holds her hands high to deflect the quick, providing some help to the middle. She either follows and blocks the hitter opposite her or crosses the court to double-block with the non-following, outside blocker (**382**).

The Non-following, Outside Blocker. The outside blocker with no responsibility to follow read-blocks. She stays in her zone. She may double with the committing middle blocker but she does not cross the middle (**383**). She performs as she does in the read-block scheme, except that she expects little help from the middle blocker.

Like the reader, the non-following outside blocker starts either near the sideline or near the commit-blocker. She starts near the sideline when her primary responsibility is the sideline attack; she starts near the commit-blocker when her responsibility is both to help with the quick and to block on the sideline.

* * * * *

The blocker designated to stack gives each commit scheme its name. When the left blocker stacks, the scheme is referred to as left-stack (**381**); when the right stacks, the scheme is right-stack (**384**); when both stack, the scheme is double-stack (**385**).

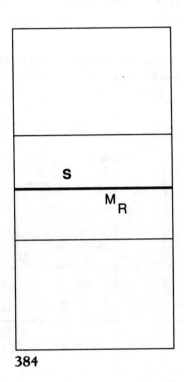

384

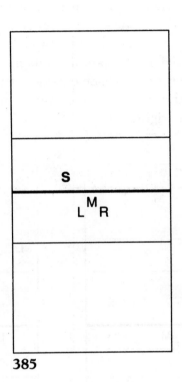

385

Left-Stack. The most common commit scheme is left-stack, in which the middle commits, the left follows and the right blocks on the right (**386**). The team that uses the left-stack expects the one to be set. The middle blocker usually starts to the left of the center of the court, near the attack point for the one. The left starts slightly behind, and to the left of, the commit-blocker (**386**).*

Any set by the opponents, other than the one, means trouble for the left-stacking defense. It encounters its least trouble when the opposing middle approaches to attack the one or the back one and the set is delivered near the quick attacker (**387**). The commit-blocker may be able to jump twice on these attacks.

The defensive team faces its most trouble when the opposing middle approaches to attack the three and each outside hitter approaches on a sideline (**388**). The follower must block, in this instance, one-on-one on the left sideline. A low set to the right sideline likely isolates the right, too.

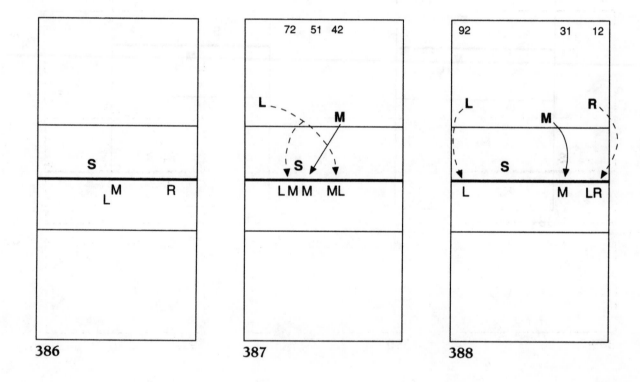

386   387   388

---

*The left stacks on the right shoulder of the commit-blocker when the opponents' attack pattern calls for it. The blocking scheme remains left-stack. She is the left blocker and her responsibility is to follow.

Right-Stack. The defensive team uses the right-stack when it expects the three to be set.

The middle blocker usually starts near the attack point for the three. The right starts slightly behind, and to the right of, the commit-blocker (389).

Any set, other than to the three hitter, means trouble. The defense encounters its least trouble when the middle approaches to hit the three and the set is delivered near the three-hitter (390). The commit-blocker may be able to jump twice on these attacks.

The defense faces its most trouble when the middle approaches to hit the one or the back one and the set is delivered to the right of the middle (391). The left likely helps the middle with the quick and the right is isolated against the two outside attackers.

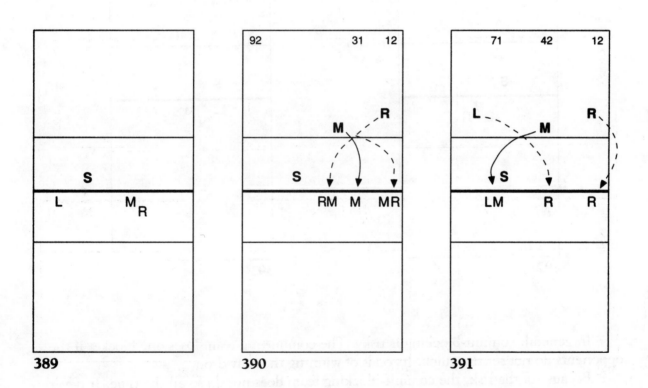

389   390   391

Double-Stack. The double-stack blocking scheme is a combination of the left- and right-stacks (**392**). The middle blocker commits to the quick. The outside blockers stack near the left and right shoulders of the commit-blocker. The left blocker follows when the middle approaches to hit the one; the right blocker follows when the middle approaches to hit the three.

The defensive team uses the double-stack blocking scheme when it expects the one or the three to be set and the outside attackers to approach near the quick hitter. Because most offenses spread the defense from sideline to sideline, the double-stack is rare.

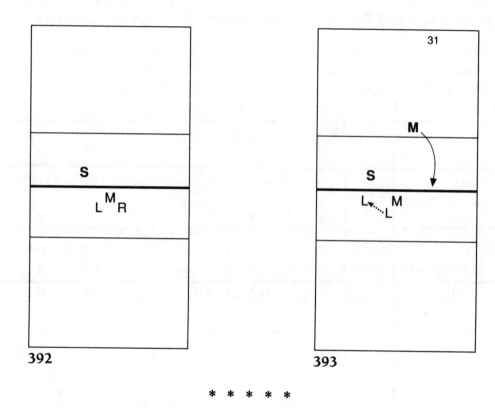

392   393

* * * * *

In general, commit-blocking is risky. The committing team loses one blocker if the opponents do not set the quick. Its odds of winning the rally drop.

Because of the risk, the commit-blocking team does not do so all the time. It never commits on a bad pass. It may limit its commitment to certain rotations and/or times.

Advanced teams use safeties. This means that the defense changes its scheme in mid-rally when it confronts a play that attacks its weak point.

The most common change is from commit to read. If the defensive team, for example, stacks its left blocker and the opposing middle approaches to hit the three, the defense read-blocks (**393**). The change occurs in mid-rally but is predetermined by the defense.

The team may implement a comparable change when it stacks its right blocker and the opposing middle approaches to hit the one.

The defense may also change from one follower to two. If the defense stacks its left blocker, for example, and the right hitter crosses the middle hitter, the right blocker may follow the right hitter (**394**).

358

* * * * *

Commit-blocking does not pose much risk when the opponents attack with only two players. In this case, one blocker stuffs the quick while the other two blockers double the combination (395).

Few commit-blocking teams face only two hitters. Teams that run the quick well all use a back-row attack that adds, at least, a third hitter.

The committing team disguises its deployment. If the offense knows what commit scheme is to be deployed, it can respond with a play that insures its success.

When does the coach choose commit-blocking?

1. When the team's blockers are experienced and mobile. The commit system requires all blockers to make dramatic movements. Safeties require mid-rally changes in scheme and communication among the blockers.

2. When the opponents pass well. Accurate passing brings an increase in quick sets, which the commit system is designed to stop.

3. When the opponents' quick hitter is tall and/or jumps high. The reading middle blocker, who must stay near the floor, has difficulty resisting quicks that are attacked high.

4. When the team recovers quickly after being attacked. Commit-system blockers often switch positions and then run their offense from the new positions. Commit-system blockers hit all sets.

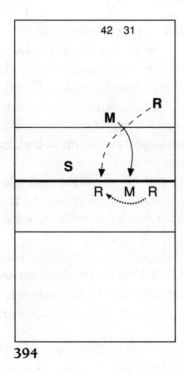

394

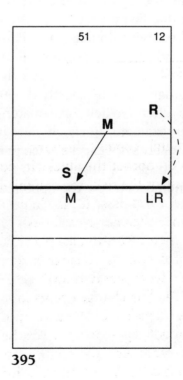

395

The block chart depicts the team's deployment of blockers against 27 plays, ten of which are two-hitter (no back-row) attacks, seventeen of which are three-hitter attacks.

The block chart does not include all plays that the defense may confront. The chart presents a range, from simple, two-hitter attacks to double crosses.

Four blocking schemes are included: read, left-stack, right-stack and double-stack.

The blockers' movements on the chart strike a balance between what the blockers would like to do and what they can do. The blocker who commits three or more zones from the combination attack does not form a double-block on the chart (although she may, in rare cases, do so).

The block that succeeds part of the time is shown in gray, rather than black. The read blocker confronting the quick is shown in gray (396); so is the commit-blocker who, after jumping against the quick, jumps a second time one or two zones away (397).

The blocker with more than one responsibility appears on the court more than once. The middle blocker reading a quick hitter and two sideline hitters, for example, appears in three locations on the court, in front of each attack (396).

The stars note the blocking schemes that have a good chance of stopping the attack it confronts. One star means that the defense fronts the quick with at least one blocker and double-blocks the combination attacks. All of the read-block deployments exhibit one star (396).

The commit scheme that has a good chance of success offers greater resistance than the comparable read scheme. The middle in the commit scheme jumps to stuff the quick, rather than waiting to see. The single-stack commit schemes that front the quick with one blocker and double the combination exhibit two stars (398). The exceptions are the patterns in which the middle jumps twice, which exhibit one star.

The qualifying double-stacks exhibit only one star, even though they, like the single-stacks, include the committing middle. The stack blockers in the double have greater difficulty covering an outside attack than the stackers in either of the single-stack schemes. Even the single stars are mostly theoretical indicators of the double-stack's effectiveness.

Some offensive/defensive match-ups on the chart are extreme. The committing defense, for example, likely changes its scheme in mid-rally when it confronts a double-quick. It also does not expect to face a two-hitter attack because most teams at this level use at least one back-row attacker.

The numbers below the opponents' baseline specify the opponents' attack patterns.

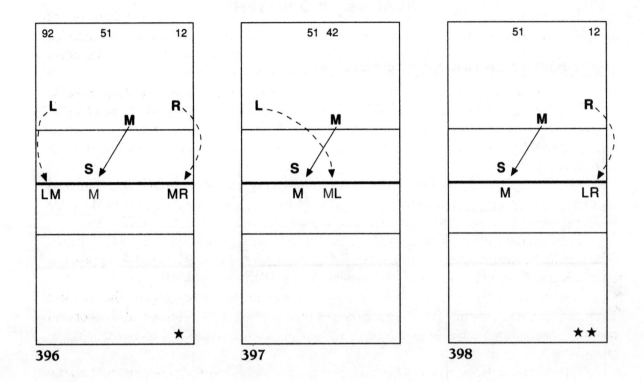

92	51	12		51 42			51	12
L		R		L	M			M	R
	M								
	S			S			S	
LM	M	MR		M	ML		M	LR

396

397

398

★

★★

READ vs. TWO HITTERS

Gray letters represent possible, but difficult blocks.

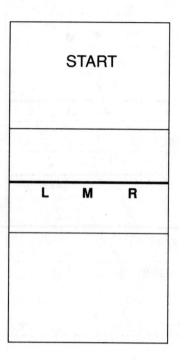

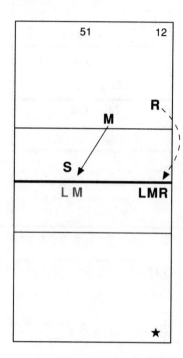

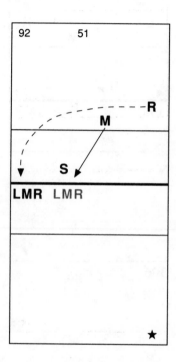

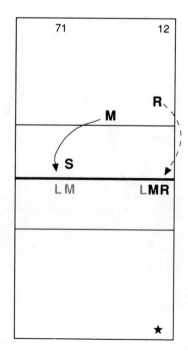

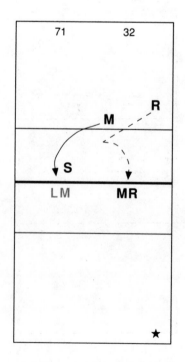

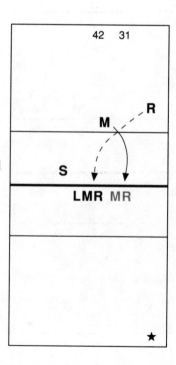

READ vs. TWO HITTERS

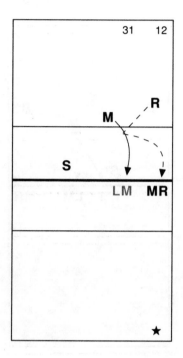

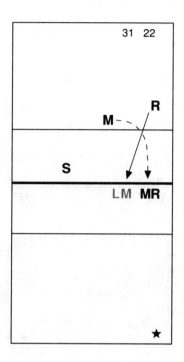

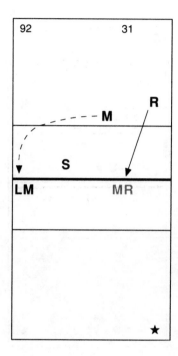

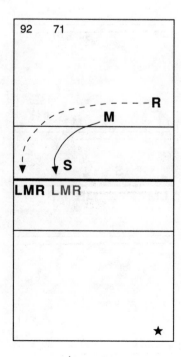

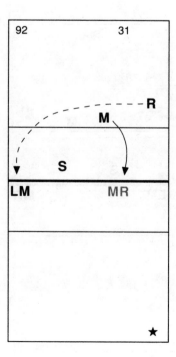

READ vs. THREE HITTERS

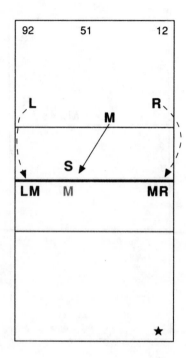

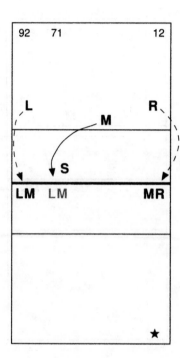

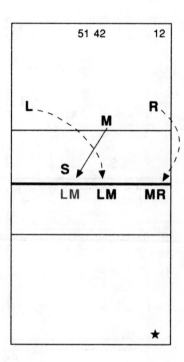

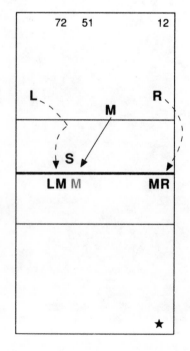

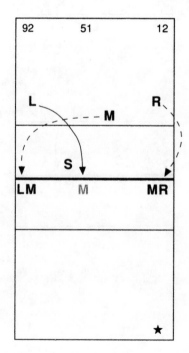

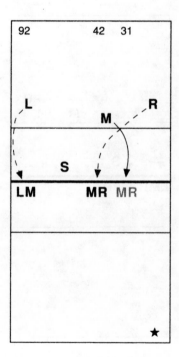

READ vs. THREE HITTERS

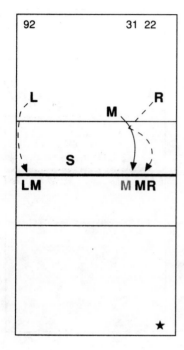
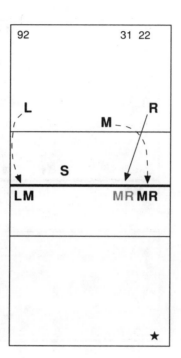

READ vs. THREE HITTERS
Quick/shoot, Double-quick Combinations

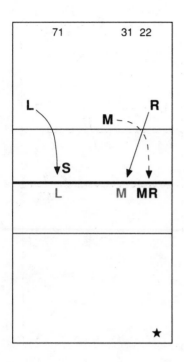

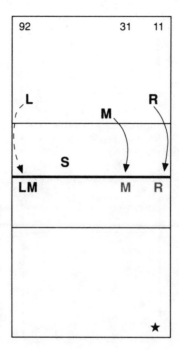

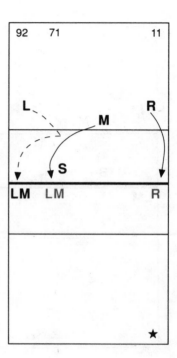

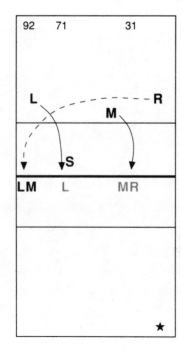

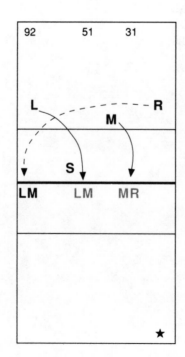

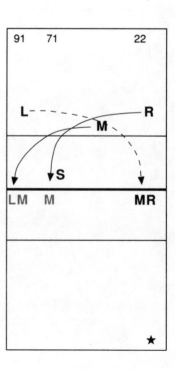

READ vs. THREE HITTERS
Quick/shoot, Double-quick Combinations

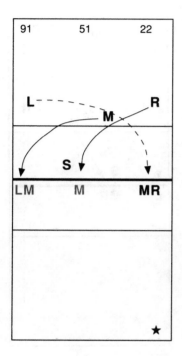
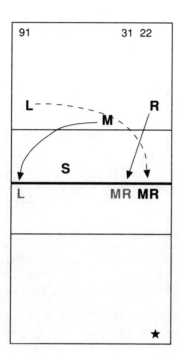
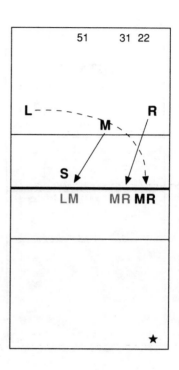

LEFT STACK vs. TWO HITTERS

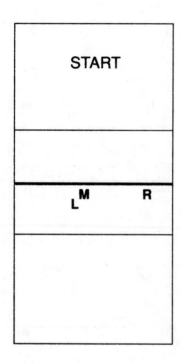

START

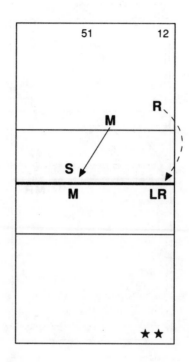

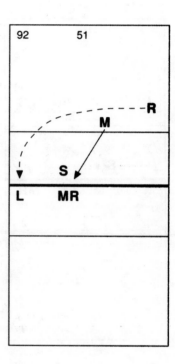

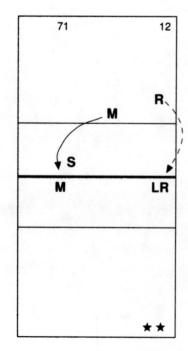

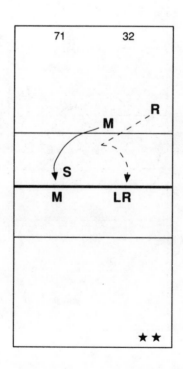

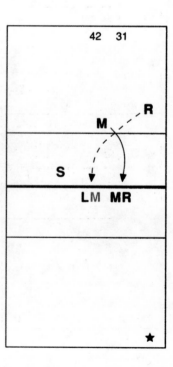

LEFT STACK vs. TWO HITTERS

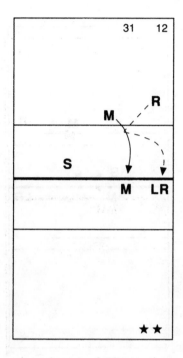

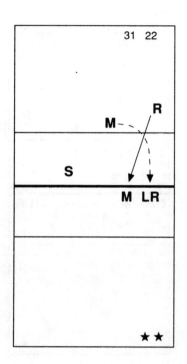

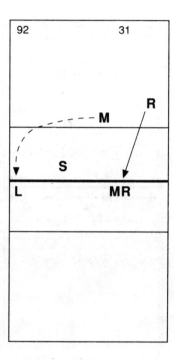

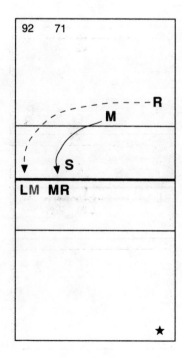

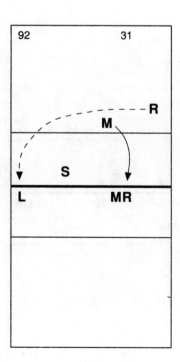

LEFT STACK vs. THREE HITTERS

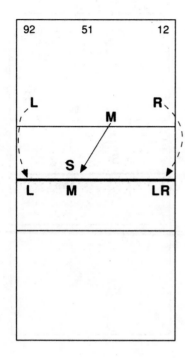

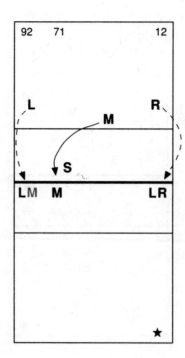

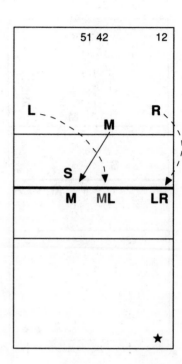

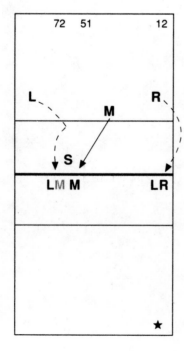

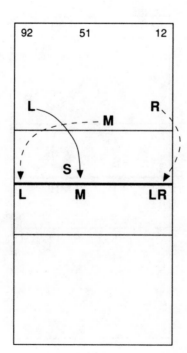

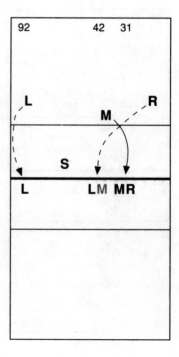

LEFT STACK vs. THREE HITTERS

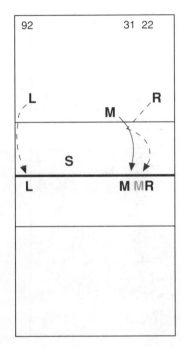
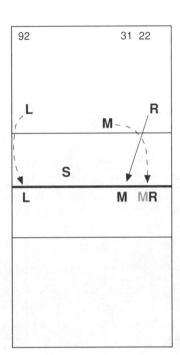

LEFT STACK vs. THREE HITTERS
Quick/shoot, Double-quick Combinations

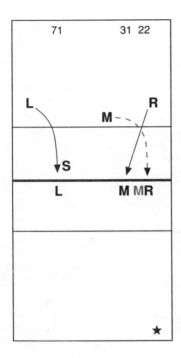

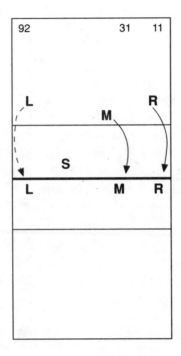

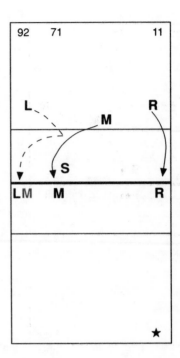

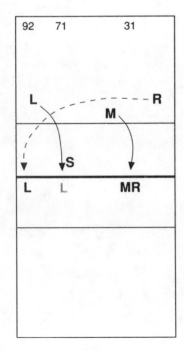

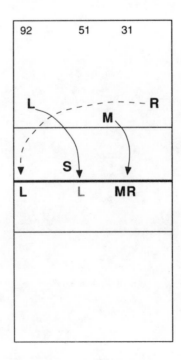

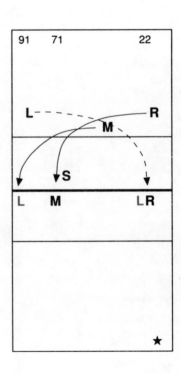

LEFT STACK vs. THREE HITTERS
Quick/shoot, Double-quick Combinations

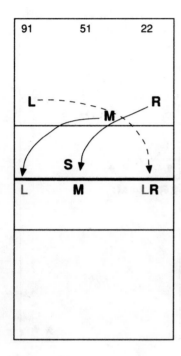

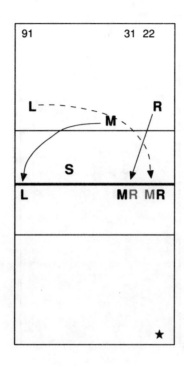

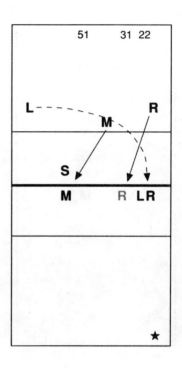

RIGHT STACK vs. TWO HITTERS

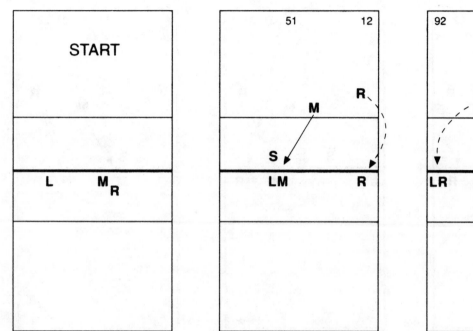

START

L   M R

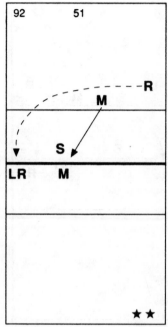

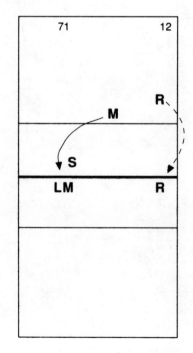

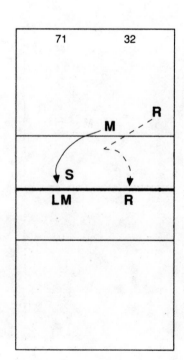

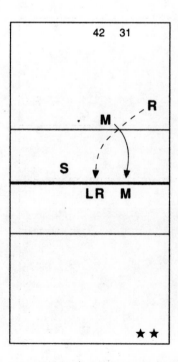

RIGHT STACK vs. TWO HITTERS

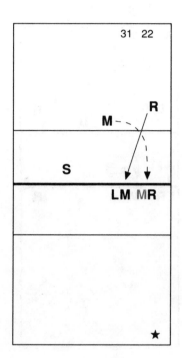

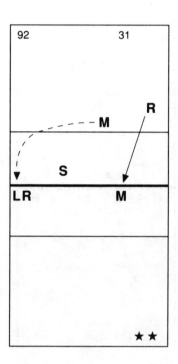

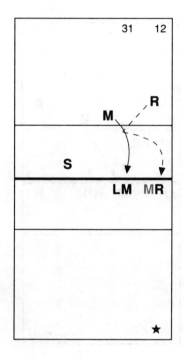

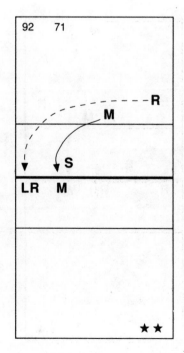

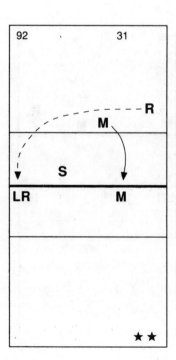

RIGHT STACK vs. THREE HITTERS

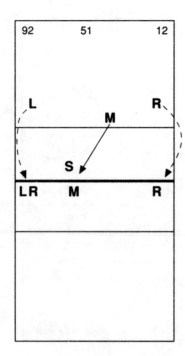

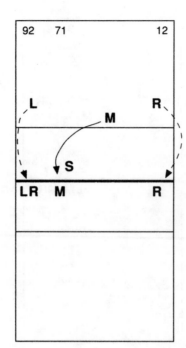

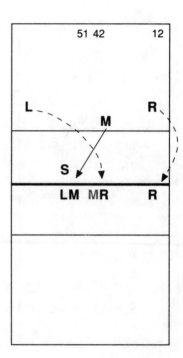

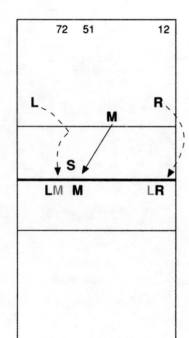

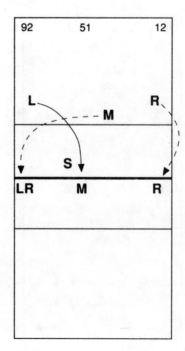

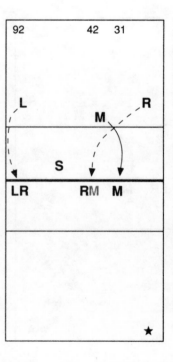

RIGHT STACK vs. THREE HITTERS

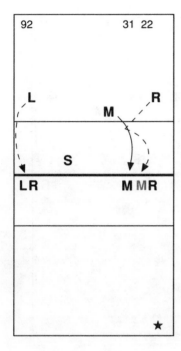
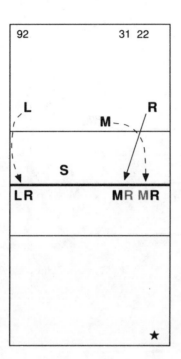

RIGHT STACK vs. THREE HITTERS
Quick/shoot, Double-quick Combinations

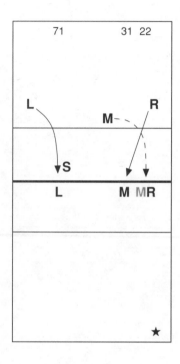

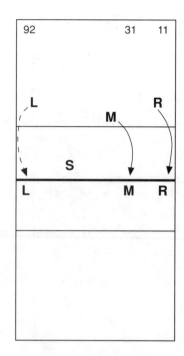

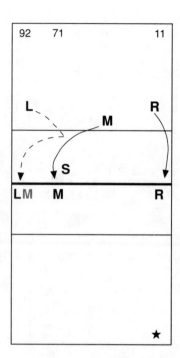

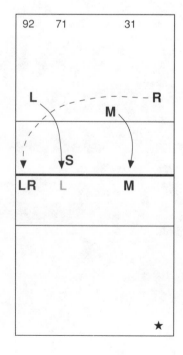

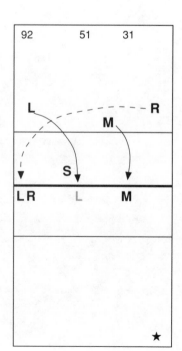

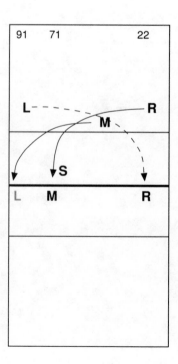

RIGHT STACK vs. THREE HITTERS
Quick/shoot, Double-quick Combinations

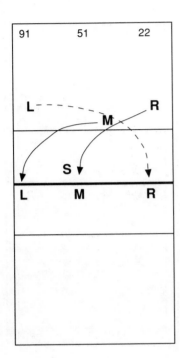
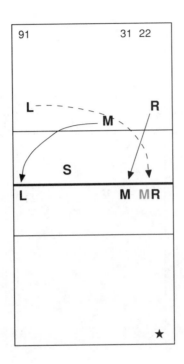
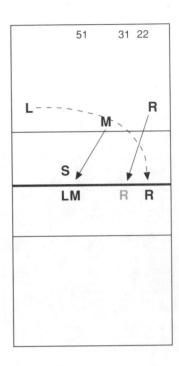

DOUBLE STACK vs. TWO HITTERS

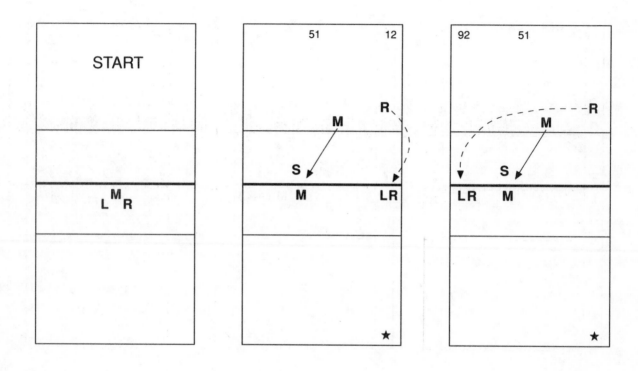

START

L M R

51   12

M → S

R

M   LR

★

92   51

R

M → S

LR   M

★

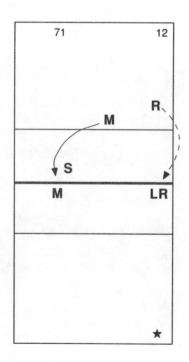

71   12

M

R

S

M   LR

★

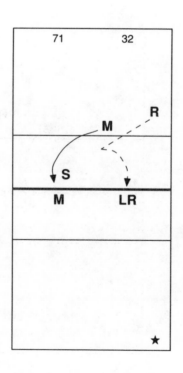

71   32

M   R

S

M   LR

★

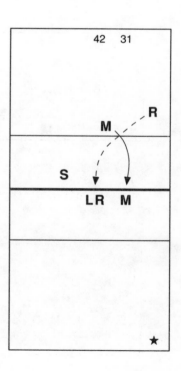

42   31

M   R

S

LR   M

★

DOUBLE STACK vs. TWO HITTERS

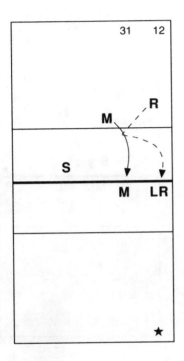

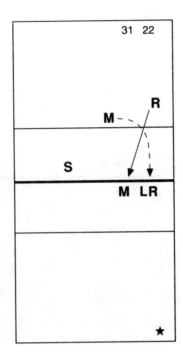

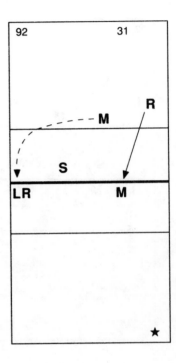

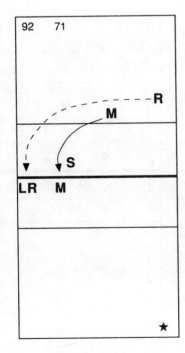

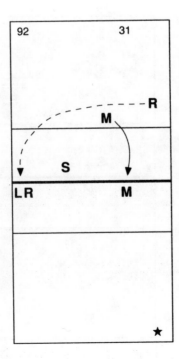

DOUBLE STACK vs. THREE HITTERS

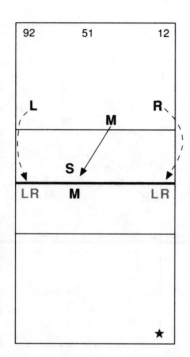

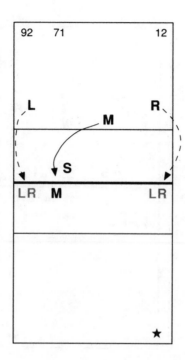

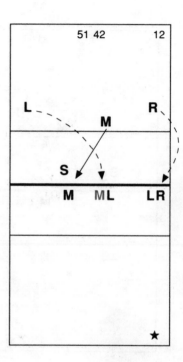

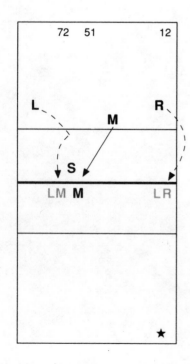

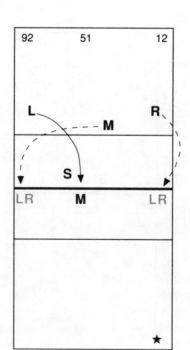

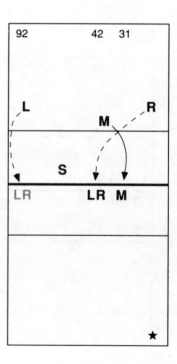

DOUBLE STACK vs. THREE HITTERS

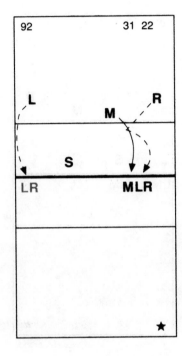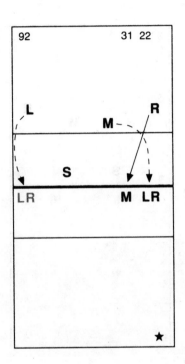

DOUBLE STACK vs. THREE HITTERS
Quick/shoot, Double-quick Combinations

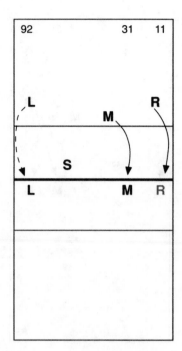

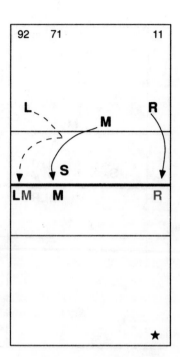

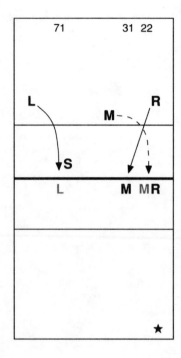

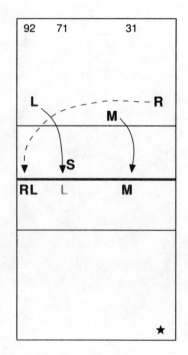

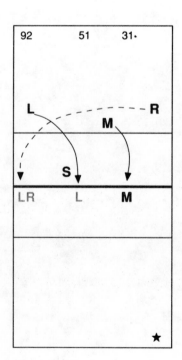

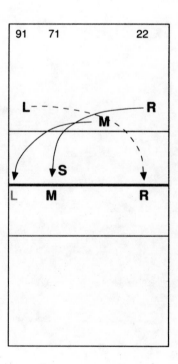

DOUBLE STACK vs. THREE HITTERS
Quick/shoot, Double-quick Combinations

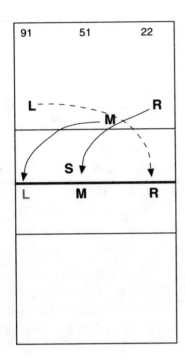
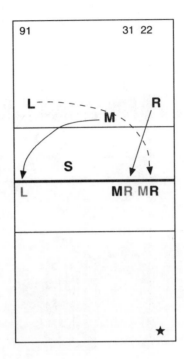
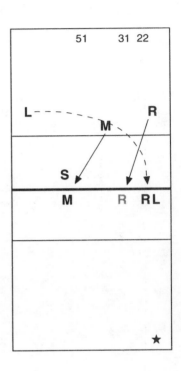

The Backcourt

The coach has settled on a blocking scheme, or schemes, for his team. He turns his attention to the backcourt.

The coach chooses among four schemes: perimeter, rotate, counter-rotate and middle-up (the middle-up is covered in Chapter 4). Matched with an advanced blocking scheme, each creates a coherent defensive system.

* * * * *

The block influences the positions of the backcourt players, regardless of the scheme. The backcourt players arrange themselves differently for one, two or three blockers; they make final adjustments according to the position of these blockers.

The following discussion matches each backcourt scheme—the perimeter, the rotate and the counter-rotate—with single, double and triple blocks. The blocks, and the attacks from which they arise, take place on the right sideline, the center of the net and the left sideline.

* * * * *

The team starts with its players distributed symmetrically about the perimeter of the court (399). This starting arrangement allows each player to move quickly to her final defensive position, regardless of the team's backcourt scheme.*

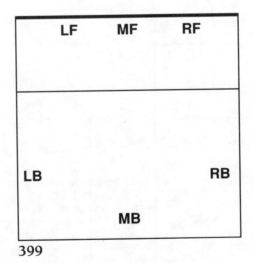

399

---

* The exception is the middle-up, which benefits from its middle backcourt defender starting closer to the net.

Perimeter

Most attacks in international play arrive near the borders of the court. The most common backcourt scheme at the advanced level is the perimeter (**400**).

The strength of the perimeter is in covering the hard spike with four diggers. The weakness is in its susceptibility to tips, especially those arriving in the center of the court.

The final positions in the perimeter accord with principles that are common to all backcourt schemes.

1. The player who finds herself with the attack aligned between two blockers holds her position. She adjusts herself to the seam, the midpoint between the blockers. She covers the attack that goes through, or over, the block. In the perimeter, the seam defender is the middle-back (**400**).

2. The player closest to the seam defender positions herself so that she can see the ball outside the blocker's hand. She covers the attack that goes around the block. In the perimeter, the deep wings defend outside the block (**400**).

3. The defender cannot always position herself outside the blocker's hand; sometimes she meets the sideline first. In this case, she faces the attack and readies herself to dig. Like the outside-the-block defender, the digger who meets the sideline is usually a deep wing (**400**).

4. The fourth defender, the off-blocker, positions herself near, or deeper than, the attack line. She adjusts to the midpoint of the area bounded by the attacker's sharpest angle and her deeper teammate (**400**).

As the attack moves toward the center of the net, the line digger moves forward. The other defenders adjust according to the principles (**401**).

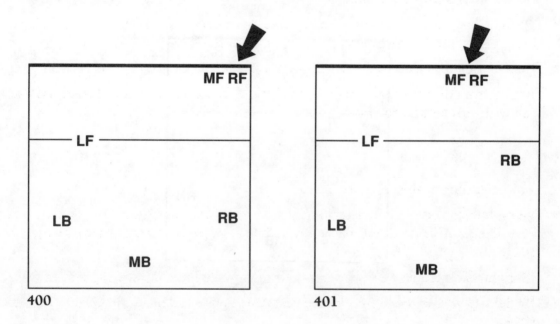

400   401

For the center attack, the team designates which outside player forms the double-block with the middle. The left usually does so, since she may start nearer than the right to the center of the net. The right moves away from the net to defend in the backcourt (**402**).

When the team triple-blocks, the middle-back aligns herself with the center of the block. The deep wings align themselves according to the principles (**403**).

When the second blocker cannot arrive to block, she moves away from the net to cover the tip. The other backcourt defenders adjust to her presence (**404**).

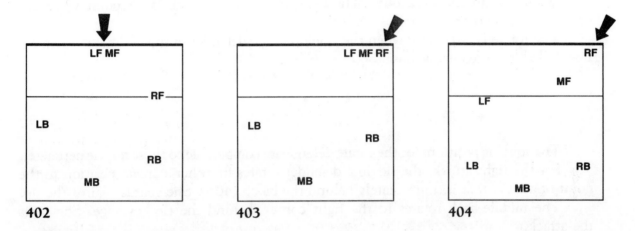

402   403   404

In defending against a right attack,* the responsibilities for each backcourt player in a perimeter scheme include:

- The middle-back covers the baseline, from its center to the corner behind right-back. She has no shallow responsibilities (**400**).

- The right-back covers the sideline from about six meters deep to immediately behind the block. She shares responsibility for the center of the court with the off-blocker (**400**).

- The left-back digs the angle just outside the block, often called the "hot corner" (**400**).

- The left-front digs the sharp angle and covers the center of the court; she helps the right-back with tips behind the block (**400**).

* * * * *

In defending against a center attack:

- The middle-back covers the seam between the blockers, as she does for a sideline attack. When the seam is closed, she moves left, in order to even her coverage with the right-back (**402**).

- The right-back protects the area between the middle-back and the right-front (**402**).

- The right-front and the left-back cover the sharp angles and tips in the center of the court (**402**).

*The defensive positions for the left attack—and for attacks between the left and the center—are mirror images of those for the right.

Rotate

The rotate backcourt scheme, a variation of the perimeter, rotates the defenders toward the attack. Its final arrangement includes two defenders on the line, one immediately behind the block and one near the baseline (405).

The rotate defense complements a tall block that covers the cross-court attack. The block eliminates attacks to center-back, where the rotate positions no diggers. The block may not cover the line, where the rotate positions two defenders.

The strength of the rotate is in covering the line and the tip. The weakness is in having one less digger in the backcourt. The team must consider the latter point when the opponents spike over the block.

The rotate is often used when the would-be line defender in the perimeter scheme is not skilled in backcourt defense.

* * * * *

The starting positions for the rotate defense are comparable to those for the perimeter.

For the right attack, the sideline defender rotates from her starting position to the point of attack, that is, immediately behind the block (405). She guards against the tip.

The middle-back rotates to the right corner, behind the tip coverage. She faces the attack.

The left-back positions herself in the corner, covering the deep angle.

The off-blocker moves away from the net, deepening more than she does in the perimeter scheme. She leaves the sharp angle open.

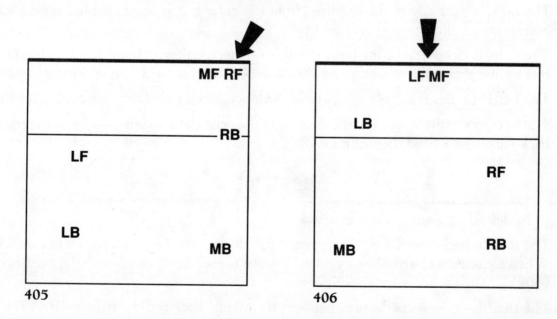

405   406

On a center attack, the left-front blocks with the middle (406). The left-back rotates forward to cover the tip; the middle-back rotates left. The right-back stays in the corner. The right-front deepens, positioning herself outside the right blocker's hand. She digs the sharp angle.

When the rotating team triple-blocks, it loses another deep defender. For an attack away from the center of the net, the attack-side line digger rotates into tip coverage; middle-back also rotates (**407**). The opposite wing moves to the corner. Both the deep center of the court and the sharp angle are open.

For an attack in the center of the net, the team designates which wing rotates into the tip coverage (**408**). The middle-back and the opposite wing occupy the corners.

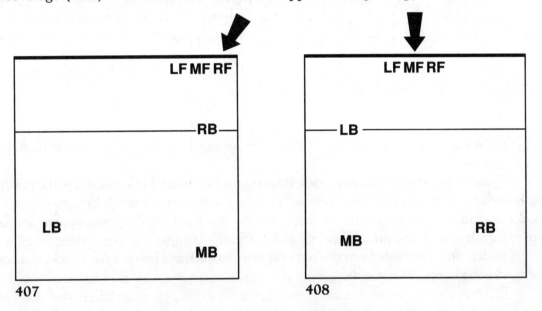

407

408

When the middle cannot block on the sideline, she moves away from the net to cover the tip; only one player blocks (**409**). The line digger tries to read the middle's change early enough to position herself about halfway between the net and the baseline; a second player in tip coverage is unnecessary. The middle-back, opposite wing and off-blocker move as if two players were blocking.

When the middle blocks singly on a center attack, the left-front covers the tip (**410**). Left-back and right-front dig the sharp angles, slightly deeper than the attack line. Middle- and right-back position themselves near the corners, leaving the center of the baseline open.

409

410

The Counter-Rotate

The counter-rotate is a second variation of the perimeter. The backcourt in this scheme rotates away from the attack.

The final arrangement of players includes one defender behind the block, as does the rotate (411). In the counter, however, the tip coverage positions herself near the center of the court instead of on the line; this places two defenders on the angle and one on the line.

The strength of the counter is in covering the tip and other attacks that fall behind the block, especially those directed toward the center of the court. The weakness, as in all tip coverage defenses, is having only three diggers in the backcourt.

* * * * *

The starting positions for the counter-rotate are the same as for the perimeter and rotate defenses.

For the right attack, the right-back stays on the sideline (411). She deepens, positioning herself a meter or two from the baseline; she has no tip responsibility.

The middle-back moves to the left corner; she covers the deep angle. The left-back moves forward, near the attack line. She digs the sharp angle.

The left-front retreats from the net and positions herself behind the block; she covers the tip in the center of the court.

* * * * *

On the center attack, the left-front blocks with the middle, as she does in the rotate (412). The right-front moves behind, and to the right of, the blockers. The right-back positions herself to dig outside the block, between the attack line and the baseline. The middle-back adjusts to the seam. The left-back moves to dig outside the block, near the attack line.

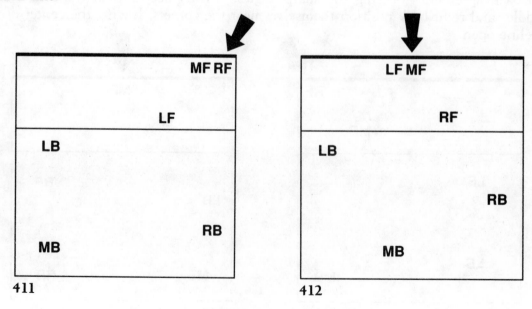

411   412

392

The counter-rotating team that triple-blocks positions the deep wing, either right- or left-back, in tip coverage. The cross-court wing covers the tip: left-back on a right attack (**413**) and vice-versa. The right-back does so on a center attack (**414**).

The remaining two deep defenders position themselves in the corners (**413, 414**).

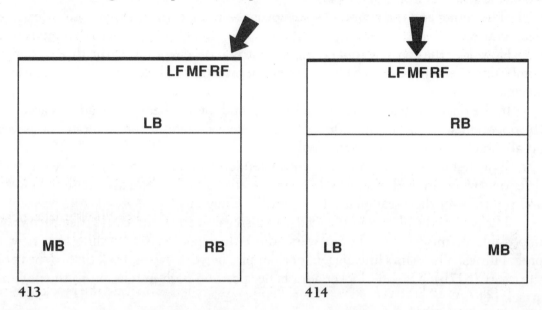

413   414

When the middle cannot arrive to block on the sideline, she covers the tip in the location designated for the left-front (**415**). The team tries to adjust to this mid-rally change. If it succeeds, the left-front digs the sharp angle and the other defenders distribute themselves about the perimeter of the court. If it does not, the middle- and left-fronts cover the same area and the center of the baseline is open.

When the middle single-blocks, right-front covers the tip on the right shoulder of the middle (**416**). Left-front and right-back dig the sharp angles; left- and middle-back cover the deep corners.

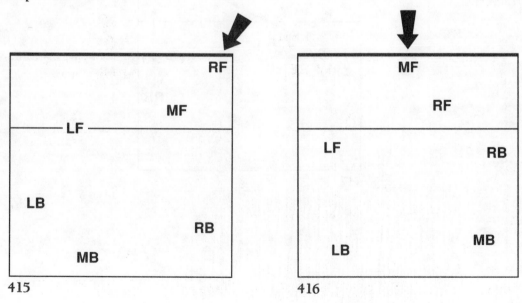

415   416

The Ideal

The perimeter, rotate and counter-rotate schemes strengthen certain areas of the court at the expense of others. The perimeter's strength is in defending against the hard spike, especially those directed toward the court boundaries. It is vulnerable to tips, off-speed shots and dribbles from the block.

The rotate and the counter-rotate cover the tip but, in doing so, lose a digger in the deep court.

How does the coach reconcile the strengths and weaknesses of the three schemes? By combining them into one. The coach implements what could be called the read backcourt scheme.

In the read, the team starts in a perimeter and then either stays or adjusts according to the opponents' attack. In the latter case, the defense rotates, counter-rotates or moves into an alignment that is not conventional.

This system requires skilled, mobile defenders. It requires, perhaps more importantly, defenders who can read, that is, see the opponents' attack unfold and sense the movement and positions of their teammates (Section III, Chapter 2).

The goal of the players in the read is to disregard certain attacks as they become either impossible or improbable. The players adjust their positions according to a new set of probabilities. The team's line digger, for example, moves forward, back or into the center of the court (417b). The off-blocker adjusts her position both in relation to the net and the attack (417a).

The deep diggers respond to the movements of their teammates. If, for example, the line digger moves forward, the middle-back may cover the deep line. Or she may not; no team member is locked into a pattern.

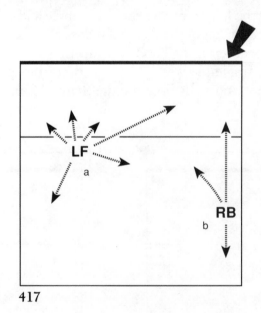

417

* * * * *

The best way to understand the reading team's movements is to watch it responding to an opponent's attack. The example that follows includes an attacker who telegraphs her intentions. This is not realistic, particularly at high levels of play, but is demonstrative. The attacking team, Western Union, opposes a read defensive team, the Seers.*

The Western Union setter delivers a medium-height set to the right hitter. It is slightly inside. As the ball leaves the setter's hands the Seers' right and middle-front players move into position to double-block. Its backcourt arranges itself according to the perimeter defense facing a right attack (418).

The Union hitter approaches to attack. As the inside set becomes clear, the Seers' right-back disregards the line shot which, with the block in position, is sure to be stuffed. She adjusts (419b).

The Union hitter turns her back to the net on her plant to jump. The Seers' outside blocker sees that the attacker, if she is to spike, must direct the ball on the sharp angle. The blocker stays down and retreats from the net (419a).

The attacker turns her back to the net because she has overrun the ball. From this position, she cannot deliver a hard spike, which the defense now disregards.

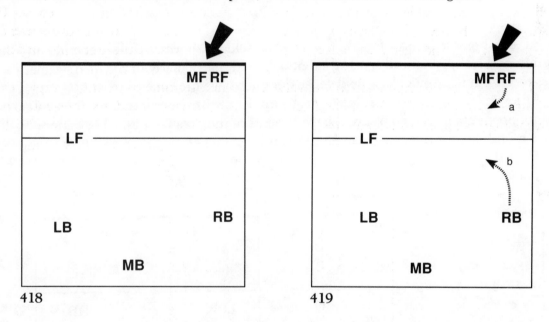

418   419

---

*Narration cannot capture the fluidity of the players' actions. Neither can illustrations. Micro-seconds time the events on the court.

It is clear that the attacker must tip or make an off-speed shot on the sharp angle. The Seers adjust again, with the left-front moving toward the attacker (**420a**).

The left-back senses her teammate's movement and shifts behind her, thereby positioning another defender on the sharp angle (**420b**). The middle-back adjusts left and forward (**420c**).

The ball is tipped, clearing the blocker's left hand. The left-front rolls to her right, away from the net. She deflects the ball toward the baseline at a height of about twenty centimeters from the floor (**421a**).

The middle-back, who has seen her teammate reach for the ball, heads for the floor herself. At her teammate's touch of the ball, she starts to dive. Sensing the presence of her teammate, the left-back, she sweeps the ball to her left (**421b**).

The left-back fires the ball over the net with the thumb and forefinger of her right hand (**421c**).

* * * * *

At the highest levels of play, the defense seldom moves as the Seers do in the illustration. The opponents disguise their attacks and, particularly in the men's game, the spikes reach the floor quickly. The defense does not have the time to react.

At lower levels, there is a different problem: the players can neither see the evolution of their opponents' attack nor sense the movements of their teammates. They cannot read. This is a problem for the coach; he must teach his players how to see and how to move.

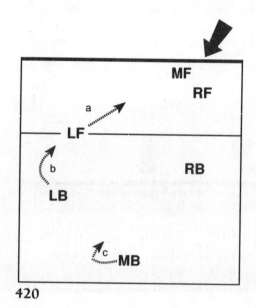

420

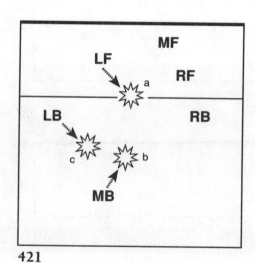

421

PERIMETER

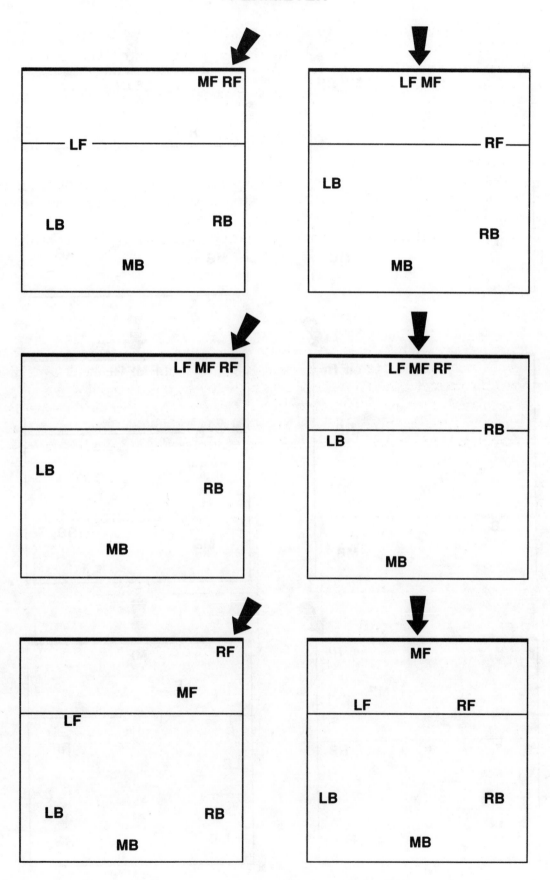

ROTATE

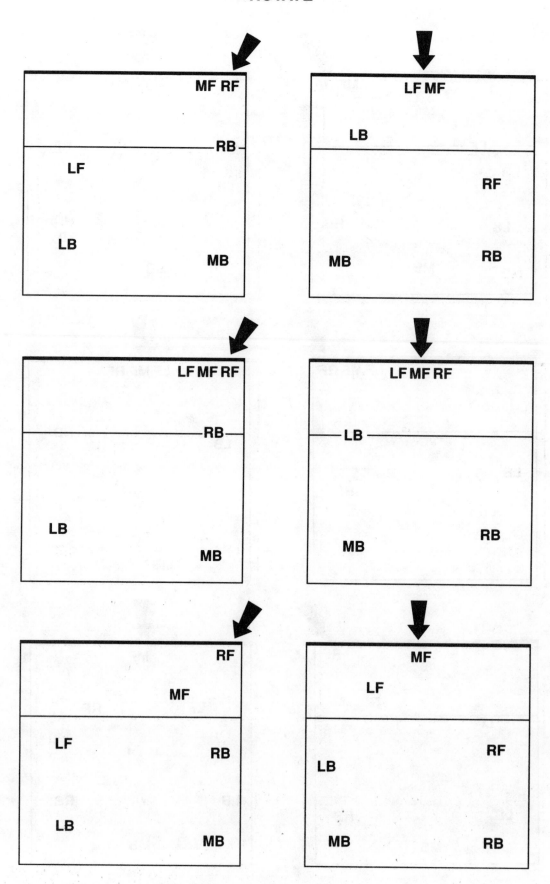

COUNTER-ROTATE

Situations

The defense confronts certain situations that are outside the responsibilities of the standard blocking and backcourt schemes. These require planned changes.

The Free Ball

The team's free-ball formation may include five, four, three, two or one receiver. At advanced levels, the team uses no more than two.

When the team sees that the free ball is imminent, the setter heads to the net and the left-front and the right-front retreat (422). The middle-front may stay at the net until the ball has been passed. This insures that her presence does not distract the back-row receivers.

The front-row players, especially the middle, try to avoid handling the ball; passing interferes with hitting. They must guard against shallow shots, however, before they ready themselves to attack.

The left-back and the middle-back divide the responsibilities in the deep court, both in two-and three-hitter rotations (422). They handle the ball whenever possible with an overhand pass, which is more accurate than a forearm pass.

It is not unusual for the highest-level teams to assign one player the responsibility for covering most, if not all, of the court. This player is the best ball controller and usually the middle-back.

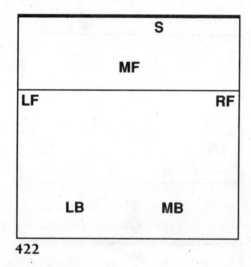

422

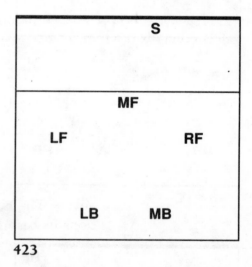

423

The Down Ball

Sometimes the attacker is not in position to deliver a hard spike, but not so far out of position that she must deliver a free ball. She can attack, but not hard enough to warrant blocking. The team calls "down ball." The "down" refers to the blockers, who neither jump nor raise their hands above the net. Blockers' hands offer a target to the attacker.

The down ball differs from the free ball in that all five players try to cover the backcourt and receive the attack. The ball may be delivered crisply; the formation compares to the five-passer serve-receive (423).

When the blockers do not have the time to join the formation, as is often the case, they stay at the net. The backcourt adjusts.

The Back-Row Attack

The main considerations in confronting the back-row attack are whether to block and, if so, how to do so. The defense uses three main patterns, depending on the effectiveness of the attack.

1. The defense does not block the ineffective attack. Its back row digs and its left- and right-front players cover the shallow court.

2. The defense blocks when the opponents attack with an effective, but infrequent, *D*.

    The blockers first concentrate on the front-row hitters, who receive the majority of the sets. They shift their focus to the back-row attacker after the ball has been set.

    A typical pattern aligns the team's left blocker near its middle to help with the quick. When the opponents set the D, the left and the middle block cross-court. Two back-row defenders cover the line **(424)**.

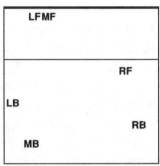

424

3. When the back-row attack is formidable and frequent, the defense blocks as if it were facing a three-hitter, front-row attack. It likely uses a read-blocking scheme. The team may load, that is, confront the opponent's best hitter with its best blocker.

    The blockers delay their jump on the back-row attack. The backcourt defenders generally position themselves deeper in the court.

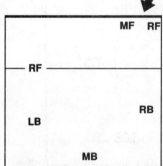

425

The Split Block

Occasionally the defense confronts an attacker whose favorite shot is the sharp angle, either left or right. The spike from this player goes around the block.

The defense splits its blockers, covering the sharp angles. The blockers leave a gap, where the backcourt positions its best digger **(425)**. The split block either stuffs the attack or forces the attacker from her favorite shot.

The Deep Set

On a deep set, a front-row player usually attacks the ball cross-court. Because a left/right mistake is magnified, the spiker avoids the line, where there is little margin for error.

The defense, on a deep set, forms its block farther inside than usual. It may adjust its line diggers toward the center of the court, particularly if it uses the read scheme **(426)**. When the front row blocks, the back row does not disregard the line; the ball may ricochet from the blockers' hands.

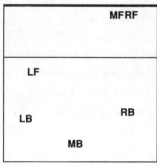

426

Defensive Strategy

Defensive strategy asks the same questions as offensive: "what plays?" "who runs them?" and "when are they run?" The defense, however, asks them about the opponents. It must predict the opponents' attack.

Defense is reactive. The team cannot choose what its opponents run. It must formulate plans to resist all attacks.

* * * * *

The advanced defensive team, in general, has several goals. It wants to double-block the combination attack; to triple-block the high center attack and, perhaps, the high sideline as well; and to single-block, at least, the quick attack.

Regardless of the number of blockers with which the team confronts the attack, it wants its blockers to touch every ball. The touched ball moves more slowly than the untouched, giving the backcourt a greater chance to control it.

The team wants no tips to reach the floor. The opponents must spike if they are to win the rally.

* * * * *

The advanced team chooses from two main blocking schemes, read and commit. The latter includes three patterns, left-, right- and double-stack, totaling four basic blocks.

Each of the four basic blocks allows triple-blocking the high attack left, center and right and doubling the high center. Each may be deployed to cover angle or line attacks on the outside. Three triples, one double, two angles and two lines total eight variations. Four schemes multiplied by 8 variations equals 32 blocking possibilities.

The team chooses among the perimeter, the rotate, the counter-rotate and the middle-up backcourt schemes. The former three can be applied discretely to left, right and middle attacks. Thirty-two blocks multiplied by 3 backcourts and again multiplied by 3 attack points equals 288 block/backcourt permutations.

Each permutation can be applied by rotation: $288 \times 6 = 1728$. The team may choose the middle-up backcourt,* adding another 32 possibilities for a grand total of 1750 possible defensive arrangements.

* * * * *

The team determines which of the 1750 permutations it employs by considering the opponents' offense and its own personnel. The team usually organizes its defensive schemes by rotation. Which opponent in each rotation is the most effective hitter? The second most effective? What percentage of the sets does each hitter receive? Where does each like to direct the ball? Tips? Do the opponents attack from the back row? If so, who hits and from where?

For each rotation, the team applies both a blocking pattern and a backcourt arrangement to a particular attack. On a right attack, for example, the team may use a standard double-block (neither oriented toward the line nor toward the angle) and defend with a perimeter backcourt arrangement. On a left attack, it blocks the angle and rotates its backcourt defenders. On a high middle attack, it triple-blocks.

---

*The middle-up, by virtue of its back-row player positioned near the net, must be applied to all attacks or not at all.

* * * * *

The team's first decisions regard its block: on outside sets does it cover the line or the angle? In double-blocking center attacks, does it cover the left, right or straight-ahead shot? The team decides on the basis of its scouting report and the skills of its backcourt.

The position of the block may change from rotation to rotation; it may change by the distribution of the opposing spikers within one rotation; it also may change from left to right attack.

The Block

Does the team read or commit? The criteria for making this decision are set forth on pages 350 and 359. If the team decides to commit, it must determine when to do so. In some rotations, the team may not commit at all. In others, it may commit on every good pass. In still others, it may turn the commit on and off either by rally or within a single rally.

In order to turn the commit on and off by rally, the team decides upon the scheme before the serve. It continues the scheme throughout the rally.

In order to change the scheme within the rally, the team calls audibles. Or its system includes safeties, which are invoked by the patterns of the opponents.

The left blocker confronting a back one, for example, may be assigned to commit. If the opponents run a different quick, she reads. The team may commit on the opponents' first attack, when the pass is likely to be good, and read throughout the rest of the rally.

If the opponent alters its attack to the defense's disadvantage, the defense, in turn, alters its scheme. If the committing team faces double-quicks, for example, it switches to reading. Or it commits two blockers. When the set goes to the non-quick hitter, one of the blockers must jump twice.

* * * * *

The team may load its blockers. When the team positions its two best blockers on the most effective hitter, one of the opponents' attackers faces little or no resistance. Two blockers on one hitter is referred to as "trap" blocking.

The team that arranges its blockers according to the opponents' positioning does so at the possible expense of its transition attack. For some teams, whose hitters are accomplished at hitting all sets, the trade-off is a good one. Whoever is in the best position after blocking fills the nearest attack lane. Other teams cannot give up the specialization of their players on offense.

In general, the best blocker confronts the best hitter, without regard to where the best blocker must go in order to do so. The exception is the setter. She usually does not block left because she has difficulty running the attack from there.

* * * * *

It is not unusual for the most effective hitter to be on the right, as the defense faces the opponents. The read-blocking team loads its best blocker in the middle or on the right. The right is preferred when the opponents shoot or when the best blocker does not move quickly.

The read-blocking team may position its two best blockers in the middle and on the right, provided (usually) that the arrangement does not leave the setter on the left.

The commit-blocking team may position its best blocker on the right, as a non-following blocker. The second-best blocker follows and the weakest blocker commits.* When the follower has a stack-man assignment, the team traps the opponents' right.

The best blocker may be assigned to follow with stack-man responsibility. She must be mobile. The second best blocker positions herself on the right as the non-follower. Once again, the weakest commits.

In either of the commit schemes, the follower may stack/read. This does not trap the right. It gives the follower, however, the flexibility to determine where she blocks.

* * * * *

Sometimes the opponents' most effective attacker hits quick. This arrangement is ideal for commit-blocking.

The best blocker commits. The second best blocker positions herself to help the commit-blocker, that is, left if the opponents set predominately the one and the back one, right if the opponents set predominately the three.

The read-blocking team makes a comparable arrangment: the best blocker positions herself in the middle and the outside blockers position themselves to help.

* * * * *

When the opponents' best hitter is left, the read-blocking team positions its best blocker either left or middle. It may position its two best blockers in these positions. The stronger may be in either spot.

The team probably does not commit when it intends to stop the opponent's left hitter. Committing against the quick makes double-blocking the X series, in which the left hits the play set, difficult.

* * * * *

The team disguises its blocking scheme, that is, it waits to show its blockers' intentions. The best teams do not show until the opponents pass. This means that the opposing setter has difficulty seeing the defensive arrangement.

The players usually show one scheme all the time, regardless of how the team intends to block. Starting in a stack is common. Players find it easier to step toward the net than away from it.

---

*Sometimes the blocker who has difficulty moving outside, adjusting her position and timing her jump can commit-block effectively.

The Backcourt

The perimeter defense offers the best coverage for a team of skilled defenders. "Skilled" means that the backcourt players can dig the ball, read the opponents and move. These skills are especially important for the left-back and the right-back.

The perimeter distributes four diggers about the backcourt; the others distribute three. The fourth digger near the center of the baseline is especially beneficial when the opponents hit over the block. The middle-back in this instance receives a large number of spikes.

If the opponents tip, and the left- and right-backs cannot see the shot in time, the team must consider one of the tip-coverage schemes. There are two main differences in these defenses: the location of the tip coverage and the origins in the rotation of the players that occupy the positions.

The team that uses a tip-coverage scheme accords its back-row setter special consideration. It prefers a defense that positions her near the net, allowing an easy transition to the setting spot. The middle-up, with the setter covering the tip, is a good choice. It can be applied to all attacks. The rotate offers a comparable benefit on a right attack and the counter-rotate on a left attack.

The rotate is not a good choice on a left attack. The setter plays the deep right corner in this scheme, positioning her far from her setting spot. The same is true of the counter-rotate on a right attack.

* * * * *

The team switches its setter to the right-back defensive position, as mentioned. It may switch other players where they most benefit the team. In the perimeter, for example, the best, most mobile defender often positions herself at middle-back. She roves the baseline.

The back-row setter normally positions herself on the right. When the setter is in the front row, the best back-row attacker plays on the right.

The poorly-skilled player may dictate the team's backcourt plan. The player who cannot dig, read or move usually moves into tip coverage.

Afterword to Section I

The idea of "perfect technique" is anathema to some. Teams that have been strongly taught and that perform the skills similarly are considered mechanical and lacking in spontaneity. Players should be allowed to develop their own ways—what is most natural—according to this school of thought. There is no such thing as "perfect technique."

The problem stems from volleyball's newness. The sport is still rapidly evolving, particularly at the lower levels of play. The forearm pass for example, is only about 35 years old. Other skills, notably the chip and the collapse, are younger still.

In contrast is the game of golf. Historical records show that people played the game before the time of Columbus, meaning that the golf swing is more than 500 years old. By the middle of the 20th century (and perhaps considerably earlier), the best golfers had gained a clear idea of how to swing a golf club: they gripped the club by pressing their palms together, rotated their hips into the ball and shifted their weight from back to front foot. In 1957, these ideas were disseminated in a book entitled *The Modern Fundamentals of Golf* by Ben Hogan. From that point on, golfers at all levels of play could understand what had previously been known by only the few: the elements of the perfect swing.

Volleyball skills can be compared to the golf swing in mid-century: the best players in the world have a clear idea of how to do them. Their bodies, through repetition, have *found* the most effective ways. Thus, forearm passers at the international level hold their heads still and their feet side-by-side; international setters position their hands wide in order to squeeze the ball; spikers finish with their bodies straight (except when they are off balance or desperate). Asian serves are common, particularly among the women.

Unfortunately, the techniques shared by the best players in the world are not common among the many. Club and school players still straighten their legs in forearm passing; a commanding arm squeeze on the set is rare; few amateurs are able to hit without a pike. The biggest omission is the Asian serve: there is only one team in the USA that uses it exclusively—and with dominating success.

APPENDICES

Appendix to Section I, Chapter 1

A child has little ability to see an object and move herself or her hands to it. A thrown ball bounces from her chest before she can catch it. The ball moves too fast for her to see.

The inexperienced passer has a similar problem. She can see the ball but has trouble judging its location. She cannot tell whether the ball has been served high or low, left or right until it is near. She moves late.

The inexperienced passer's problem is not an inability to move or a lack of being ready, but of judging the location of the ball. And yet coaches often respond to this inability to judge by teaching their players to move—usually their feet—at ready. This is a mistake. Any movement other than a slight swaying for balance increases the player's reaction time by interfering with her vision. The inexperienced passer needs to watch more serves, not dance at ready.

* * * * *

Individual player movement is sacred to some volleyball coaches. In their opinions, a moving body or a moving player is always better than one that is still. This applies to the pass: a position that is solid or stable cannot be good. There are, however, many examples in sports of the benefits from quieting the head and the body—especially in hand/eye movements.

The sacrifice bunter in softball wants to contact the ball squarely. She turns to face the pitcher and holds her head and body still as she watches the ball. Her vision is sharp. During the bunt, she moves only her bat. She is usually successful in making contact. The drag bunter, in contrast, wants not only to contact the ball, but also to reach first base before the throw. She is moving, starting her run to first as she tries to bunt. She often misses the ball.

The receiver in football is more likely to catch the ball when he is standing still than when he is on the run. Standing still in a pass pattern is not deceptive but, like the sacrifice bunt, sure. Moreover, the receiver, like the forearm passer, can spring for the ball if needed. Being still allows him to move quickly in any direction.

Finally, the baseball outfielder does not try to time his run to a fly ball so that he and the ball arrive at the catching site at the same time. Instead, he runs very fast to the catching site, adjusts his position and catches the ball standing nearly still.

Stillness* allows the player to know where she is in relation to everything else. All of the environment serves as a reference. Her vision is at its best.

* * * * *

Ready positions are often stylized in ways that work against quick movement. Extending the arms toward the server brings an air of determination to the receiver at ready. She must bring her arms back to her body, however, before she can move. Extending the arms means an extra, unnecessary motion.

---

*"Still" must not be confused with "tight" or "tense." "Still" is not inhibiting.

Appendix to Section I, Chapter 3

"The harder the spiker hits the ball, the more his body stops at contact." This seems contrary. The observer expects the hitter's hand to follow through more quickly or completely on the hardest hits. But both the spiker and the ball are in midair. Contact between them must be seen as a collision between two bodies, each of which has no support.

The easiest way to understand the results of the collision is by making a comparison. Consider a falcon colliding with a volleyball. The falcon would not sustain much impact if it were flying at 5 mph when it hit the ball. But if its speed were increased to 100 mph, it would sustain a great impact. Its speed would decrease drastically at contact. The spiker's hand and body work the same way. The harder the spiker's hand collides with the ball, the greater the impact for the spiker. The more drastically his hand and body slow at contact.

* * * * *

"The spiker develops his greatest power when his body has returned to perfectly straight." The easiest way to consider this idea is by making another comparison.

Imagine a flexible rod suspended vertically by four cables. The cables are tight, holding the rod at the midpoint of its length. Now the top and bottom of the rod are drawn back like a bow is bent in archery. Both the top and bottom move an equal distance in the same direction.

The bent rod wants to return to its starting position, to straighten. In the language of physics, it has "restoring force" when it is bent. Now both the top and bottom of the rod are released. The rod straightens. Its speed of straightening increases as it moves closer and closer to its starting postion. The rod is moving at its fastest when it is once again perfectly straight. In the language of physics, it has "maximum velocity" at this point.

Since the rod is flexible, it does not stop when it has returned to straight. It bends in the opposite direction. The rod's speed of bending in the new direction begins to decrease until it stops, ready to straighten again in the opposite direction.

The spiker can be compared to the rod held by cables. He is suspended in midair; he bends his body to make a C; he straightens for power. But the most important comparison concerns speed: the tips of the spiker's body, like the tips of the rod, are moving at their fastest when they return to perfectly straight. One of these "tips" is the spiker's hitting hand.

Appendix to Section IV, Chapter 5

Numbering the net 1–9 is the standard practice in the world (page 302). An alternative and, in some people's minds, easier system has gained favor among a few coaches.

In this system, the net is numbered (from left to right): *5, 4, 3, 2, 1*; zero for the setter; and, behind her, *A, B* and *C*.

The combination of the numbers and the letters is easier to visualize. The zones emanate from the setter, located at zero, as do the sets themselves. The short sets have low numbers (or letters) and the long sets have high numbers (or letters). The division into numbers and letters makes a distinction between front and back sets. Finally, the system corresponds roughly with the numbers of the sets: one, two, three, and four (five is the exception).

* * * * *

The system cannot designate its back-row zones with letters since these are used in the frontcourt. It uses a combination of numbers and letters (from left-to-right): *500, 300, 100, AA* and *CC*. These parallel the front-row attack zone.

Two- and three-digit designations are more cumbersome than single digits. Some coaches find that the ease of imagining the front-row zones (which are more widely used than those in the back) outweighs the burden of more-than-single-digit back-row zones.

GLOSSARY

A: a back-row attack near the left sideline.

Angle: cross-court.

Antenna: the pole that rises above the net to delineate the sideline boundary.

Attack line: a line three meters away from, and parallel to, the net. A back-row player cannot legally attack the ball above the net unless he takes off on his jump from behind this line.

Audible: a play called in mid-rally.

Auxiliary setter: the player assigned to set when the designated setter cannot; usually the right-front.

B: a back-row attack between the left sideline and the midline of the court.

Back row: the three players whose court position, according to the official scorekeeper, is near the baseline.

Back set: a set delivered behind the setter.

Back slide: a quick slide behind the setter.

Baseline: the back boundary of the court.

Break: an abrupt change of direction in the attacker's approach.

Break point: the spot where the attacker changes direction.

Broad jump: a forward jump in the attacker's approach.

C: a back-row attack between the right sideline and the midline of the court.

Centerline: the line, under the net, that divides the court.

Chain of command: the levels of authority on the team.

Combination: an offensive strike that includes two or more players who attack in concert; a play.

Commit: a blocking scheme in which one player, usually the middle, jumps with, and attempts to stuff, the quick attacker.

Complementary set: a medium-height set that combines with a quick set.

Counter-rotate: a backcourt defense in which the off-blocker moves near the block and the middle-back moves to the cross-court corner.

Cover the hitter: to retrieve rebounds from the opposing blockers.

Creep: to move stealthily so as to escape notice.

Cross: a combination in which the path of one attacker crosses the path of another.

D: a back-row attack near the right sideline.

Deep: away from the net, toward the baseline.

Double-block: a block formed by two players.

Double-quick: a play including two quick sets.

Double-stack: a commit-block scheme in which both the left and the right start behind the middle in order to follow the crossing attacker.

Down ball: an attack, neither a hard spike nor a free ball, which the defense tries to field with its back-court players only.

Fake cross: a play that starts as a cross but changes the direction of its play-set hitter with a veer.

Fake X: a play in which the right fake-crosses the one-hitter and then attacks to the right of the setter.

Five: a medium-height set on the the right sideline.

Flair: a play in which the right fakes-crosses the one-hitter and then attacks on the right sideline.

Floater: a serve that moves in an unpredictable path.

Follow: to move with, and then block, an attacker, often changing positions with another blocker in the process.

Follower: the outside blocker who crosses the commit-blocker.

Four: a low, fast set that is attacked near the left sideline.

Free ball: a slow, arcing shot that the receiving team is "free" to attack as it likes.

Front: to position oneself, in order to block, in front of the attacker.

Front-row: the three players whose court position, according to the official scorekeeper, is near the net.

Front slide: a quick slide in front of the setter.

Game plan: the team's offensive and defensive emphases for a particular opponent, usually organized by rotation.

Glide: a long, smooth run that precedes a spike.

Inside: toward the center of the net.

Isolation: a single-player combination in which the attacker fakes hitting a quick and then hits a medium-height set.

Jump serve: a serve in which the player jumps and attacks the ball as in spiking.

Kinesthesia: the sense that allows the player to know the position or the movement of his body.

Left-stack: a commit-block scheme in which the left starts behind the middle in order to follow the crossing attacker.

Line: a straight-ahead, sideline attack.

Lineup: the players' serving order, which reflects their starting locations on the court.

Load: to arrange the blockers so that the team's most effective confronts the opponents' most effective attacker.

Loop: a curved approach to attack.

M: a back-row attack on the court's midline.

Middle: either the middle-front or the middle-back player.

Middle-up: a backcourt defense in which the middle-back takes a shallow position in front of the attack.

Midline: (1) an imaginary line drawn equidistant from the sidelines, that is, lengthways, on the court; (2) an imaginary line drawn vertically on the player's body that divides it into comparable left and right parts.

Multiple-attack: an offense consisting of plays in which two or more players attack at different places on the net at different times.

Off-blocker: the outside blocker not included in the double-block.

Off-hand: a set delivered from the left side of the right-handed spiker and vice-versa.

Off-speed: an attack that is intentionally slow.

One: a low, quick set that is attacked either directly in front of, or behind, the setter.

One-footed slide: an approach to attack that includes a one-footed jump along the net.

On-hand: a set delivered from the right side of the right-handed spiker and vice-versa.

Open-up: to step away from the ball's path in receiving serve.

Opposite: (1) three positions away in the line-up; (2) the player opposite the setter.

Outside: toward the sideline.

Outside-in: defending, either at the net or in the backcourt, from the sideline to the interior of the court.

Overlap: a foul in which one player is out-of-position in relation to another when the ball is served.

Overpass: a ball that is passed across the net.

Overset: a ball that is set across the net.

Pancake: a technique in which the player flattens his hand against the floor in order to save the ball.

Pace: the overall rhythm of the team or of a player.

Pass: (1) the first contact of a served ball; (2) a forearm pass.

Perimeter: a backcourt defense in which four players arrange themselves near the boundaries of the court.

Play: an attack with a planned fake, usually including two or more hitters; a combination.

Play set: a medium-height set that, when combined with a quick set, constitutes a play.

Point: a front-row position in the serve-receive formation.

Post: the standard that supports the net.

Pump: a play in which an attacker fakes spiking a quick set and then spikes, at the same location, a medium-height set.

Push: to lengthen a set.

Quick: a low, fast, inside set.

Quick/shoot: a play that includes both a quick set and a shoot set.

Quick slide: a quick attack that includes a two-footed take-off and a broad jump along the net.

Read: (1) to determine what event will take place before it occurs; (2) a blocking scheme in which the front-row players watch the setter in order to determine where to block; (3) a backcourt defensive scheme based on all players reading their opponents and their teammates.

Release: (1) a high set, usually delivered to the left sideline, that serves as an outlet when the play goes awry; (2) a block pattern in which an outside blocker fronts the quick hitter as the middle double-blocks on the sideline.

Reverse: a combination in which the usual quick hitter attacks a play set and the usual play-set hitter attacks a quick set.

Right-stack: a commit-block scheme in which the right starts behind the middle in order to follow the crossing attacker.

Rotate: (1) to advance one position in the line-up; (2) a backcourt defense in which the line defender moves near the block and the middle-back moves behind the line defender.

Rotation: the players' locations on the court, according to the scorer.

Safety: a planned change in the blocking scheme used when the team confronts an attack it cannot cover.

Seam: the mid-point between two players.

Specialize: to concentrate efforts on one part of the game.

Spike: to hit the ball forcefully into the opponents' court.

Split block: a double-block that leaves a space between its blockers.

Shallow: near the net.

Shank: a severely misdirected forearm pass.

Shoot: a low, fast set to an attacker who is away from the setter.

Slide: an attack approach that includes a last minute move along the net.

Soft block: a technique in which the blocker angles his hands backward in order to deflect the ball and slow its speed.

Stack-man: a commit-block scheme in which the follower is assigned to block one attacker only.

Stack-read: a commit-block scheme in which the follower determines, by reading the setter, whom he blocks.

Step-around: a one-footed slide in which the attacker moves around the setter.

Step-in: a one-footed slide in which the attacker moves toward the setter.

Step-out: a one-footed slide in which the attacker moves away from the setter.

Stuff: to block the ball to the floor.

Swing: to move from one sideline to the other, usually in approaching to attack.

Switch: to change positions on the court.

Tandem: a combination in which one player attacks immediately behind another.

Tape: the top of the net.

Telegraph: to show one's intention to the opponents.

Three: a low, fast set that is attacked between the setter and the left sideline.

Three-meter line: a court line that is parallel with, and three meters from the net. A back-row player cannot legally attack the ball above the net unless he takes off behind this line.

Touch: a player contacting the ball.

Transition: the change from defense to offense.

Trap: (1) a set close to the net that gives the blocker the advantage; (2) to concentrate the block on one hitter, ignoring another.

Triple-block: a block formed by three players.

Two: a medium-height set that is usually attacked near the center of the net.

Veer: to change direction sharply during a spike approach; to break.

Wing: the player located on the extreme right or left of the formation.

W: a serve-receive formation with three players in the front row, two in the back.

X: a cross in which the middle attacks a front one and the right attacks a two to the left of the middle.

31X: a series of plays in which the middle attacks the three (31) and the left crosses or fake-crosses the three-hitter.

51X: a series of plays in which the middle attacks the one (51) and the right crosses, fake-crosses or flairs from the one-hitter.

4-2: an offense with four spikers and two setters.

5-1: an offense with five spikers and one setter.

6-2: an offense with four spikers and two spiker/setters.

BIBLIOGRAPHY

Bertucci, Bob, *Championship Volleyball (by the Experts)*, Leisure Press, West Point, New York, 1979.

Bertucci, Bob, *The AVCA Volleyball Handbook*, Masters Press, Grand Rapids, Michigan, 1987.

Coleman, James E., & Taras N. Liskevych, *Pictorial Analysis of Power Volleyball*, Creative Sports Books, Carmichael, California, 1976.

Dunphy, Marv, & Ron Wilde, *Volleyball Today*, West Publishing, St. Paul, Minnesota, 1991.

FIVB Coaches Manuel 1, Federation Internationale De Volley-ball, Lausanne, Switzerland, 1989.

Gozansky, Sue, *Championship Volleyball Techniques & Drills*, Parker Publishing, West Nyack, New York, 1983.

Hare, Dennis (with Jill Esteras), *The Art of Beach Volleyball*, Hogar Publishing, San Bernardino, California, 1981.

Hebert, Mike, *Insights and Strategies for Winning Volleyball*, Leisure Press, Champaign, Illinois, 1990.

Herzog, Karl, *Volleyball, Movements in Photographic Sequence*, Team-L Volleyball, Dulman, Federal Republic of Germany, 1975.

Jerome, John, *The Sweet Spot in Time*, Summit Books, New York, 1980.

Keller, Val, *Point, Game, and Match*, Creative Sports Books, Hollywood, California, 1968.

Kiraly, Karch, *Karch Kiraly's Championship Volleyball*, Simon and Schuster, New York, 1990.

Matsudaira, Yasutaka, Naohiro Ikeda, & Masaru Saito, *Winning Volleyball*, Canadian Volleyball Association, Vanier, Ontario, Canada, 1977.

Morehouse, Laurence E., & Leonard Gross, *Maximum Performance*, Pocket Books, New York, 1977.

Neville, William J., *Coaching Volleyball Successfully*, Leisure Press, Champaign, Illinois, 1990.

Prsala, Jan, & Jim Hoyle, *Volleyball for Everybody*, Dalhousie University, Halifax, Nova Scotia, Canada, 1982.

Scates, Allen E., *Winning Volleyball*, Allyn & Bacon, Boston, Massachusetts, 1976.

Schaafsma, Frances, & Ann Heck, *Volleyball for Coaches and Teachers*, Wm. C. Brown Co., Dubuque, Iowa, 1971.

Selinger, Dr. Arie, & Joan Ackermann-Blount, *Arie Selinger's Power Volleyball*, St. Martin's Press, New York, 1986

INDEX

About the Author

Jeff Lucas has played in more than 125 U.S. Volleyball Association tournaments in the past 15 years, including five National Championships. One of his national tournament teams included U.S. Olympic gold medal winning coaches Doug Beal and Bill Neville.

Lucas has coached volleyball for 15 years. In eight years of coaching at Wenatchee, Washington, High School, his teams played in the AAA State Tournament five times, finishing fourth and third before winning the championship in 1983. He received second degree coaching certification—the highest available—from the International Volleyball Federation in 1980.

Lucas has a B.A. in history from Stanford (1968) and did graduate work in business at Columbia.

About the Artist

Artist Stuart Moldrem paints oil portraits and teaches fine art at the Moldrem Atelier School of Art in Seattle, Washington. He is listed in *Who's Who in American Art*. For 35 years, Moldrem had a drama and sports feature in the *Seattle Post-Intelligencer*. In the U.S. Army he was the only artist on the staff of the *Stars & Stripes* newspaper.

Moldrem received international recognition in 1967 by the *Salon Internationale de la Caricature* for achievement in journalistic art. He was cited for "Excellence in Journalism" by Sigma Delta Chi in 1965, '66, '74, '75 and twice in 1977. Moldrem is a tournament tennis player and a volleyball fan.